'This thoughtful and practical text will be critically important for all social workers, probation officers, psychologists, police and other professionals involved with decision making concerning parental capacity to protect. It also makes a significant contribution to the literature on protecting children from sexual abuse.'

– *Stuart Allardyce, Children's Service Manager,*
Barnardo's and Chair, NOTA Scotland

'Written by an experienced practitioner, this practical guide combines theory and useful models to assist those faced with the difficult task of assessing mothers of sexual abused children and partners of offenders. This difficult area of practice has long suffered from an absence of practical literature and *Assessment and Intervention with Mothers and Partners Following Child Sexual Abuse: Empowering to Protect* is therefore to be welcomed.'

– *Marcus Erooga, Independent Child Safeguarding Consultant*

'Jenny Still responds to some of the key questions posed by practitioners working with partners of sex offenders – Did they know? Why did their child not tell them? Why do some not believe their child's allegations? Are they safe? What will help? She provides a format for assessment and intervention with practical advice on how to enhance partners' understanding of risk in order to help them protect their children and meet the child's recovery needs. Importantly it also helps practitioners identify where protection cannot be provided and where alternative care and intervention is required. This book is an essential resource for all those involved in assessment, intervention, case management and supervision.'

– *Robert Tucker, Independent Social Work Consultant,*
RGT Training and Consultancy

'Jenny states "My aim throughout the book is to provide a basic grounding in understanding sex offenders and to weave that knowledge much more into our understanding of mothers and partners". For me the book does exactly that. It deals with what can be some potentially emotive issues with great care, whilst ensuring that the practitioner has a clear understanding of why things should be done in the way Jenny suggests. The work is based on theory but it is also firmly based on Jenny's excellent knowledge and understanding of the subject area. All in all it weaves theory with the knowledge and skills required to achieve the aims and objectives of the intervention, while illustrating practice application. The book is a "must-read" for all those who are involved in this area of work as well as those who assess children and families in other situations.

– *Trevor Evans, Registered Social Worker, Consultant*
Trainer and Associate Lecturer, The Open University

Assessment and Intervention with Mothers and Partners Following Child Sexual Abuse
Empowering to Protect

Jenny Still

Jessica Kingsley *Publishers*
London and Philadelphia

First published in 2016
by Jessica Kingsley Publishers
73 Collier Street
London N1 9BE, UK
and
400 Market Street, Suite 400
Philadelphia, PA 19106, USA

www.jkp.com

Library of Congress Cataloging in Publication Data
Names: Still, Jenny.
Title: Working with mothers of sexually abused children : did she know and
can she protect? : assessment and intervention for partners and mothers /
Jenny Still.
Description: Philadelphia : Jessica Kingsley Publishers, 2016. | Includes
bibliographical references and index.
Identifiers: LCCN 2015038784 | ISBN 9781785920202 (alk. paper)
Subjects: LCSH: Mothers of sexually abused children. | Family counseling.
Classification: LCC HQ759.914 .S75 2016 | DDC
362.82/86--dc23 LC record available at
http://lccn.loc.gov/2015038784

British Library Cataloguing in Publication Data
A CIP catalogue record for this book is available from the British Library

ISBN 978 1 78592 020 2
eISBN 978 1 78450 266 9

Printed and bound in Great Britain

MIX
Paper from
responsible sources
FSC
www.fsc.org   FSC® C013056

CONTENTS

INTRODUCTION

Background to the book

My aim in writing this book is to present a new approach to understanding, assessing and working with women who are caught up in situations of child sexual abuse by an adult male in a family or similar situation: the mothers of children or young people who have been sexually abused and/or the partners of men who are suspected of such abuse, or of men who are known as sex offenders to the authorities. It is based on research and empirical evidence as well as on my clinical experience in working with both children and families and with sex offenders and paedophiles.

Having worked in child sexual abuse with children and families for many years, I accepted an offer to help set up a clinic working with sex offenders as part of a small multi-disciplinary team for two reasons. The first was the fact that, at that time, whilst the needs of children were being recognised, the need to do something about the cause of the problem – the offender – was in its infancy. Seeing more and more children and young people being referred for sexual abuse led me to want to do something about the cause of the problem. Fortunately, research and clinical practice related to sex offending have developed immeasurably since that time. The second reason for agreeing to work with perpetrators was that I found myself looking for a greater understanding of the responses I was seeing in the children, mothers, partners and families with whom I was working, beyond what was then available in the relevant literature. We all have times when we are working 'by the book' using established knowledge and methods yet we are left wondering 'what am I doing wrong?' and 'why is it not working?' My hypothesis was that a better understanding of sexual perpetrators would help. My hypothesis was borne out more than I had hoped. Every day of working with sex offenders seemed to produce a 'eureka' moment when I would think '*now* I understand why that particular child/mother/partner acted or reacted in that way'. This led to a continuation on my part in joint work with social workers in sessions with children, mothers and families, putting this knowledge of sex offenders to practical use.

About the book

Aims

My focus in this book on mothers and partners is because of their pivotal role in child protection and therefore child protection decision making. The book draws on research and empirical evidence, including the many hours I have spent with women in one-to-one and group work, as well as the many joint sessions with known and suspected offenders and their partners or significant others. My aim throughout the book is to provide a basic grounding in understanding sex offenders and to weave that knowledge much more into our understanding of mothers and partners. It is not to excuse failure to protect but to understand it more. I understand the difficulties those working with victim of abuse may have in reading about the perpetrators. I hope I have presented it in a way that is approachable and interesting, and which highlights why such information is relevant in order to help us a) to maximise the woman's ability to understand risk, to protect and to meet the needs of the child and family; and b) to be more precise in identifying those situations where that cannot be done and where children need to be protected by other means. In the last two chapters I bring it all together to create a practice guide for assessment and intervention with mothers and partners. Whilst this is the primary focus, I hope it will also be of use to those working with the child and/or family.

Who the book is for

It is written for social work practitioners, supervisors and managers as well as any other individual or agency involved in working with child sexual abuse, as well as for students in training. Given the heavy demandson busy professionals' time it is designed in a way that provides easy reference to issues along with practical solutions. Chapters are cross-referenced throughout. It builds on the existing knowledge, training and expertise of social workers and other child protection professionals whilst also recognising the needs of those who are less experienced in working with child sexual abuse. Case examples are used to highlight relevant points and in some instances exercises are offered for the reader to consider either on his or her own or with colleagues.

The title

In the title I have used the phrases 'Did she know? Can she protect?' because whilst there are many questions to be asked, this one is at the heart of our work with mothers and partners. The welfare and safety of the child is paramount but research has repeatedly highlighted the importance of the mother not only to the child's future safety but also to the child's healing process. Therefore whilst our primary goal is to keep the child safe we should also endeavour, where appropriate, to maximise the chances of the mother/partner providing the child with that support. However, as we examine in Chapters 1 and 2, we are often faced with a dilemma. On the one hand, the general view is to keep mother and child together and to remove the known or suspected offender; on the other hand, there is often doubt and suspicion that she must have been more aware or even collusive in the abuse, particularly but not exclusively if the abuse was by her partner, of her child and in the family home. This is often exacerbated by the difficulty of working in cases where child sexual abuse is alleged or suspected but there is no conviction. The stakes are high. Sometimes it is necessary and appropriate to remove someone from the family home, whether it is the known or suspected offender or the child who is deemed to be at risk. However, there are also less clear situations where our fear of getting it wrong and leaving a child exposed to further abuse can lead us sometimes to 'play safe'; if the appropriate person cannot be removed then we need a child protection plan, which can involve rigid rules being set within the home as to who can do what, where and with whom, which can be bewildering for the family. We need as much information as possible to ensure they are the right rules for the particular situation.

Why do we need a new approach?

Within the child protection community we have become accustomed to using generic formulae in assessment designed for use with a wide range of child- and family-related issues and with different forms of child abuse and other children's needs. However, child sexual abuse is a complex subject and whilst there are some similarities with other forms of child abuse such as physical abuse, neglect and emotional abuse there are many ways in which sexual abuse is different. My thesis is that whilst such generic protocols are invaluable in providing a wealth of information, there are limitations in the extent to which they assess either sexual risk or a woman's ability to protect, because they remain rooted in a historical perspective focusing on the child and family, which does not utilise current levels of knowledge of sex offenders. My arguments for the need for a more focused approach specific to sexual abuse are made in Chapter 10, along with explanations of some other forms of sexual risk assessment in common usage.

How did we get to where we are now?

This book builds on existing knowledge and literature. Because sex offenders commonly stay silent, in denial and/or give minimal information about their offending, historically our understanding of child sexual abuse developed around this information vacuum. It was first understood by child protection professionals in terms of the family dysfunction and this provided the framework for assessment and the focus for intervention. For example, Jones and Ramchandani (1999) summarised the research findings of common characteristics of family dysfunction and sexual abuse as being 'rigid family belief systems, dysfunctional adult partnerships, parental neglect and unavailability, and inability to nurture autonomy in their children' (p.13). This was initially interpreted in terms of patterns of communication and family conflict resolution (Furniss 1983). The systemic family therapy approach to sexual abuse was developed which saw causality as 'circular' rather than 'linear', seeing individuals as being 'caught in a dance with one another' (Bentovim *et al.* 1988, p.41). Similarly, Trepper and Barrett (1989) devised the Multiple Systems Model in which intra-familial sexual abuse was seen as a reflection of the family's vulnerability to incest. This has been complemented by a vast increase in our knowledge of the short- and long-term effects of sexual abuse on children and young people.

However, it has now been recognised that a family-based approach to understanding child sexual abuse skews responsibility for the abuse and does not sufficiently relate the problem to its cause, which is *the offender.* As early as 1984 Wolf presented the concept of grooming (Wolf 1984). In 1992 Bentovim examined a link between the dysfunctional family system and the offender in his concept of 'trauma organised systems'. Still (1995) and Eldridge and Still (1998), whilst acknowledging the importance in understanding family dynamics, have argued that in cases of child sexual abuse there should be a greater emphasis on the fact that 'dysfunctional family dynamics don't cause sexual abuse; rather, sex offenders wilfully exacerbate or create such dynamics' (Eldridge and Still 1998, p.48) in order to abuse and prevent discovery and he should be *central* to our understanding of them. This requires an understanding not only of children and families in relation to child sexual abuse but also of sex offenders.

Other works have recognised this. For example, Salter (1995) argued to great effect that therapists working with adult survivors need to have an understanding of sexual perpetrators in order to understand the impact on the survivor and his or her response to the abuse. Calder and Peake (Calder, Peake and Rose 2001, pp.115–116) also provide invaluable information about some of the links between perpetrators and mothers of children who are sexually abused. However, in wider everyday practice most child protection professionals either do not have this information or do not use it to maximum benefit. Whilst the current wider recognition of the concept of grooming is to be welcomed, this only scratches the surface of the large amount of information that is now available on sex offenders and paedophiles in terms of research, assessment and clinical practice. However, most of this information is invested in those working with convicted sex offenders in the criminal justice system and is for the most part not available to child protection practitioners unless specialist additional training is sought. Despite progress having been made through organisations such as NOTA (National Association for Treatment of Sex Offenders) in the UK and ATSA (Association for the Treatment of Sexual Abusers) in the USA in addressing issues relating to both offenders and victims and their families, the gap persists today.

How do I know the approach I am proposing works?

It has been used successfully by me for many years in specialist work for social services departments and family court cases throughout the UK and well received in training. It was developed further at the instigation of the UK government Home Office as a group work programme for partners of sex offenders convicted of abusing children and/or young people, to run in tandem with Home Office accredited sex offender treatment programmes throughout the south of England (Still, Faux and Wilson 2001). Specific training was provided, to include both probation officers and social workers, but only for those who would be using the programme. Those social workers recognised the value of the work and began to adapt it to their own wider practice in working with mothers of children as well as with partners of offenders, in cases of suspected as well as known abuse and where there was no involvement from the criminal justice system beyond investigation. This in turn led to the creation of an integrated mother and child intervention programme for Essex County Council (Tucker and Still 2009) in association with women attending the Essex Partners' Programme. My hope is that in writing this book it will reach a wider audience.

Providing wider important contextual information

I have included a chapter to provide a basic grounding of information on the development of research, assessment and treatment programmes for work with sex offenders. Sex offenders are arch manipulators and child protection professionals need the means to counter this. We may also be asked to explain to mothers and partners the basis for our concerns about a known or suspected sex offender and how particular conclusions are drawn, for example, as to why we think someone does or does not present a sexual risk, to what extent and to whom.

I have included also a chapter addressing multi-agency working, with particular emphasis on the different language and terminology used within the child protection system, the legal system and the criminal justice system and how we may believe we are talking the same language when we are not. This may seem harmless – what difference do words make? Yet in practice it can interfere with good insight, mutual understanding and decision making and cause utter confusion when used in conversation with mothers and partners.

Last but not least

I make no apology for drawing on the human context and looking at the situation from the mother's and partner's perspective. Whilst I have referred to research and literature throughout, the book is based also on the responses I have seen and heard from the many mothers and partners with whom I have worked over the years. In our concern as managers and practitioners to protect the child I sometimes think we expect superhuman responses from these women: immediate and consistent belief of and support for the child and a total and permanent rejection of the known or suspected offender. Whilst this does happen, it often does not. Denial, disbelief, inappropriate blame and anger displaced onto the authorities are all the kind of reactions and behaviours that ring alarm bells, which can shout out that the woman is unsafe as a protector. But how would we react in her situation? None of us is immune to being targeted by a sex offender even if we do this work and sex offenders and paedophiles are master manipulators at persuading other people of their innocence, especially their partner or the child's mother. Key questions for us in working with mothers and partners are: 'can she be a safe protector in future?' and 'how can we help her achieve that goal?' And if we were in that situation, once we were persuaded of his wrongdoing one of the first questions we would want answered would be 'how did he do that to me, and to the child?' And if we knew about sex offenders we could find the answers and therefore the way forward.

References

Bentovim, A. (1992) *Trauma-Organized Systems: Physical and Sexual Abuse in Families.* London: Karnac Books.

Bentovim, A., Elton, A., Hilderbrand, J., Tranter, M. and Vizard, E. (1988) *Child Sexual Abuse Within the Family.* London: Wright Butterworth.

Calder, M.C., Peake, A. and Rose, K. (2001) *Mothers of Sexually Abused Children: A Framework for Assessment, Understanding and Support.* Dorset: Russell House Publishing.

Eldridge, H.J. and Still, J. (1995) 'Apology and Forgiveness in the Context of the Cycles of Adult Male Sex Offenders who Abuse Children.' In A.C. Salter *Transforming Trauma: A Guide to Understanding and Treating Adult Survivors of Child Sexual Abuse.* Thousand Oaks, CA: Sage.

Eldridge, H.J. and Still, J. (1998) 'Building Networks: Phase 1.' In H.J. Eldridge (ed.) *Therapist Guide for Maintaining Change: Relapse Prevention for Adult Male Perpetrators of Child Sexual Abuse.* Thousand Oaks, CA: Sage.

Furniss, T. (1983) 'Family process in the treatment of intra-familial child sexual abuse.' *Journal of Family Therapy 4,* 263–279.

Jones, D.P.H. and Ramchandani, P. (1999) *Child Sexual Abuse: Informing Practice from Research.* Abingdon: Radcliffe Medical Press.

Salter, A.C. (1995) *Transforming Trauma: A Guide to Understanding and Treating Adult Survivors of Child Sexual Abuse.* Thousand Oaks, CA: Sage.

Still, J. (1995) 'An Overview.' In A. Hollows (ed.) *Rebuilding Families After Abuse: Papers from conference at the National Children's Bureau.* London: NCB.

Still, J., Faux, M. and Wilson, C. (2001) *The Thames Valley Partner's Programme.* The Home Office, London. Crown Copyright 2001.

Trepper, T.S. and Barrett, M.J. (1989) *Systemic Treatment of Incest: A Therapeutic Handbook.* New York: Bruner Mazel.

Tucker, R. and Still, J. (2009) *Staying Safe: Focused Intervention for Children and Young People who Live in Families who Have Been Affected by Sexual Abuse. Facilitator's Manual.* Essex: The Lucy Faithfull Foundation and Essex County Council.

Wolf, S. (1984) 'A multifactor model of deviant sexuality.' Third International Conference on Victimology, Lisbon.

CHAPTER 1

THE COMPLEXITY OF ASSESSING NON-OFFENDING MOTHERS AND PARTNERS

The law states that the child's welfare is paramount. This requires us as child protection professionals to do our best to ensure that is the case and to protect the child from further abuse, as well as any other child who is exposed to the same risk. However, child protection risk assessment can never be an exact science. With consistently low conviction rates, most child sexual abuse is dealt with not in the criminal justice system but in the child protection system and family courts, where the standard of proof is based on the balance of probabilities. Without a conviction, the assessor is commonly left working with minimal information from the known or suspected offender who in order to protect himself remains silent or tells as little as is necessary. It can be difficult gaining detailed information from the child, due to his or her age-related limited cognitive ability, the trauma resulting from the abuse and as a result of the offender's grooming to ensure silence. Problems can be compounded further by legal constraints on the types of communication we are allowed to use with the child or young person.

Such risk and safety assessments are therefore often fraught with difficulties. In this information vacuum it is necessary to turn to other sources of information. Over time, assessment formats have developed based on factors relating to the context of family dynamics and other social factors, with the non-offending parent placed in a key role:

- as a potential source of additional contextual information
- in child protection decision making
- in the child's healing process.

In the absence of information from other sources, child protection agencies often rely heavily upon judgments of maternal attitudes, responses and support (Adams 1982; Coohey 2006; Everson *et al.* 1989; Reidy and Hochstadt 1993). This can impact on decisions regarding:

- legal interventions or not
- who leaves the family home and who stays
- what type of clinical intervention.

Empirical evidence suggests also that such judgements can impact also on decisions regarding:

- whether or not we share information with a mother about what goes on in her child's therapy
- to what extent we involve her in her child's therapy
- contact with the known or suspected offender, e.g. for other children in the family
- possible family reconstruction.

The importance of the mother to the child

Whilst there is a duty to protect there is also the need to consider other aspects of the well-being of the child and it can be difficult to juggle the two.

Research over the years has repeatedly highlighted the importance of the non-offending parent to the child, even suggesting that the ability of the non-abusing parent to provide support following disclosure is a critical factor influencing the child's post-abuse psychological adjustment and recovery (Adams-Tucker 1982; Conte and Schuerman 1987; Esparza 1993; Everson *et al.* 1989; Feiring, Taska and Lewis 1998; Lovett 1995; Ruggiero, McCleer and Dixon 2000; Tremblay, Hebert and Piche 1999). More specifically, research suggests that:

- there is a strong correlation between a warm and supportive relationship with a non-offending parent and the resilience in the child (Spaccarelli and Kim 1995)

- maternal support may be a better predictor of the child's psychological adjustment than abuse-related factors (Johnson and Kenkel 1991 and Spaccarelli and Kim 1995).

This would suggest a preferred option in meeting the child's needs should be to keep mother and child together and remove the known or suspected adult male offender. However, it is often not that simple, because whilst research highlights the importance of the mother to the child it also suggests that what we commonly see in mothers and partners at the time of disclosure does not inspire confidence.

Common dilemmas in assessment and decision making

The impact of disclosure on the non-offending parent

Children need strong protectors and carers. However, not surprisingly, research shows that the discovery of child sexual abuse has a negative impact on non-offending mothers/partners. For example:

- Non-offending mothers of sexually abused girls showed a heightened level of depression and anxiety (Kim *et al.* 2007; Lewin and Bergin 2001) and heightened levels of general symptoms of distress (Deblinger *et al.* 1993; Newberger *et al.* 1993).

- Mothers found talking to their daughters about sexual abuse to be highly stressful, with a common response being that no one else could understand what they were experiencing (Hill 2001).

- The mother–child relationship is often jeopardised by behaviour problems in the child and parental exhaustion, insecurity and lack of confidence as parents try to manage this situation (Plummer and Eastin 2007).

- Non-offending mothers commonly experience considerable psychological distress related to wider familial and social challenges following disclosure of their child's abuse (Avery, Hutchinson and Whitaker 2002; Kim, Noll, Putnam and Trickett 2007).

None of this is likely to leave the mother/partner in the best position to help and support the child and family.

Furthermore, her difficulties can have a less than helpful impact on the child. Research suggests, for example, the following:

- The non-offending parent's inability to understand the problem and provide appropriate support to the child has been found to have a negative effect on the child's well-being post disclosure (Everson *et al.* 1989; Spaccarelli 1994).

- A lack of perceived support from the non-offending parent has been found to make younger children and those abused by a parent figure more likely to retract (Malloy *et al.* 2007).

Responses to disclosure

The non-offending parent or carer has a crucial role in the future protection of the child. But if she failed to protect in the past, how can we be sure she will do so in future? This worry can be exacerbated by her response to disclosure. In assessing the woman's ability to protect it would be made easy if we saw perfect responses from the mother or partner, with her totally and consistently believing the child and immediately banishing the offender for good. However, that is often not the case and her responses can be troubling. In most cases of child sexual abuse there is no medical evidence to confirm or refute the child's allegations so it comes down to who she believes is telling the truth. It is not uncommon to see the mother in a state of confusion and ambivalence, swinging on a pendulum between believing the child completely one minute and not the next, or believing some but not all of it: 'I can believe this but I cannot believe that.' All of this is likely to be compounded by the alleged offender trying to persuade her he is a good man who would never do such a thing.

Did she know? Can she protect?

This can be exacerbated by the question of 'did she know?' In the absence of robust information there can be the niggling worry: how could she not have known? This is especially so if the perpetrator was her partner/close relative/friend and even more so if the abuse took place in the family home. In worst case scenarios this can lead to a suspicion that she was at least collusive if not directly involved. The same question can arise where the known or suspected offender is her partner but the allegation is not from within the family: if she lives with him and is his sexual partner, how could she not have suspected or known? And if the woman herself is a survivor of childhood sexual abuse such suspicions can become cranked up: with her experience, how could she not have seen something was wrong? This leads to the next question: 'is she a safe protector?'

Problems for the mother/partner

Research suggests that non-offending parents experience overwhelming emotions and conflicts with child protection investigations, which they find difficult and intrusive (Tuttle *et al.* 2007). The non-offending parent can have problems in that if she did not know or have any suspicions about the abuse in the past and thinks she is being doubted or disbelieved, this is likely to make her angry, upset and potentially hostile toward the agencies that are assessing her. Similarly, a woman who is genuine in her commitment to protecting her child in the future and who is convinced of her ability to do so, is likely to become angry and frustrated with agencies and professionals who doubt her.

It is not difficult to see how this can make her less willing to cooperate, which in turn can increase the perception that she is unsafe. This in turn can make her more mistrustful and even less willing to cooperate, which in turn can increase the perception that she is unsafe. As a result, we and sometimes the courts, can become ambivalent in our approach to the mother or partner and what should or could be a working partnership between us and the mother/partner becomes fraught with difficulty and goes on a downward spiral of mistrust.

The absence of offender information and knowledge

One of the difficulties is that with little or nothing coming from the known or alleged offender we are often working in an information vacuum. This deprives us of the context of the abuse and therefore the context of the woman's responses.

With little or no information coming from the criminal investigation it has to be sought through the child protection process, where assessment of the known or suspected offender falls to social workers. But even the most competent social worker is placed at a disadvantage because whilst probation officers and police officers are trained in the techniques of interviewing sex offenders, social workers are not, and the skills and procedures that can be applied with success in interviewing children and families do not translate across to interviewing offenders, who are well practised in the art of lying and manipulation. To complicate matters further, if no charges have been brought against him, or were brought against him and he was found not guilty, this boosts his insistence that he poses no risk to a child, even if he does.

Furthermore, with the generic child- and family-based approach to assessment that is in common usage, a sex offender can afford to be responsive, cooperative and compliant because he is unlikely to be questioned in a manner that will dent his denial or his ability to give minimal information about his actual offending. This gives the child protection assessor two further dilemmas:

- First, his cooperation with the authorities does not necessarily mean he did not do it, or that he did it but is low risk – but it may do.

- Second, someone who is *not* an offender and who is trying to be helpful and demonstrate he is *not* a risk is likely to present in a similar way. But if we do not have and apply knowledge of how sex offenders operate, how can we tell the difference?

How can we understand the woman's responses if we cannot put it in the context of the offender?

Whilst a generic approach to assessment can produce a wealth of invaluable information, the value of that information in relation to the specific issue of child sexual abuse is limited if it is not then analysed and interpreted using knowledge about sex offenders in general and, where available, specific information about a known or suspected offender. Knowledge of offenders raises questions not just of 'what did he do?' but also: 'how did he do what he did? What did this particular individual do to enable him to abuse and prevent discovery? Why did it have that particular effect on this child, this mother/partner and other family members? How is he still manipulating the situation? How likely is he to do it again? How appropriate and relevant to him are any protective strategies that have been put in place? And if there is no longer contact with him, how is his legacy still affecting everyone's responses to this painful situation?

Conclusions

As there is no such thing as a risk-free environment, we have the task of balancing a) maximising the child's safety with b) a mother or partner's previous failure to protect and c) with the child's emotional need for a parent. How can we help maximise the woman's ability to protect in future and to meet the child's needs? If we are concerned, how does that weigh up against any potential harm to the child in removing the child from her care? And with a paramount duty to protect the child, how can we avoid the trap of becoming overly careful in our child protection decision making, for example, in limiting the woman's involvement in the child's therapy where it may actually be helpful, in the rules we set for contact arrangements, or even separating mother and child? Sometimes that is an obvious need but it is also often a grey area which we must negotiate our way through.

References

Adams-Tucker, C. (1981) 'A socioclinical overview of 28 sex-abused children.' *Child Abuse and Neglect 5*, 3, 361–367.

Adams-Tucker, C. (1982) 'Proximate effects of sexual abuse in childhood: A report on 28 children.' *American Journal of Psychiatry 139*, 10, 1252–1256.

Avery, L., Hutchinson, D. and Whitaker, K. (2002) 'Domestic violence and intergenerational rates of child sexual abuse: A case record analysis.' *Child and Adolescent Work Journal 19*, 1, 77–90.

Conte, J.R. and Schuerman, J.R. (1987) 'Factors associated with an increased impact of child sexual abuse.' *Child Abuse and Neglect 11*, 210, 201–211.

Coohey, C. (2006) 'How child protective services investigators decide to substantiate mothers for failure-to-protect in sexual abuse cases.' *Journal of Child Sexual Abuse 15*, 61–81.

Deblinger, E., Hathaway, D.R., Lippman, J. and Steer, R. (1993) 'Psychosocial characteristics and correlates of symptom distress in nonoffending mothers of sexually abused children.' *Journal of Interpersonal Violence 8*, 155–168.

Esparza, D. (1993) 'Maternal support and stress response in sexually abused girls ages 6–12.' *Issues in Mental Health Nursing 14*, 85–107.

Everson, M.D., Hunter, W.M., Runyon, D.K., Edelson, G.A. and Coulter, M.L. (1989) 'Maternal support following disclosure of incest.' *American Journal of Orthopsychiatry 59*, 2, 197–207.

Feiring, C., Taska, L.S. and Lewis, M. (1998) 'Social support and children's and adolescents' adaptation to sexual abuse.' *Journal of Interpersonal Violence 13*, 240–260.

Hill, A. (2001) '"No-one else could understand": Women's experiences of a support group run by and for mothers of sexually abused children.' *British Journal of Social Work 31*, 385–397.

Johnson, B. and Kenkel, M. (1991) 'Stress, coping, and adjustment in female adolescent incest victims.' *Child Abuse and Neglect 15*, 293–305.

Kim, K., Noll, J.G., Putnam, F.W. and Trickett, P.K. (2007) 'Psychosocial characteristics of non-offending mothers of sexually abused girls: Findings from a prospective, multigenerational study.' *Child Maltreatment 12*, 4, 338–351.

Lewin, L. and Bergin, C. (2001) 'Attachment behaviors, depression, and anxiety in nonoffending mothers of child sexual abuse victims.' *Child Maltreatment 6*, 4, 365–375.

Lovett, B.B. (1995) 'Child sexual abuse: The female victim's relationship with her nonoffending mother.' *Child Abuse and Neglect 19*, 729–738.

Malloy, L.C., Lyon, T.D. and Quas, J.A. (2007) 'Filial dependency and recantation of child sexual abuse allegations.' *Journal of the American Academy of Child and Adolescent Psychiatry 46*, 2, 162–170.

Newberger, C.M., Gremy, I.M., Waternaux, C.M. and Newberger, E.H. (1993) 'Mothers of sexually abused children: Trauma and repair in longitudinal perspective.' *American Journal of Orthopsychiatry 63*, 92–102.

Plummer, C.A. and Eastin, J. (2007) 'The effect of child sexual abuse allegations/investigations on the mother/child relationship.' *Violence Against Women 13*, 10, 1053–1071.

Reidy, J.R. and Hochstadt, N.J. (1993) 'Attribution of blame in incest cases: A comparison of mental health professionals.' *Child Abuse and Neglect 17*, 371–381.

Ruggiero, K.J., McLeer, V. and Dixon, F.J. (2000) 'Characteristics associated with survivor psychopathology.' *Sexual Abuse Characteristics Associated with Survivor Pathology 24*, 951–964.

Spaccarelli, S. (1994) 'Stress, appraisal, and coping in child sexual abuse: A theoretical and empirical review.' *Psychological Bulletin 116*, 340–362.

Spaccarelli, S. and Kim, S. (1995) 'Resilience criteria and factors associated with resilience in sexually abused girls.' *Child Abuse and Neglect 19*, 1171–1182.

Tremblay, C., Hebert, M. and Piche, C. (1999) 'Coping strategies and social support as mediators of consequences in CSA victims.' *Child Abuse and Neglect 23*, 929–945.

Tuttle, A.R., Knudson-Martin, C., Levis, S., Taylor, B. and Andrews, J. (2007) 'Parents' experiences in child protective services: Analysis of a dialogical group process.' *Family Process 46*, 3, 367–380.

CHAPTER 2

DID SHE KNOW?
CAN SHE PROTECT?

The circumstances behind an assessment of a mother or partner vary. For example, it may be that:

- her child has disclosed sexual abuse within the home by a family member
- her child has disclosed abuse outside the home by an outsider
- her partner has been accused of abuse either within or outside the family
- she has just been informed by police or social workers that her partner has a conviction for a sexual offence(s).

Whatever the situation, given the number of pitfalls outlined in the previous chapter, a major function of any assessment must be to gain a deeper understanding of her situation both at the time of the assessment and at the time of the abuse. In this chapter we consider the range of possible responses from mothers and partners, an examination of denial and disbelief, potential impact issues for the mother/partner and potential additional issues for women who are adult survivors of abuse.

Belief, Disbelief and Denial

As seen in Chapter 1, research and experience suggest the professional child protection community is often ambivalent in its approach to non-offending parents. On the one hand, the general view is to keep mother and child together and remove the known or suspected offender; on the other hand, there is often doubt and suspicion that she must have been more aware or even collusive in the abuse, particularly but not exclusively if the abuse was by her partner of her child and in the family home. How could she not have known? This is an important question in terms of:

- the woman's future ability to act as the safe protecting parent against the same or any other sexual predator

- her role in the healing process of the child: if she knew of the abuse prior to disclosure, or even if the child *thinks* she knew, this is likely to cause mistrust on the part of the child and a painful rift between mother and child, which a sex offender would also be quick to spot and use to his own advantage

- the possibility of any family reconstruction.

What the women say

Table 2.1 shows a spectrum of responses I have heard from the many mothers and partners with whom I have worked about what they did or did not know about the abuse prior to disclosure which must be considered within the context of the offender grooming her out of a position to protect (see Chapter 6).

TABLE 2.1 SPECTRUM OF NOT KNOWING–KNOWING

1	She didn't know anything
2	She knew something was going on but had no idea it was that
3	She knew something was wrong and wondered, suspected sexual abuse but found nothing to confirm that
4	Active collusion – knowing it was sexual abuse but convincing herself nothing was going on
5	Co-offending - active participation either willingly or coerced
6	Offending (independently)

Most put themselves at points 1 or 2 but said they felt the agencies and professionals with whom they were involved did not believe them, either overtly or implied.

Women on point 3 commonly said they knew *something* was wrong and had read/heard about child sexual abuse, for example, in the media but saw or heard nothing to validate their concerns and there were other valid explanations for increased stress and tension. For example, in the child they may have interpreted it as relating to school problems, the 'terrible twos' behaviour of a toddler, expected difficulties in adolescence and so on and in the adult they may have thought any tensions were related to financial worries, work stress, relationship difficulties and so on.

For the women on points 2 or 3 the most common reasons given for not realising it was sexual abuse were that prior to disclosure they firmly believed they would know if anything was wrong and, if they missed it, that their child would tell them.

Some women placed themselves higher up the spectrum at point 3 but in most instances further examination suggested this was based on a chronic sense of guilt and self-blame at failing to protect, endlessly re-running scenarios in their heads: 'I *must* have known...I *should* have known...it must have been when...', especially when the message implied by others was 'you must have known', when in fact they did not. Those women who placed themselves at point 3 often felt disgusted with themselves for even thinking their partner/relation/close friend could do such a thing when they could find nothing to substantiate their worries: there are many other potential causes of everyday stress in families without it being sexual.

A minority of women should have placed themselves higher up the spectrum but failed to do so, either initially or at all.

Some authors (Chaffin 1996; Salter 1995; Still 1995; Still *et al.* 2001) argue that there is no research to support the notion that women in general know and/or collude in the child's abuse. Conversely, when Danish researcher Inebe Jonker (1999) asked a sample of 180 women if they knew about their child's abuse, 95 per cent said they did not (personal communication: Rudd Bullen 2001).

Denial and disbelief

In a perfect world we look for the perfect child protection response from the non-offending parent: that is, to immediately and unwaveringly support the child and banish the known or suspected offender. Some women are able to do that. Many are not. The woman may believe some of it but not all of it, or all of it one minute and none the next, and every variation in between.

It is worrying when a mother fails to totally believe and act on a child's allegation and where that happens it can have a devastating impact on the child. This cannot be excused but the background and context need to be understood. We should also expect what may be seen as some initial natural human responses.

EXERCISE
(CAN BE DONE INDIVIDUALLY
OR WITH COLLEAGUES)

Imagine you do not work in child protection and have unrelated lives and jobs. Then imagine this situation. There are no right or wrong responses. We are all different.

Consider/share the following script:

'Today is an ordinary day and you're enjoying your normal, everyday life. You have the usual minor domestic crises experienced by most other people and families. You're looking forward to doing something nice this evening. Life is rumbling along. You go home and you receive a telephone call from a friend who says she is sorry but there's something she thinks you need to know.'

Then ask, in this order:

- Your husband/partner/relative is having a sexual affair with another woman. What might you think? How might you feel?
- Not with just any woman but a woman you know. She is your best friend who you have known for years and you meet up regularly.
- This other person is not an adult but a child; your husband/partner is having sex with a child.
- This is a child who is known to you.
- This child is your brother's child or your sister's child.
- Your child.
- What might you think? How might you feel?

Observations

There can be no comparison in the seriousness and legality of scenarios relating to adults and children. However, the type of emotional responses all these situations provoke is likely to be surprisingly similar whoever you try it out on. In the earlier adult scenarios responses commonly vary from total belief accompanied by 'I'd kill him!', 'I'd throw him out!' and/or 'what's wrong with me?' through to total disbelief with 'we have a good relationship', 'he wouldn't do that to me' and 'I'd know if he was having an affair' and all points in between. These typically include doubt as to the truth of the allegation, wanting to ask a barrage of questions and/or challenge the recalcitrant partner, not wanting to ask questions or challenge anyone for fear of the answer, indignation, rage toward their partner, rage toward the other woman, questioning the motives of the messenger, shooting the messenger, blaming the other woman, self-doubt and a whole lot more. Some may say they would wish to throw him out, others may wish to work it out and stay together. Not unreasonably, many say they would want some kind of proof or verification that it is not all a fabrication by someone stirring up trouble. However, without exception as the third party scenarios in this exercise shift from adult to child, and from a child who is a stranger to one who is close to them, whilst the emotional responses remain similar there is a profound increase in intensity of impact caused by disgust at the very idea of sexual behaviour toward a child, culminating in individual and collective silence, shock and incredulity. Reasons commonly given are that they know their partners, they are his sexual partner and therefore his interest is in adults not children, they know about sex offenders and he's 'not like that'.

The relevance to non-offending parents

Most important to note is that these are the same responses described by many partners of suspected sex offenders and mothers of children who have been sexually abused. Such responses could be considered normal human behaviour and therefore would not necessarily make the woman a bad mother or unsafe for the future.

Absence of proof

The problems of the non-offending mother or partner are compounded by the fact that in child sexual abuse there is often no proof in terms of physical evidence so she is confronted with a situation where it is the child's word against that of the alleged offender. From a child protection viewpoint the child's word should be good enough. But life is not that simple. We know that in reality children and young people are rarely able to give a clear and consistent account of events, whether due to their age, cognitive and/or linguistic ability, emotional trauma and whatever threats have been made in grooming to maintain their silence. Whereas sex offenders, for their own self-preservation, are highly adept in the art of denial, manipulation and deceit and well-practised in portraying themselves as good people who would never do such a thing as sexually abusing a child and presenting a hundred and one 'reasons' why the child is wrong, mistaken, misguided or trouble-mongering. The closer the relationship between the woman and the alleged offender the harder it can be to see through such persuasive arguments.

Messages from children

The problem is often exacerbated by the responses we see in children. Whilst in my experience most women want to make a commitment to their child(ren) to keep them safe in future, this picture is not always reflected in the perception of victims of abuse. For example, Monck (1996) at the Institute of Child Health in London found in a sample of child sexual abuse victims:

- only one third perceived their maternal carers as truly believing them

- one third as disbelieving them

- one third felt doubtful of their mother's support.

This mismatch can sometimes be explained by the ambivalent responses in the non-offending parent as previously explored. Similarly, it is not uncommon for a child who is being sexually abused to think their mother knew when she did not.

Case example: Naomi

When I asked twelve-year-old Naomi if she thought her mother knew her father was sexually assaulting her, which I knew both from the mother and the offender that she did not, Naomi replied that she thought her mother did know but did nothing about it. When asked why, Naomi looked at me as if this was a ridiculous question and replied: 'She's mum and married to dad'. This assumption that everything was shared between parents was a perfectly reasonable response from an adolescent perspective, albeit incorrect because it failed to take into account the power of the offender in manipulating the situation to ensure mother did not know.

In addition, children are not immune from the attitudes of others. On seeing their mother being assessed and possibly being excluded from certain information or intervention, and/or banned from supervising contact and/or being taken to court, it can create mistrust: 'others don't trust her so maybe I shouldn't'. And if children doubt their mother's ability to protect, we will too.

Children can also become protective of the non-offending parent, sometimes to the point of retracting an allegation, either because of the distress caused to her by the disclosure or because of threats that have been made by the offender at the time of the abuse: 'If you tell, this/ that will happen to you mother…'

Every situation is different. All of this makes it vital that in assessment we try to gain some understanding of what is going on in every individual case.

Denial in a human context

Disbelief and denial are deeply worrying responses and even more so when they persist in the face of professional opinion. However, whilst we acknowledge the effect of the abuse on the victim can be profound at the same time we should not underestimate the impact on a non-offending parent, as seen from the research in Chapter 1. This is not to minimise or excuse either failure to protect or denial but to understand both more, in the interests of making appropriate decisions about child protection and therapeutic intervention.

The price of belief

One of the most helpful questions to ask a mother or partner who cannot accept an allegation when it is believed by experienced child protection professionals is: 'what would it mean for you if you allowed yourself to believe it is true?' As one woman said: 'It's like being asked to jump off a cliff not knowing if there's any safety net at the bottom.'

When beginning an assessment it is helpful to give some thought to the possible impact of the abuse on the non-offending parent. The following are lists of issues raised by the hundreds of women with whom I have worked either individually, in group or in family sessions (adapted from Still, Faux and Wilson 2001).

Common issues for the woman in her relationship with the victim (where the victim is her child or in a close relationship with her)

- Who to believe?

- Who to blame?

- A sense of guilt, self-blame and responsibility for failure to protect (e.g. 'I should have known'; 'what did I miss?'; 'I'm a bad mother'; 'I should have stood up to him more when he was difficult/violent'; 'I should have known what he was like from our own sexual relationship').

- A sense of divided loyalties between the child and the alleged offender.

- Fear of losing either: loss, grief, a sense of bereavement.

- Coping with the child's response to the abuse: trying to understand the emotional, behavioural and cognitive effects of the abuse on the child – how to cope?

- Her overt/covert responses to the child, e.g. feeling closer? Protectiveness? Warmth? Love?

- A sense of guilt if she experiences any negative feelings toward the child such as anger, jealousy ('I'm his sexual partner'), scapegoating or emotional rejection, even if she knows it is irrational. 'Why can't I be perfect?'

- Is she aware or unaware of the appropriateness or inappropriateness of some of her responses?

- The dangers of over-protectiveness: 'I'll never let my children out of my sight'.

- Fears for the future, e.g. 'Will my child be OK? Or be abused again? Or become an abuser?'

Common issues for the woman in her relationship with her own children (if the alleged/known offender is her partner) or the victim's siblings (if the victim is her child)

- Did he abuse them too?

- Might he in future?

- Will I lose them too?

- If they say they weren't abused does that mean it didn't happen or that they are covering it up?

- Am I the only one who didn't know?

- Are there any more secrets?

- Understanding and coping with sibling responses to her, e.g. anger at her failure to protect, mistrust.

- Understanding and coping with their responses to the victim, e.g. are they supportive or do they blame him/her for the abuse and/or the loss of father/stepfather/grandfather/friend from their lives?

- Anxieties about the consequences for them, e.g. 'might my son become an abuser too?'

- Dangers of over-protectiveness.

Common issues for the woman in her relationship with the alleged or known offender

- Belief versus disbelief.

- Confusion: 'why did he do it?', 'how could he?'

- Loss, grief, sense of bereavement (whether or not he's left – everything has changed).

- Sense of betrayal: 'nothing was real'.

- Fear: 'he's violent, what will he do to me or my child if I believe it/tell the truth/support the victim/don't have him back?'

- Anger but directed at whom?

- Ability/inability to express anger; displacing anger elsewhere.

- Self-blame: 'I must have let him down'; 'if I'd been a better sexual partner he wouldn't have done it'; 'if I'd been more supportive…'

- I chose him as my partner so what does that say about me?

- Feeling a fool for being conned by him.

- Our future relationship: the abuse versus his positive pro-social qualities, e.g. good father to her other children who still love him, good provider.

- Issues of trust, of him or any other man.

- The implications of staying together: the maternal belief in her power and determination to protect her child(ren) now she knows (except she knows nothing about sex offenders).

Common issues for her with extended family, friends, colleagues and/or her local community

Where the sexual abuse is public knowledge the woman may receive some support but she may also be the target of:

- curiosity and gossip

- blame

- derision

- insults such as 'paedophile lover'; verbal and physical threats or actual abuse

- ostracism.

Where the abuse is kept secret the woman may be:

- keeping it secret to survive

- at odds with child care workers who may be encouraging her through their work with the victim to dispense with secrecy
- isolated by the secrecy.

Common issues for her relating to her faith, culture, social values and beliefs

- I made a vow before God that we will stay together until death, come what may.
- If I believe it I shall want to leave him and that will make me a bad Christian/Muslim/Hindu/any other faith.
- If it is true then I and my children could be ostracised from our local faith group and community and we have nowhere else to go. That would damage all my children.
- I was taught to believe in forgiveness. If I cannot forgive then my faith is wrong.
- He is the head of the house and I have been taught to obey.
- If I believe the allegation and act on it and it becomes public knowledge, it will damage my child's marriage prospects.
- The authorities consist mostly of western white people and they won't understand.
- We do not talk about things outside our faith or ethnic group so I can't talk even if I want to.

Common issues for her as a woman

- Surviving the crisis.
- The pain of recognising the problem.
- Secondary victimisation (as a mother/partner, and her exposure to outside agencies and the investigative child protection process).
- Bewilderment, e.g. 'How did this happen?', 'I promised myself that would never happen to my child', 'My child would have told me…'
- Conflicting role demands.
- Loss of autonomy.

- The acceptance of outside intervention (proof that the problem really is that bad).

- Loss of a sense of self as a woman/partner/parent (e.g. her life was not what she thought it to be).

- Poor self-esteem and self-confidence.

- Social isolation (caused by the offender's grooming tactics; caused by her avoidance of family, friends and local community post-disclosure due to the stigma).

- Dealing with bereavement and loss (the loss of the relationship she thought she had with the offender/her child; the actual loss of offender and/or child).

- Possible survivor issues from her own abuse.

- Sexual issues for her (e.g.'Was it because I wasn't good enough sexually?', 'Was it because I wouldn't do that particular sexual act?'; 'What does it say about me? – I chose a child molester/rapist!?').

- Attitudes to men in general.

- Trust/mistrust: 'I'm never going to have another relationship with any man.'

- Practical consequences – single parent, financial consequences, etc.

- Her role at the centre of family life, dealing with the responses of other family members, extended whole family and peers.

- What to tell people?

- Disentangling lies and cover-ups since disclosure to protect her family from hostile outside attitudes: 'What have I said and to whom?'

- Dealing with a possibly hostile community where the abuse is known, or fears that the community may become hostile if they find out (ranging from fears of their children being teased or picked on by other children to fears of being driven out of the family home by hostile crowds 'naming and shaming').

- Possible clinical depression and/or anxiety.

- Coping mechanisms (functional or dysfunctional?).

And at a time when even the strongest, most capable parent is at what is likely to be one of the lowest points in their lives they are confronted by police, social workers and others asking – directly or otherwise – 'Did you know? Are you safe?'

Case example: Angela

Angela was a warm, loving mother who worked as a school nurse and had been married to Jim for nine years. She thought they were a happy family until her six-year-old daughter Kylie gave a partial disclosure that Jim was sexually abusing her. Angela found this hard to believe because Jim was a kind and loving father and husband and she saw nothing to suggest he was a child molester. It was the kind of thing that happened to other people, not to her family. Further details emerged during investigation, which, whilst not giving a complete picture, led her to believe it was true. During one of our sessions as she grasped the full implications of what Jim had done, Angela sobbed that 'it would have been better if he'd ki...', before stopping midsentence, horrified at what she had been about to say. It was obvious that she did not mean literally that it would have been better if he had killed her daughter. In her deep distress she explained that what she meant was that if as a mother your child dies there are accepted social mores and rituals to guide you through the morass of emotions: the love and support of family and friends, encouragement to believe that although you will never forget, time will help to heal. Angela described how her own reaction to the abuse was like a death but that the social stigma of sexual abuse was such that she did not trust herself to talk about it to family, friends or colleagues. She felt isolated, alone and had no idea how to cope with the pain, both in terms of what happened to her daughter and the loss of the man she thought she knew. What she was saying was that where there is a death there is a 'map' toward some kind of recovery and in her situation there was no such map and she had no idea how to cope with her feelings.

Issues for mothers and partners who are survivors of sexual abuse

There can be additional issues for adult survivors. For example, many women in this situation had promised themselves they would never let such abuse happen to their child, they would know if it did and anyway they would make sure their child would tell them. The trouble is this does not take into account the power of the offender in manipulating the child and grooming him or her into compliance and silence. Furthermore, many such women believe they would recognise a sex offender when they see one and would never let him near any of the children. The trouble here is that whilst sex offenders have many things in common every sex offender is different and so will not look at all like her own abuser. Consequently, whatever other reasons she may have for disbelieving that a current partner, close friend or relative is a sex offender can be compounded by her genuine belief that: 'I know sex offenders and he's not like that.'

When assessing mothers and partners in relation to safety and risk for the future we need to consider their reactions and responses within this normal human context.

Other common issues for survivors of sexual abuse

Whilst it is not true in every situation, research (e.g. Kreklewetz and Piotrowski 1998) suggests that a high proportion of adult survivors experienced problems connected with their abuse in their everyday parenting. Rumstein-McKean and Hunsley (2001) observe that adult women survivors experience more relationship problems and more problems in sexual functioning, marital functioning and attachment. They also argue that further research was required into the impact on maternal functioning. However, for a woman in this situation, the suggestion that her child has been sexually abused and/or that her partner or someone close is allegedly a sex offender is not going to make it any easier, all of which can create problems for a survivor in addition to those already described, for example:

- an enhanced sense of guilt that she has failed to protect when she promised herself she would do so

- reliving her own abuse, complete with flashbacks and associated trauma

- the possibility that this may be the first time she has ever spoken of her own abuse with the associated anxiety and possible trauma

- a fear that disclosure of her own history of abuse will be seen as increasing our perception of her as a vulnerable/weak/unsafe mother

- being limited and stuck in defining abuse only in terms of her own experience, which may make her resistant to hearing different information.

How might an offender use this situation to his own advantage? It is a sad fact of life that some sex offenders target women in whom they recognise a vulnerability that they can manipulate to their own advantage. This does not automatically equate to her being a weak, bad or unsafe mother. On the contrary, many survivors have a heightened motivation to protect. But it highlights the need for all these factors to be considered in our assessment of her, not in terms of blame but in terms of focusing subsequent recommendations for intervention to her particular needs.

Do women readily disclose to us any of the above difficulties they may be facing?

The simple answer to this question is no, because other things can get in the way of them doing so. For example:

- *Some women are afraid to tell us.* We ask 'how are you doing?' and she replies that she is 'fine, absolutely fine', when she is not fine at all but fears that if she admits it, it will be interpreted as her being weak and unable to protect. What she is really thinking is 'don't take my children away' even when that is not our intention because she knows child protection professionals have the power to go to the courts to do so.

- *Some women are resistant to hearing new information about the abuse and about why we are concerned.* What this may be is the woman is really thinking 'if I believe all of this then that means it is as bad as for my child as they say it is and I don't want it to be that bad for him/her'.

- *Some women do not tell us because our responses close her down.* The woman says directly or indirectly 'what about me?' because she is all at sea with conflicting thoughts and feelings. She knows she needs help but it is interpreted as her being preoccupied with self-interest when she should be thinking only of the child.

As one competent, loving and caring mother who had been floundering in her ability to cope said to me several months after her assessment: 'If at that time the social worker knew what I was really thinking and feeling she'd have taken all my children away.'

Understanding and working with denial

Denial is defined as: 'An unconscious defence mechanism used to allay anxiety by denying the existence of important conflicts, troublesome impulses, events, actions, or illness' (Farlex Partner Medical Dictionary 2012).

Similarly: 'From a trauma processing perspective, features such as denial, unfocused anger, minimisation of the problem, and ambivalence toward both the alleged victim and abuser should be considered par for the course, rather than evidence of toxic parenting or deep seated psychopathology' (Chaffin 1996, p.113).

None of this is helpful to the child. Parents are not perfect and children pick up on their parent's anxiety at this time. The purpose of assessment is to identify the specific issues at the root of ambivalence, denial or disbelief so that they may be addressed positively and by mutual agreement with the mother/partner through an appropriate intervention plan.

Persistent disbelief and denial

Concern is naturally increased when the woman is confronted with more substantial evidence to support the child's story but still refuses to believe it. However, the same presenting problem can represent different underlying stories, which can either increase or decrease concern. Consider the following.

Case example: Mrs A

A 14-year-old girl tells her teacher that her stepfather is raping her. There is medical evidence of penetration. In assessment interview the mother, Mrs A, continues to disbelieve the allegation.

- When asked why she does not believe it Mrs A said 'she would have told me if he'd done it and she did not (she told the teacher), so it's not true'. Many good and loving parents genuinely believe their child would tell them but in this instance there is medical evidence. What of that?

- Mrs A then moved on to accepting that her daughter had been abused but said it must have been a babysitter who came in some time ago to look after a younger brother. She had heard a rumour that he had been sexually abused and that victims often went on to be abusers. Closer examination showed this did not make sense.

- Mrs A then accepted that her daughter must have had sex with a boy her own age and lied to cover it up. When asked what she thought about 14-year-old girls having sex with boys Mrs A said she considered them to be 'promiscuous sluts, slags, whores'.

- This begged the question put to Mrs A: 'why is it easier for you to think of your daughter as being promiscuous rather than as a victim of sexual abuse?'

This is a case of a woman whose head is firmly buried in the sand and determined to keep it there, with additional concerns about the attitudes to young people, and her daughter in particular, which she chooses to adopt to maintain her denial. If she remains entrenched in this view despite efforts to help then she is clearly potentially unsafe as a protecting parent.

Case example: Ms C

Ms C's husband was alleged to have abused young children outside the family. There was a decision not to prosecute due to lack of viable evidence but the allegation was believed by the child protection agencies and Mr C was told to leave the family home, which he did. He was granted supervised contact with his children, which he accepted and at which Ms C was present. Ms C was recognised as a good and loving mother but a difficult woman to work with: she had a fiery personality and constantly railed against the intrusion of the authorities into the lives of herself and her children. She was furious with her husband for his offending but considered herself capable of protecting her children. This was doubted by the authorities because of her insistence that she continue her relationship with her husband although she insisted she only did so away from the family home in order not to break conditions imposed by social services.

On balance it was decided she could not be trusted and the case was successfully taken to court for a Care Order. She subsequently arrived for one joint clinical session with her husband dressed provocatively as what she described as 'a tart', which was totally out of character. Her argument was that if the authorities were going to make her feel like a tart by making her sleep with her husband away from the family home, it was reasonable that she should dress like one. On one level her act of defiance was seen as a further sign that she could not be trusted, but on a human level her behaviour could be seen to be congruent with her situation. Ms C caused further consternation by continuing to fight the Care Order tooth and nail. However on the day it was finally revoked, on leaving the court she told her husband the relationship was over and she never wanted to see him again. Her argument was that she always believed the sexual allegations against him but she wanted it to be *her* decision to tell him to leave and not something to be decided by other people.

Conclusions

Whatever the woman's position on the spectrum of knowing – not knowing and whatever her responses may be to disclosure and allegations, it is important that we consider it in the context of what the known or suspected offender is doing to groom her into maintaining her position of disbelief or her reluctance to accept any allegations. That does not make the woman weak or stupid but reflects offenders' ability to manipulate and deceive even the most intelligent and capable mother/partner. The dilemma for those of us working in child protection is that any effort to point this out to the woman is likely to be met with cries of indignation from the offender and accusations that *we* are the manipulative ones who are trying to turn the woman against *him*. These issues are addressed in more detail in Chapters 6 and 12.

References

Denial (n.d.) *Farlex Partner Medical Dictionary*. Available at http://medical-dictionary.thefreedictionary.com/denial, accessed on 2 February 2016.

Chaffin, M. (1996) 'Working with unsupportive mothers in incest cases.' 12th Annual Midwest Conference on Child Sexual Abuse and Incest, Madison, WI.

Jonker, I. (1999) Personal communication: Ruud Bullens, 2001. Clinical Psychologist and Psychotherapist. De Waag Amsterdam and Diagnostic Expertise Centre (DEC). Amsterdam.

Kreklewetz, C.M. and Piotrowski, C.C. (1998) 'Incest survivor: protecting the next generation.' *Child Abuse and Neglect 22*, 12, 1305–1312.

Monck, E. (1996) *Child Sexual Abuse: A Descriptive Study and Treatment*. Studies in Child Protection. London: HMSO.

Rumstein-McKean, O. and Hunsley, J. (2001) 'Interpersonal and family functioning of female survivors of childhood sexual abuse.' *Clinical Psychology Review 21*, 3, 471–490.

Salter, A.C. (1995) *Transforming Trauma: A Guide to Understanding and Treating Adult Survivors of Child Sexual Abuse*. Thousand Oaks, CA: Sage.

Still, J. (1995) 'An Overview.' In *Rebuilding Families After Abuse*. Papers from conference at the National Children's Bureau 1995. London: NCB.

Still, J., Faux, M. and Wilson, C. (2001) *The Thames Valley Partner's Programme. The Home Office, London*. Crown Copyright 2001.

CHAPTER 3

THE ADDITION OF THE OFFENDER PERSPECTIVE TO OUR UNDERSTANDING OF MOTHERS AND PARTNERS

In this chapter we look at why we need to understand about sex offenders, illustrated by a long case example.

Sex offenders commonly stay in silence or denial or, at best, minimise the extent of their offending for their self-preservation. Child protection professionals have therefore had to develop an approach to assessing alleged and known child sexual abuse in an information vacuum and to devise other ways of making sense of it. This is a genuine difficulty and goes back to the systemic problem that although most cases of child sexual abuse are dealt with through the child protection system, most of the training on understanding and interviewing men who sexually abuse children and young people is focused on those working within the criminal justice system. This leaves social workers and others in the unenviable position of being at a considerable disadvantage when expected to evaluate situations involving offenders who are highly adept at deceit and manipulation. Also, the absence of a good working knowledge about sex offenders and how they operate places an over-reliance for children's protection on the mother/partner who also generally lacks good information and on children having to learn how to protect themselves.

However, all is not lost. A good working knowledge of sex offenders provides us with another tool to add to our existing skills by helping piece together how it was for this particular mother, child and family. As we shall see in Chapter 4, whilst men who sexually abuse a child or young person have some things in common every offender is different, therefore the experience of every woman, child and family is unique to them.

The benefits of applying offender knowledge

It helps provide the answers to important questions, for example:

- Did she know and is she safe? (This is discussed in Chapter 2).

- How did she not know?

- Why can she not totally believe or accept it?

- If she believes the child and rejects the (alleged) offender how much can we trust that to continue?

- If she is still supporting the known or alleged offender – why?

- If she believes the allegations and rejects the offender can we trust that response?

It helps us to understand the nature of her relationship with her child and how it became that way. For the child it can help answer the questions: 'Did my mother know? How could she not have known? Why didn't she do something?'

Knowledge empowers the mother by enabling her to gain a better understanding of her situation – 'how did he do that to me?' – and to explore other important questions, for example:

- How did he do what he did?

- What did he do to enable him to abuse and prevent suspicion or discovery?

- What effect did that have on the child, the mother/partner and other family members?

- Is he still manipulating the situation? If so, how?

- If there is no longer contact with him, how is his legacy still affecting everyone's responses to this painful situation?

Knowledge of sex offenders, both in general and in particular:

- provides a basis for assessment and intervention, which places responsibility with the adult who committed the abuse, or is suspected of the abuse, whilst still enabling us to consider the mother/partner's failure to protect

- enables mothers, partners, agencies and family courts to make a more accurate risk assessment and more informed decisions about child safety

- enables child protection plans and conditions of contact or residence to be more focused and relevant to the individual situation

- enables the creation of an individualised intervention programme that relates more to the specific type of sexual risk

- all of which ensures an appropriate use of resources.

How do we know this approach works?

This approach combines experience in working with children and families and with sex offenders. It has been used at expert witness level in specialist work for social service departments and family courts throughout the UK. It formed the basis for the Partners' Programme (Still, Faux and Wilson 2001) devised for the Home Office to run in tandem with the new sex offender treatment programmes across the south of England and was developed further as part of an integrated mother and child intervention programme for Essex County Council.

Why we might not want to apply the offender perspective

Before looking at a case example to show how this approach does work, let us consider what kind of attitudes might get in the way.

'Sex offenders are nothing to do with me. I work with children and families'

This is a view often heard from social workers and other child protection workers and is usually based on an understandable revulsion at what sex offenders do, particularly when they are working with the trauma and distress caused by the abuse. However, we need to manage those feelings so they do not impede the task in hand; appropriate supervision and support are vital to doing this work effectively and maintaining one's own equilibrium. If that is not possible then it should be possible for any individual to consider whether this particular kind of work is right for them and whether they could use their professional training and skills to good effect elsewhere, without any inappropriate negative consequences from management.

'It would be unethical and break confidentiality'

Some professionals have argued they would be betraying the child to 'get involved' with anything connected to the offender beyond the information acquired during investigation. Others have argued, both from the probation and the social work side, that it would be a breach of confidentiality to share any information, for example, if the offender is in therapy. However, if we are to make the best decisions in the best interests of the child, when doing any assessment with child or family we need as much information as we can acquire.

Note: it should be clear that this traffic of information is one way. Whilst we need to have maximum information about the known or suspected offender, he does not have the right for reciprocal information about the child, for example, from the child's therapy, which could then be used to reinforce abusive fantasy and masturbatory practices and to continue to exercise control.

'They're all the same' – the difficulties of over generalised views of sex offenders

With sex offenders giving minimum information and in the absence of offender-specific training, child protection workers can feel there is no option but to 'play safe' in order to protect the child and so take a hardened view of the known or suspected offender. Commonly held assumptions include, for example, 'if he's done this he must have done that' and 'if he hasn't done it yet he probably will do it in the future', which may not be true. This can lead to difficult and sometimes inappropriately harsh decisions that can impact negatively on the child, especially when there are other strong arguments in favour of a known or suspected offender remaining in contact or in some family situation, in the interests of the child(ren).

An over-emphasis on what he did, rather than how he did it

With the need to consider whether or not to go to law, whether criminal or civil, there can often be a preoccupation with questions about 'what did he do, when and for how long?' But sexual abuse is not an act or an incident but the corruption of a relationship. Failure to look at *how* he did it can deprive us of valuable information in understanding the child, the mother and the whole family dynamics and their consequences.

Most sex offenders are adept at spotting these vulnerabilities as well as lack of knowledge. As one sex offender put it to me: 'social workers know a lot about kids and families but they don't know anything about me', thus giving him both the ammunition and the confidence with which to groom and manipulate the worker to his own advantage.

Why this is important

- Whilst sex offenders have many things in common every sex offender is different, therefore every mother, partner and carer's experience is unique to them.

- A key question is what is known about the offender: not only what did he do but, as importantly, *what kind* of an offender is he, which informs *how* did he do it?

How does it work?

Consider the following case example and the extent to which the offender perspective is relevant. The family dynamics post-disclosure of Family B are similar to those commonly seen in cases of child sexual abuse.

EXERCISE
FAMILY B

Alex and Annie had been married for 18 years. Alex sexually abused his daughter Suzy from the age of 12 to 14 including rape. He denied the abuse but was charged, convicted and sent to prison. On his release Alex was referred to a sex offender treatment programme, the first part of which was a detailed specialist risk assessment. While Alex was in prison social workers worked with Suzy, her mother, Annie, and three younger half siblings, none of whom said they had been abused by Alex and who described him as a kind and loving father. Although this support eased some of the family tensions many of the post-disclosure relationship dynamics persisted.

At first Annie had difficulty believing the allegations but came to do so and was supportive of her daughter. However, their previously good relationship had already become more distant and although mother and daughter now wanted things to be better the improvement was marginal. Suzy was dealing with the trauma of the abuse, the investigation and her father's incarceration. Individual therapy for Suzy helped but she persisted in believing the abuse was her fault, despite social workers telling her it was not, with the associated negative impact on her. Annie continued to feel guilty for failing to protect and Suzy was angry with her mother for not protecting her and, even worse, as the abuse happened in the family home she could not believe her mother did not know. The younger children mourned the loss of their father and refused to believe he did it. They either blamed Suzie angrily for attention seeking and making it up, or said that if he did do it, it must have been her fault.

As someone who had always been what she thought to be a good and conscientious mother, Annie had difficulty struggling both with the involvement of outside agencies and as a now single parent of four children. In addition, she was trying to cope with the many conflicts and tensions that arose whilst trying to support Suzy and the other children at the same time as coming to terms with what her husband had done, as well as his subsequent departure.

When Alex was released from prison the younger three siblings, to whom he had otherwise always been a good father, wanted contact and an assessment was required of Annie as to her ability to protect the children.

Questions

- How and why did the family dynamics present in this way?
- Had the family reached its optimum level of healing?
- Or was work blocked and if so, why in these specific areas?
- What would help move things on?

Applying offender knowledge

Let us re-examine the family dynamics in the context of what we know from Alex's pre-therapy assessment: what he did and how he did it. Although Alex was a strict father he was also fun and there was natural sibling rivalry for his attention. However, Suzy was always 'Daddy's favourite', thus incurring the jealousy and resentment of her siblings, which led to arguments and them ganging up on her. Alex always stepped in to rescue her. Unbeknown to anyone, Alex had been aroused specifically to Suzy since she was eight. When she reached puberty he wanted to put his fantasies into practice. He was a seductive type of offender, building on his established role of loving father. He developed distorted thinking to justify and excuse it: 'it would not have been OK when Suzy was younger but it's OK now'; 'it's because I love her'; 'we've always been close, she loves me, she'll want it too'; 'I'd never hurt her'.

How did he get Suzy alone in an overcrowded family home? As the eldest, Suzy was the first to lose interest in after school clubs and so every day, late afternoon she and her father were at home on their own. Mother was at work. When they are alone in the house he suggested 'making love' because that is what fathers do when they love their daughters so much. She said no and thought she must have misheard. Alex did not pursue it further but Suzy noticed that when her siblings picked on her, her father no longer came to her rescue. She felt rejected and wanted 'loving Dad' back. She put two and two together and so *she* went to *him* and said yes. He declined, saying he did not want her to do anything she did not want to. The third time she 'asked' he said OK. Suzy did not want to do it but was relieved to have loving Dad back, hoping it was a one-off. But Alex wanted more. Realising the tactic worked he started subtly to provoke sibling arguments against Suzy whilst continuing to withdraw his support. Suzy was miserable and isolated. Alex won. Suzy was trapped in a cycle of abuse for the next two years until she told a friend, who reported it.

While Alex was in prison Suzy's therapy was blocked because when social workers told her she was not to blame she did not believe it. All she remembered was that *she* asked *him* for sex – repeatedly. She did not know or understand how her father had groomed her via an elaborate cat and mouse game.

The impact on the mother–daughter relationship

Whilst some sex offenders have low and occasional illegal arousal, Alex had high levels of arousal and a need to abuse on a regular basis, so needed Annie out of the house on a regular and predictable basis when he knew he could offend. Alex worked an early shift so he persuaded Annie to take a late afternoon/evening cleaning job while he did the after school child care. This meant he was seen by others as a supportive husband and father.

Also, although Alex knew Annie was a strong, competent, capable woman he led Suzy to believe she could not tell her mother because her mother was weak and vulnerable, that she would not be able to cope and it would kill her if he were sent to prison. (It did not. She coped admirably.)

When Suzy was asked what impact this had on her relationship with her mother, Suzy said she loved her mother but began to resent her to the extent of seeing her almost as a co-abuser because 'if my mother wasn't so pathetic, I could tell her'. Mother therefore went up in Suzy's mind in terms of culpability and down in terms of respect as a parent. This was exacerbated by Suzy's sense of guilt about having 'asked' her mother's husband for sex, although Suzy also thought her mother must have really known what was going on. When asked why she thought this, she said 'because she's Mum and married to Dad' and clearly considered it to be a silly question.

Sibling responses

A similar dynamic was true for Suzy's siblings. Any message from the social workers that the abuse was not their sister's fault had limited impact when counteracted deliberately by subtle or overt messages from Alex to the contrary, especially when they desperately wanted to still see him as a wonderful father.

Initial outcome

In the absence of information for the family and social workers alike as to how Alex manipulated the whole family situation, work with Suzy, Annie and the siblings remained blocked and an undercurrent of blame, resentment and recrimination persisted.

Assessment of Annie: the bonus of knowing what Alex did and how he did it

- The case illustrates the potential complexity of the nature of grooming.

- In assessing Annie a major bonus was to apply knowledge of the 'cat and mouse' entrapment of Suzy and the manipulation of his wife and children in order to be able to abuse without discovery in an otherwise unbelievable situation.

- For Suzy, it unblocked her sense of guilt and blame, having been unaware of the complicated lengths her stepfather went to in grooming her for abuse.

- It provided the foundation for progress on the mother–daughter relationship, which both wanted so much.

- It enabled recommendations to be made by the social worker as to the specific nature of intervention that would empower Annie to protect and the type of focused intervention that could address all these subsequent issues relevant to this particular set of circumstances, both for Annie and Suzy and for other family members.

- It provided Annie with information on which to make her own decisions for the future in relation to Alex and laid the foundation for a genuine partnership between Annie, the family and the child protection workers.

- It informed the Care Plan by pinning down more specifically how potential risk should be managed should contact between Alex and the younger children be agreed and avoiding limited resources being wrongly allocated. For example, if it were considered to be in the younger siblings' best interests to have contact with their father it would be usual for such contact to be supervised by a social work assistant or someone similar.

However, this would be a costly exercise and unsustainable in the longer term. It would also give the message to the children that their mother cannot be trusted and is 'unsafe'. Conversely, it would be more empowering for Annie to be able to safely monitor the situation herself. Her ability to do so would be enhanced by having more knowledge and insight into Alex's pattern and style of offending so that she would know not just the 'what' but also the 'how' she was protecting them from.

The social worker's response

Memorably, the social worker involved expressed the wish that during the assessment of Annie there had been more insight into the nature of Alex's offending from the beginning because it would have informed the nature of subsequent intervention and put the family on a positive healing course sooner. Resource-wise, it would have diminished the length of time she was involved with the family. A subsequent time-limited action plan involved one-to-ones with Suzy using the information about Alex's offending profile, dual sessions with mother and daughter and a small number of carefully managed family sessions to address the wider dynamic and to allow a safe outlet for individual and collective feelings.

Other feedback comments from social workers in training have commonly included comments such as 'a light bulb went on in my head' and that without adding the offender perspective it was 'like working blindfold with both hands tied behind my back'.

Conclusions

Where a known or suspected offender has been formally assessed and/or is attending a therapy programme, child protection workers should seek out all information regarding the 'how', as well as the 'what' and the 'when'.

In cases of allegation or suspicion where there is no conviction and/or no formal assessment available, we can apply general but informed knowledge of sex offenders to inform what questions we pursue with the mother or partner and to help us understand her responses.

References

Still, J., Faux, M. and Wilson, C. (2001) *The Thames Valley Partner's Programme*. The Home Office, London. Crown Copyright 2001.

CHAPTER 4

UNDERSTANDING SEX OFFENDERS
HOW MUCH DO WE NEED TO KNOW AND WHY?

The good news is that it is not necessary for us to know everything in the same way as do probation officers, police investigators and those working in the criminal justice system: the aim of this book is to provide sufficient information about sex offenders and paedophiles to inform work in assessment and intervention with mothers and partners, with the additional benefit of informing our work with children and families. The purpose of this chapter is to provide:

- general guidelines for understanding sex offenders and paedophiles and our use of terminology

- a basic overview of how an understanding of sex offenders and paedophiles has developed

- a consideration of how an understanding of sex offenders has informed assessment of sexual risk, sex offender therapy and our understanding of internet offenders.

Some general guidelines
What is meant by the term 'child sexual abuse'?
There have been many definitions over the years as knowledge, experience and practice have evolved. The following definition was provided by HM Government in 2010:

Sexual abuse involves forcing or enticing a child or young person to take part in sexual activities, not necessarily involving a high level of violence, whether or not the child is aware of what is happening. The activities may involve physical contact, including assault by penetration (e.g. rape, or oral sex) or non-penetrative acts such as masturbation, kissing, rubbing and touching outside of clothing. They may also include non-contact activities, such as involving children in looking at, or in the production of, sexual images, watching sexual activities, encouraging children to behave in sexually inappropriate ways, or grooming a child in preparation for abuse (including via the internet). Sexual abuse is not solely perpetrated by adult males. Women can also commit acts of sexual abuse, as can other children. (HM Government 2010, p.38)

This incorporates internet offences and 'grooming' introduced in the UK in the Sex Offences Act 2003, where the age of consent is 16.

Sex offenders who come from ethnic minorities often argue that in their country of origin and/or faith and culture some of these activities would be legal. That may or may not be true, depending on the activity and the age of the child. However, it is the law of the land in which they reside which applies.

Dispelling some common offender myths and stereotypes

Sex offenders are not all the same.

- Some offenders have abused one child and some many.

- Some have a pattern of abusing a child as a 'one-off' then move.

- Some abuse the same child over a long period of time.

- Some do both.

- Some are risk takers, others are not.

- Levels of arousal vary (from occasional to more persistent).

- Patterns of arousal vary: only to children, only to one child, arousal to adults and to children.

- There are different 'styles' of offending, from seductive to physically threatening and violent.

- Some offenders are thinking about offending much of the time but many are not.

- Some drift in and out of offending at different times in their lives.

Using accurate labels and terminology

It is important to use accurate terminology otherwise our credibility is undermined. Also, we need to be clear about what other people mean when they use specific words otherwise we may think we are all talking about the same thing when we are not (see Chapter 10). Whilst there are many different academic definitions, the following are useful guidelines for child protection professionals based on everyday practice.

Paedophile

This term is in popular usage to describe any adult who is known or suspected of having sexually abused a child or young person under the age of 16 years. However, it should be noted that as a medical term there has been an emphasis on paedophilia relating, for example, to 'a paraphilia in which an adult has recurrent, intense sexual urges or sexually arousing fantasies of engaging or repeatedly engages in sexual activity with a prepubertal child' (Dorland's Medical Dictionary for Health Consumers 2007).

Sex offender/child molester

The above definition helps us also to differentiate between two different general patterns of offending. For example, in sex offender literature the term paedophile is commonly applied to an offender, for example, who is highly aroused to a particular type of child or young person outside the home either within a local community or the offender's work place and who has maybe hundreds of victims over a long period of time. However, as a general rule it is not true of most adults who abuse children within a family context. Whilst the latter may, for example, have intense and recurring fantasies about a specific child and go on to abuse that child multiple times, in many cases his illegal sexual fantasies are intermittent, occasional and even rare, along with his acts of abuse. It is more appropriate to describe such a person as a *sex offender* or, as in American literature, a *child molester*.

Hebephile

This term relates to those who target adolescents as opposed to pre-pubescent children. It is in less common everyday usage and is most commonly used in research literature on offenders where there is a need to have a more detailed classification for academic and/or statistical purposes.

For example, if we relate this to our case of Family B in Chapter 3, Alex was not a paedophile but an offender or child molester. In terms of direct sexual risk, whilst the younger siblings were adversely affected by the aftermath of their father's abuse of their older sister, younger daughters were not at risk of direct sexual abuse by their father because he was obsessively fixated specifically on Suzy. Similarly, sons were not at direct sexual risk because Alex's sexual arousal was clearly to a pubescent girl and there was no indication of arousal to boys. However, consideration was clearly necessary as to the impact of Alex's attitudes and beliefs about sex and sexuality on his sons and other daughters.

Internet sex offender

With the arrival of child sexual abuse via the internet there is a further distinction between *contact and non-contact sexual offenders,* with some but not all crossing over between the two (see Chapter 4).

There is no single profile of a sex offender

It is important to note that there is no such thing as 'a sex offender profile' because whilst there are some things that are known to be common among men who sexually abuse children, every sex offender is different. This means also that the experience of every non-offending mother/partner, child and family is unique to them.

Defining the word 'risk'

When we say someone is or is not a risk this word means different things to different people depending on whether they work with children and families or within the criminal justice system and also how risk is assessed (see Chapter 10).

Risk of likely significant harm

This is the legal definition used by child protection agencies and family courts.

Risk of reoffending

This is a term used primarily by child protection agencies meaning 'will he do it again?' When related to alleged or suspected abuse this term is more difficult: we talk about 'will he do it again?' when actually we do not know for sure that he has already offended, which is a value judgement based on a belief of the child and other presenting information.

Risk of recidivism

This is how risk is assessed by those working in the criminal justice system with convicted sex offenders and when used by police, probation officers, psychologists and therapists on sex offender treatment programmes who use assessment protocols based on convicted sex offenders, the term 'reoffend' usually relates specifically to the risk of recidivism, that is, not only reoffending but being caught and being reconvicted (see Chapter 8).

The limitations of psychometric testing

Whilst it would be wonderful if there were one psychometric test that could tell us whether someone is or is not a sex offender that is not the case. Psychometric testing is of great value when working with sex offenders but its primary value is in testing an individual's progress in treatment and complex batteries of psychometric tests have been devised and researched specifically for that purpose.

What research and theory into sex offenders tells us: a basic overview

It is not the purpose of this book to address offender assessment in detail but to look at which are the most helpful models to apply when assessing and working with non-offending mothers and partners. In order to put that in context, let us consider briefly the overall development of research into adult males who sexually abuse children and young people and its impact on practice.

A note of caution

When looking at the research it is important to be aware of the following:

- Research is based necessarily on convicted offenders as information would not be forthcoming from those who have abused but not been convicted, because that would require a degree of admission. Caution must therefore be used when applying research to suspected or alleged perpetrators.

- Such research is helpful in identifying trends, not individuals. Therefore whilst there may be, for example, a 60 per cent chance of something being the case, there is also a 30 per cent chance of the same thing not being the case.

- Research into internet offending is in its infancy and studies can produce a range of conflicting results depending on the nature of the sample group and the type of methodology used.

However, taking that into consideration, the following are examples of progress made that have led to some of the key theoretical models, which have been applied widely in practice by those working with sex offenders and paedophiles.

Some common themes

Since the late 1980s there has been a proliferation of research into the subject of paedophiles, sex offenders and child molesters, much of which has focused on looking at contributory factors to the development of deviant and abusive sexuality and factors that can assist in risk assessment. Common themes arising from this research include issues such as negative developmental experiences in childhood, factors such as loneliness, problems with intimacy, attachment issues, low self-esteem, poor social skills, poor emotional control mechanisms, an over-identification with children, the development of deviant sexual interests and distorted thinking.

Some examples of models that have informed practice for those working with sex offenders

The 1980s saw researchers and practitioners trying to understand the *process* of child sexual abuse and produced two important theoretical models: Finkelhor's *'four preconditions'* to offending (1984, 1986) and Wolf's concept of *'cycles'* of offending (1984). This was further refined by Eldridge (1998) to differentiate between inhibited, continuous and short circuit cycles.

There have been several approaches to bring together the various strands of research into *one integrated theoretical model*, for example, Marshall and Barbaree (1990), Marshall and Marshall (2002) and Ward and Beech (2006). Ward and Beech (2004) also provided an integrated theory *linking roots of offending to risk assessment.*

Hall and Hirschman (1991) aimed to capture *different types of offenders abusing children* by looking at combinations of the individual's physiological state, distorted thinking, emotional self-management and problematic personality traits.

Hudson, Ward and McCormack (1999) advanced the early work of Finkelhor, Wolf, Hall and Hirschman and Marshall and Barbaree and highlighted the concept of *different routes into sexual offending.* Ward and Siegert (2002) took this *pathways* model further and produced a model based on the combination of early experiences, biological factors and cultural influences that could lead to the development of deviant sexual preference, problems with intimacy, inappropriate emotions and/or distorted thinking. They differentiated between historic (distal) factors in the longer term lead up to offending and the more immediate (proximal) factors that tip an individual into actual offending.

Thornton (2002) looked at *factors that could change* with clinical intervention and reduce risk of reoffending, informing both risk assessment and therapy needs. He divided these into four domains: deviant sexual interest, distorted attitudes, poor socio-affective functioning leading to difficulty in forming emotional intimacy with adults and an excessive emotional over-identification with adults and self-management problems.

There has been considerable interest both in theory and practice in the areas of *cognitive distortions,* that is, the distorted thinking that enables a sex offender to do what he does (e.g. Gannon, Ward and Collie 2007).

Ward and Keenan (1999) identified a series of common *schema* of over-arching core beliefs that underpin the distorted thinking connected with child sexual abuse. These were identified most commonly as: a) children being seen as sexual beings b) notions of entitlement c) notions of a dangerous world d) sex being seen as uncontrollable and e) a distorted view of the nature of harm (Beech and Mann 2002).

Development of risk assessment

There are different kinds of risk assessment, each with their own merits and emphasis. The two most common are:

- *structured clinical risk assessments,* which are based on the assessor's own judgement drawing on research and theoretical models to consider the extent to which there may or may not be combinations of factors that cause concern

- *actuarial risk assessments,* which are based on the use of research findings to formulate models based on predictor variables and statistical probability to calculate the risk of recidivism, i.e. the risk of re-offending and being reconvicted, in terms of low, medium and high risk (Craig, Browne and Beech 2008).

These are discussed further in Chapter 10 in relation to the need for greater inter-agency cooperation and understanding.

Development of therapy

The concepts of preconditions to offending, cycles of offending and pathways to offending, as previously described, have all played a role in treatment programmes for sex offenders.

Eldridge (1998) developed a model for treatment of sex offenders based on *preventing relapse* into offending. Thornton (2002) looked at *factors that could change* with clinical intervention and reduce risk of reoffending, informing both risk assessment and therapy needs. He divided these into four domains: deviant sexual interest, distorted attitudes, poor social functioning leading to difficulty in forming emotional intimacy with adults and an excessive emotional over-identification with adults and self-management problems. Ward, Mann and Gannon (2007) produced the *'Good Lives'* model of rehabilitation, which suggested how basic human needs were being met through abusive sexuality and how those needs can be met in a positive, non-abusive way.

The most favoured clinical approach to treating sex offenders is cognitive behavioural therapy (CBT) because it focuses on help not just with 'what did you do and how did you do it?' but also on identifying the combinations of thoughts, feelings and behaviours that lead to offending.

Sexual offending and the internet

The possession and/or distribution of child pornography, including images of sex with children, have been illegal since 1988. Online sexual offending has presented new challenges, including examination as to the extent to which it is similar to or different from non-internet offending and research into this area is still in its infancy, relatively speaking.

Note: There have rightly been objections to the use of the term 'pornography' in this context as it is clearly a form of child abuse, in the same way as it is wrong to refer to children and young people who have been sexually abused as prostitutes. However, as this is the language commonly used in the international research and literature I will use the term pornography as that point of reference.

Not all internet abuse is about indecent images. For example, some offenders download stories rather than indecent images. Some engage in such activities as a solitary exercise and some will share them with likeminded people. Taylor and Quayle (2003) identified at least six categories of internet offences, of which two involve contact sexual abuse:

- downloading and possessing child pornography

- trading child pornographic material

- distributing child pornographic material

- engaging with seduction of children via the internet

- producing child pornographic material.

There have been numerous attempts to categorise different types of individuals using the internet to access child pornography. Elliott and Beech (2009) identified several such theories (e.g. Krone 2004; Lanning 2001; Sullivan and Beech 2003). Elliott and Beech (2009) summarise them broadly as comprising four groups:

- *periodically prurient* offenders, consisting of those who do so impulsively or out of a general curiosity, for whom this behaviour is sporadic and potentially part of a broader interest in pornography that may not be related to a specific sexual interest in children

- *fantasy-only* offenders, that is those who access/trade images to fuel a sexual interest in children and who have no *known* history of contact sexual offending (e.g. Osborn and Beech 2006; Webb, Craisatti and Keen 2007)

- *direct victimisation* offenders, consisting of those using online technology as part of a larger pattern of contact and non-contact sexual offending, including child pornography and the grooming of children online to enable contact sexual offences (Krone 2004)

- *commercial exploitation* offenders, consisting of the criminally-minded who produce or trade images to make money (Lanning 2001).

Crossover between contact and non-contact sexual offenders

As we saw in Chapter 4 not all individuals who view indecent images of children go on to direct victimisation. Research has found a particular link with issues relating to avoidance of intimacy, a lack of empathy and a lack of social skills and emotional competency in making adult relationships (Elliott and Beech 2009). The internet can meet these unmet needs from the privacy and comfort of a person's own home.

What every mother, partner and child protection professional working with this problem wants to know, is what the chances are of an individual who has accessed indecent sexual images of children going on to engage in contact sexual offending. There are conflicting findings. For example, whilst one study (Middleton 2003) found 86 per cent of a sample of UK child molesters admitted to using pornography prior to offending, another study (Gallagher *et al.* 2006) found that only approximately 7 per cent of offenders investigated for the possession of pornography were also known to have sexually abused children. Furthermore, child pornography has also been found not to be a predictor of risk for sexual reconviction (Hanson and Bussiere 1998; Hanson and Morton-Bourgon 2005). Calder (2004) and Sullivan and Beech (2003) argue that there is no suggestion that an individual who views indecent images of children will automatically engage in contact sexual offences. However, the authors emphasise that does not diminish the seriousness of viewing images, which in itself is an abuse of those children.

Overall there appears to be recognition that there can be a combination of factors such as masturbatory fantasy, cognitive distortions and other factors which can raise or diminish risk of crossover to contact offending. Others argue that more work is needed in helping us to understand further the range of different types of internet offenders (Beech, Elliott, Birgden and Findlater 2008).

Conclusions

Whilst all the above are important areas of understanding sex offenders, what is needed specifically when working with mothers and partners is a simple model that helps us to understand *how* he did what he did and the implications for mother, child and family. In the next chapter we will look at two such models and why they are best suited to our purpose.

References

Beech, A.R., Elliott, I.A., Birgden, A., Findlater, D. (2008) 'The internet and child sexual offending: A criminological review.' *Aggression and Violent Behavior 13*, 216–228.

Beech, A.R. and Mann, R.E. (2002) 'Recent Developments in the Treatment of Sexual Offenders.' In J. McGuire (ed.) *Offender Rehabilitation: Effective Programs and Policies to Reduce Reoffending.* Chichester: Wiley.

Calder, M.C. (2004) 'The Internet: Potential, Problems and Pathways to Hands-on Sexual Offending.' In M.C. Calder (ed.) *Child Sexual Abuse and the Internet: Tackling the New Frontier.* Lyme Regis: Russell House.

Craig, L.A., Browne, K.D. and Beech, A.R. (2008) *Assessing Risk in Sex Offenders: A Practitioner's Guide.* Chichester: Wiley.

Eldridge, H.J. (1998) *Maintaining Change: A Personal Relapse Prevention Manual.* Thousand Oaks, CA: Sage.

Elliot, I.A. and Beech, A.R. (2009) 'Understanding online child pornography use: Applying sexual offense theory to internet offenders.' *Aggression and Violent Behaviour 14*, 3 180–193.

Finkelhor, D. (1984) *Child Sexual Abuse: New Theory and Research.* New York: Free Press.

Finkelhor, D. (1986) *A Sourcebook on Child Sexual Abuse.* Beverley Hills, CA: Sage.

Gallagher, B., Fraser, C., Christmann, K. and Hodgson, B. (2006) *International and Internet Child Sexual Abuse and Exploitation: Nuffield Foundation Research Project Report.* Huddersfield: University of Huddersfield, Centre for Applied Childhood Studies.

Gannon, T., Ward, T. and Collie, R. (2007) 'Cognitive distortions of child molesters.' *Aggression and Violent Behaviour 12*, 402–416.

Hall, G.C.N. and Hirschman, R. (1991) 'Towards a theory of sexual aggression: A quadripartite model.' *Journal of Consulting and Clinical Psychology 55*, 662–669.

Hanson, R.K. and Bussiere, M.T. (1998) 'Predicting relapse: A meta-analysis of sexual offender recidivism studies.' *Journal of Consulting and Clinical Psychology 66*, 2, 348–362.

Hanson, R.K. and Morton-Bourgon, K.E. (2005) 'The characteristics of persistent sexual offenders: A meta-analysis of recidivism studies.' *Journal of Consulting and Clinical Psychology 73*, 1154–1163.

HM Government (2010) *Working Together to Safeguard Children.* London: Stationary Office.

Hudson, S.M., Ward, T. and McCormack, J.C. (1999) 'Offense pathways in sexual offenders.' *Journal of Interpersonal Violence 14*, 8, 779–798.

Krone, T. (2004) 'A typology of online child pornography offending.' *Trends and Issues in Crime and Criminal Justice 279*, 1–6.

Lanning, K.V. (2001) *Child Molesters: A Behavioral Analysis*, 4th edn. Arlington, VA: National Center for Missing and Exploited Children. Available at www.missingkids.com/en_US/publications/NC70.pdf, accessed on 21 January 2016.

Marshall, W.L. and Barbaree, H.E. (1990) 'An Integrated Theory of the Etiology of Sexual Offending.' In W.L. Marshall, D.R. Laws and H.E. Barbaree (eds) *Handbook of the Etiology of Sexual Assault: Issues, Theories and Treatment of the Offender.* New York: Plenum.

Marshall, W.L. and Marshall, L.E. (2002) 'The origins of sexual offending.' *Trauma, Violence, and Abuse: A Review Journal 1*, 250–263.

Middleton, D. (2003) *Assessment of Individuals Convicted of Child Pornography Offences.* National Probation Service Circular 14/2003. London: Home Office.

Osborn, J. and Beech, A.R. (2006) 'The Suitability of Risk Matrix 2000 for Use with Internet Sex Offenders.' Unpublished masters thesis, University of Birmingham, UK.

Pedophilia (2007) Dorland's Medical Dictionary for Health Consumers. Saunders, Elsevier. Available at http://medical-dictionary.thefreedictionary.com/pedophilia, accessed on 16 February 2016.

Sullivan, J. and Beech, A.R. (2003) 'Are Collectors of Child Abuse Images a Risk to Children?' In A. MacVean and P. Spindler (eds) *Policing Paedophiles on the Internet.* London: The New Police Bookshop.

Taylor, M. and Quayle, E. (2003) *Child Pornography: An Internet Crime.* London: Routledge.

Thornton, D. (2002) 'Constructing and testing a framework for dynamic risk assessment.' *Sexual Abuse: A Journal of Research and Treatment 14*, 2, 139–153.

Ward, T. and Beech, A.R. (2004) 'The Integration of etiology and risk in sexual offenders: A theoretical framework.' *Journal of Aggression and Violent Behaviour 10*, 31–63.

Ward, T. and Beech, A.R. (2006) 'An integrated theory of sex offending.' *Aggression and Violent Behaviour 11*, 44–63.

Ward, T. and Keenan, T. (1999) 'Child molesters' implicit theories.' *Journal of Interpersonal Violence 14*, 821–838.

Ward, T. and Siegert, R.J. (2002) 'Towards a comprehensive theory of child sexual abuse: A theory knitting perspective.' *Psychology, Crime and Law 8*, 4, 319–351.

Ward, T., Mann, R. and Gannon, T.A. (2007) 'The good lives model of rehabilitation of offenders: Clinical implications.' *Aggression and Violent Behavior 12*, 2, 87–107.

Webb, L., Craisatti, J. and Keen, S. (2007) 'Characteristics of internet child pornography offenders: A comparison with child molesters.' *Sexual Abuse: A Journal of Research and Treatment 19*, 4, 449–465.

Wolf, S. (1984) 'A multifactor model of deviant sexuality.' Third International Conference on Victimology, Lisbon.

CHAPTER 5

TWO SIMPLE MODELS FOR UNDERSTANDING SEX OFFENDERS FOR USE WHEN WORKING WITH MOTHERS AND PARTNERS

The welfare of the child is the paramount consideration in our practice and the needs of the child must remain central in any assessment. Research evidence highlights the importance of the mother's support to the child's recovery. Therefore it is incumbent on us not only to assess risk but also to maximise the chances of her providing that support through the best assessment possible.

As we shall see in Chapter 10 assessments of child sexual abuse undertaken by child protection practitioners are often based on a standard generic and family-based formatted approach designed for use in relation to a range of issues. Whilst such assessments of the mother or partner can produce a wealth of invaluable information, the value of that information in relation to the specific issue of child sexual abuse is limited if it is not then analysed and interpreted using knowledge about sex offenders in general and, where available, specific information about a known or suspected offender. It is like looking at only one side of a two-sided coin.

The focus of this chapter is to provide the necessary information to inform such analysis in assessment. We will look at two simple but practical theoretical models that have been developed by researchers and practitioners who work with sex offenders, which can help us also in our work with mothers and partners. In the following chapters we look in more detail at how this information can be applied to inform our understanding of mothers and partners and also children and families.

The benefits of these two theoretical models

Whilst the proliferation of offender research has proved invaluable for those working with all types of sex offenders (as seen in the previous chapter), what is needed specifically when working with mothers and partners is a simple, jargon-free model that explains the sexual offending *process*. It is this that can help answer those questions of 'how did he do that to me?' and for this we return to two early theoretical models that still hold good for our purpose.

Both models reflect the following simple premises:

- Whilst every sex offender and paedophile is different, there are also key factors in common.

- Most sex offenders and paedophiles say their offending 'just happened'. However, it does not just happen: it is planned and deliberate behaviour. For example, if you ask: 'so one minute you were sitting on the sofa with your daughter watching TV and the next minute you were touching her breasts, with no idea at all in advance, ever, of what you were doing – are you really that dangerous?' Most offenders will say it was not like that and no, they are not that dangerous.

- There are steps to offending, sometimes referred to as routes, pathways or a cycle of offending.

- There is a pattern to the offending.

- Different types of approaches by the offender mean different types of experiences for the child and for the non-abusing mother or partner. *Therefore every child, mother and partner's experience is unique to them.*

Both models have been used in Still, Faux and Wilson (2001) and Tucker and Still (2009) and are referred to by Calder, Peake and Rose (2001) in their work on mothers of sexually abused children.

Model one: Finkelhor's four preconditions to sex offending

Historically, this model (Finkelhor 1984) has been used across the range of sex offenders including child molesters, paedophiles and adult rapists. It provided the basis for many of the original community-based sex offender treatment programmes in the UK, including the Home Office accredited programmes throughout England and Wales after 2001. Subsequent research and clinical experience have highlighted the limitations of this model as being overly simplistic when working with the broad range of sex offenders, emphasising the need to take into account how factors such as motives, beliefs, strategies and goals interact as well as broader contextual cultural issues (Ward *et al.* 2006). Sex offender treatment programmes have been adapted accordingly. However, it is a helpful descriptive model and the basic principles of the four preconditions remain useful to us when working with non-abusing mothers and partners and here it is adapted to its simplest form, for that purpose.

If someone is going to sexually abuse a child or young person they will want also to avoid suspicion or discovery so it is logical that certain factors have to be in place for that to happen. Finkelhor identified four such preconditions necessary for a successful outcome. Logic also suggests that, at least initially, each precondition must occur in the stated order. Preconditions three and four are of particular importance to our understanding of mothers and partners and their subsequent relationship with the child. His theory is paraphrased here for the purpose of simplicity and avoiding jargon.

Precondition one: motivation to offend

There must be *motivation* to offend otherwise he would not do it. Motivation is a complex issue but put simply for our purposes he does it because, for whatever reason, he wants to do it: if he did not want to do it, he would not do it.

Precondition two: overcoming internal inhibitors

Many men who sexually abuse a child know that what they are doing is wrong but they want to do it anyway. In order to do the behaviour they must therefore engage in some form of thinking so as to overcome the sense of 'no I mustn't, it's wrong' and change it to 'yes, it's OK'.

Precondition three: overcoming external inhibitors

In order to offend he must gain access to the child and to do this he must bypass anyone who may get in the way between him and the child. If he cannot isolate the child from potential protectors he cannot proceed and must go elsewhere. Ask any sex offender abusing within a family context who is the most likely person to get in the way between him and the child or young person he wants to abuse and the odds are he will say it is the child's mother.

Similarly, it is not uncommon to hear mothers say that prior to disclosure they no longer had the close relationship with the child that they once did. They may have put this down to other everyday factors, such as the age of the child, the child going through a difficult phase, the child having problems at school or with friends, or other tensions within the family. Knowledge of how the offender disrupted the mother–child relationship can help to heal it as well as help to identify possible future risk scenarios when he may be doing it again.

Precondition four: overcoming the child's resistance

If he is to abuse a child he must overcome the child's resistance. In more recent years this has become recognised as grooming. He must also prevent the child from telling. Ask any such sex offender who he thinks the child is most likely to tell and it is likely he will say it is the child's mother, even if the offender is from outside the family and there is a protective father or other carer. Therefore, if he is to succeed, again he has to create a wedge between the child and his or her mother.

Some people question whether offenders of low intelligence can really be that clever and manipulative. Clinical experience suggests that whilst they may not have the cognitive ability to describe the process, the survival instinct to avoid detection requires they go through the same logical process.

A difference between sex offenders and paedophiles

Craig *et al.* (2008) describe how the need for attitudes and beliefs to justify offending behaviour (Finkelhor precondition two – thoughts of 'no, I must not do this') is well supported in research relating to child sexual abuse but less prevalent among rapists and sexual murderers (pp.97–8). Many predatory or 'career' paedophiles, who may have hundreds of victims over a lifetime, see nothing wrong with what they are doing because they have a belief system that children and young people enjoy sex with adults, that it does the child or young person no harm and that this is misunderstood by the legal, professional and political community. Therefore they bypass precondition two because there are no internal inhibitors to overcome.

It is not uncommon to see those who have abused within a family context attempting to minimise the seriousness of their offending because it is 'not as bad' as what paedophiles do, partly because usually there are fewer victims and also because they may at least have experienced feelings of guilt afterwards, which the paedophiles often do not. Media reports, which often focus on extreme cases of abuse, also encourage sex offenders who abuse within a family context to think 'I'm not like that. I'm not a pervert like them', and even enable them to express their outrage to others. Such thinking is of course erroneous and meaningless to victims of any form of sexual abuse: all offending is serious.

Model two: cycles of offending

The cycles of offending model (Wolf 1984; Eldridge 1998) adds more detail that can help us further. A question commonly asked about men who sexually abuse children is 'how can they do it?' Consider the following.

EXERCISE
WE ALL HAVE CYCLES OF BEHAVIOUR:
NORMAL PROCESS, ILLEGAL CONTENT

Behaviour becomes easier if we can convince ourselves it is normal. We all do things sometimes we know we should not do: over-eating, smoking, drinking too much alcohol, spending more money than we should, and so on. On good days it may be easier for us to resist temptation but on bad days when we're feeling low, temptation can become too great. We make excuses to ourselves: 'I've had a bad day/ I'm tired/I've been working hard/other people have been difficult'. On our way home we 'just happen' to pass the appropriate shop and tell ourselves 'I deserve it'. So we buy the goodies, do the behaviour and probably enjoy it until afterwards when we feel guilty because we know it was wrong. To dispel the guilt we tell ourselves things to make us feel better: 'it wasn't that bad/it could have been worse/at least I didn't eat the whole box of chocolates or smoke the whole packet of cigarettes'. We may tell ourselves: 'it was a one-off, I won't do it again'. Except in many instances we will do it again because we like it, so we go round the same cycle again.

Can you think of any behaviour patterns you engage in that could be considered cycles similar to those described?

Sex offenders commonly have the same kind of inner dialogue. This is not to minimise the seriousness of sex offending but to explain how the *process* of offending can feel normal to the offender. It is the *content* that is abusive and illegal.

A basic cycle of offending

Figure 5.1 is a simple version of the typical pattern of a child molester/ sex offender who is aware that what he is doing is wrong. There may be different things that trigger him into offending but this type of offender also needs an 'excuse to offend' to turn 'No, I must not…' into 'Yes, go for it'. Eldridge (1998) refers to this as an inhibited cycle.

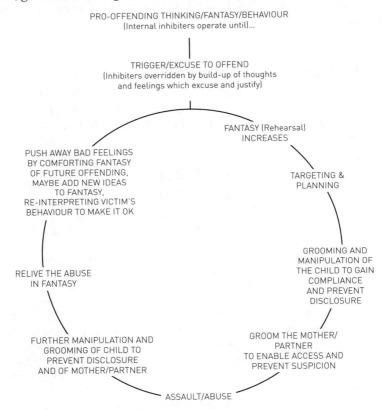

PRO-OFFENDING THINKING/FANTASY/BEHAVIOUR
(Internal inhibiters operate until)...

TRIGGER/EXCUSE TO OFFEND
(Inhibiters overridden by build-up of thoughts
and feelings which excuse and justify)

FANTASY (Rehearsal)
INCREASES

PUSH AWAY BAD FEELINGS
BY COMFORTING FANTASY
OF FUTURE OFFENDING,
MAYBE ADD NEW IDEAS
TO FANTASY,
RE-INTERPRETING VICTIM'S
BEHAVIOUR TO MAKE IT OK

TARGETING &
PLANNING

GROOMING AND
MANIPULATION OF
THE CHILD TO GAIN
COMPLIANCE
AND PREVENT
DISCLOSURE

RELIVE THE ABUSE
IN FANTASY

FURTHER MANIPULATION AND
GROOMING OF CHILD TO
PREVENT DISCLOSURE
AND OF MOTHER/PARTNER

GROOM THE MOTHER/
PARTNER
TO ENABLE ACCESS AND
PREVENT SUSPICION

ASSAULT/ABUSE

Figure 5.1 The inhibited cycle of offending
Source: Adapted from Eldridge (1998)

Variations within the cycle

Short cuts

Eldridge (1998) refers to this as an 'inhibited cycle' because such an offender knows it is wrong, as in Finkelhor's precondition two, whereas a paedophile would have what Eldridge refers to as a 'continuous cycle': he has no such inhibitions and needs no excuse to offend. A sex offender who abuses the same child repeatedly over a long period of time can eventually eliminate the targeting and grooming stages and go straight from fantasy to assault, having successfully targeted and entrapped the child. Eldridge refers to this as a 'short circuit cycle'.

Timings

The amount of time spent on each stage, and between each stage, varies from offender to offender. For example, some offenders can spend months or even years indulging in fantasy before putting the thoughts into actions whereas others can move rapidly from 'I want' to 'I take'. Similarly, some offenders spend a minimum amount of time on grooming the child whereas for others the sense of power and manipulation derived from the grooming provides its own satisfaction.

Styles of offending

For example, when someone is in his offending cycle he may present as pleasant, seductive and charming or angry, intimidating, aggressive or overtly violent. In his cycle he may be consistently one or the other or he may like to be unpredictable, sometimes being Mr Nice Guy and sometimes Mr Nasty Guy; he may be Mr Nice Guy to family, colleagues and friends and Mr Scary Guy only with the victim. He may enjoy the gratuitous use of power and manipulation or he may exert just enough for his needs. Whilst many sex offenders convince themselves they do not want to hurt the child, a minority may be termed as being sadistic, whereby the motivation to inflict pain is as important as the sexual motivation.

The style of offending is especially important in adding to the question of 'how did he do it?' and therefore helping us understand the responses not only of the mother/partner but also of the child and family because each of their experiences will vary accordingly.

Multiple cycles

Whilst many sex offenders and paedophiles stick to one pattern, some can go on to abuse in different types of situations, for example, abusing within the community as well as within the family context. They therefore have more than one type of cycle, but for our purposes the basic elements remain.

Conclusions

Both models can help us to have a greater understanding of the mother/partner, as well as of the child and family, which we will examine in more detail in the following chapter.

References

Calder, M.C., Peake, A. and Rose, K. (2001) *Mothers of Sexually Abused Children: A Framework for Assessment, Understanding and Support.* Dorset: Russell House.

Craig, L., Browne, K.D. and Beech, A.R. (2008) *Assessing Risk in Sex Offenders: A Practioner's Guide.* Chichester: Wiley.

Eldridge, H.E. (1998) *A Therapist Guide for Maintaining Change: Relapse Prevention for Adult Male Perpetrators of Child Sexual Abuse.* Thousand Oaks, CA: Sage.

Finkelhor, D. (1984) *Child Sexual Abuse: New Theory and Research.* New York: Free Press.

Still, J., Faux, M. and Wilson, C. (2001) *The Thames Valley Partner's Programme.* The Home Office, London. Crown Copyright 2001.

Tucker, R. and Still, J. (2009) *Staying Safe: Focused Intervention for Children and Young People Attending the Esssex Partner's Programme.* Essex County Council and Lucy Faithfull Foundation.

Ward, A. and Beech, A. (2006) 'An integrated theory of sex offending.' *Aggression and Violent Behavior 11,* 1, 44–63.

Wolf, S. (1984) 'A multifactor model of deviant sexuality.' Paper presented at the Third International Conference on Victimology, Lisbon.

CHAPTER 6

APPLYING KNOWLEDGE OF SEX OFFENDERS WHEN WORKING WITH MOTHERS AND PARTNERS

The focus of this chapter is to explain how a cycle of sex offending works. This forms the basis of what can be used when working in assessment and intervention with mothers and partners, as described later in Chapters 13 and 14. Every individual stage of the offending cycle is described in terms of:

- what it is

- how it supports the offending process

- how it relates to particular issues often raised for mothers/partners.

Stage one: general pro-offending thinking and/or fantasy accompanied by internal inhibitors

Sex offenders commonly exhibit underlying attitudes and beliefs, which can provide a first step to justifying their later abusive behaviour, for example, misogynistic attitudes toward some or all women and negative attitudes to children and/or young people and their developing sexuality. Comments can be heard, for example, about how some women are 'sluts', 'slags' or 'whores' and how teenage girls who wear makeup and dress 'provocatively' are 'asking for it'.

These attitudes become more worrying when combined with sexual thoughts about children or young people. If such an individual has strong internal inhibitors (Finkelhor 1984, precondition two) to tell him 'these thoughts are not OK' and the thoughts are not put into practice, they are not illegal and there is no progression to an offending cycle. However, for some, these general thoughts and beliefs may have become more entrenched and longstanding. When combined they can form the core thinking patterns or 'schema' (Ward and Keenan 1999) related to sex offending as we saw in the previous chapter.

Stage one: related issues for the mother/partner
Women can often think 'I don't believe he did it, he doesn't behave like a sex offender' or ask themselves 'how did I not see it in him?'

- Both child protection professionals and the general public alike can be misled by stereotypes of what we think a sex offender would or should look like, not least of all as portrayed in the media.

- Sex offenders are highly adept at cover-up.

- There are exceptions to most rules and many men abusing within a family context present as having positive and appropriate social attitudes, which can make it harder for the woman to believe he has a sexual interest in children. If sex offenders were easier to spot we would all be good at doing so, and we are not. Eldridge (1998, p.28) notes that Maletzky (1991) observed from a study of 5000 sex offenders that 'there has been no documentation of a typical "offender personality"… Rather, these men were characterised by their diversity' (pp.16–17). For all the helpful research into sex offenders, that remains the case.

- Conversely, we cannot assume that an adult male who exhibits negative or inappropriate attitudes to children, young people or women is a sex offender because such attitudes are not exclusive to sex offenders and/or paedophiles; whilst others may find such comments offensive they do not on their own signify that every such male is a child molester, paedophile or rapist. It is often only after the disclosure or allegation of abuse that the link to other attitudes can be made. However, given the offender's need for self-preservation and therefore deceit, he will use other means to persuade others of his innocence (see the later stage of grooming).

Stage two: excuse to offend

Child molesters/sex offenders who are aware of wrongdoing need an excuse to offend. This is the process whereby internal inhibitors are overridden by a build-up of thoughts and feelings that will be used to justify and excuse subsequent behaviour and to blame it on someone else. This also helps deal later with any sense of guilt about what they have done.

We are familiar with the idea that offenders can blame the child for the abuse, which they often do. However, when working with sex offenders it is notable how often the focus of blame is their partner and/or the child's mother. Research (Blumenthal, Gudjonsson and Burns 1999) confirms that such 'external attribution of blame' is especially common among sex offenders abusing within the family and that the most common recipient of blame is either his partner and/or the child's mother.

The following are examples of excuses to offend made by sex offenders either in assessment or in the early stages of treatment:

- 'My wife didn't love me, she only married me for a British passport…and unfortunately I came to look on my daughters as a substitute wife.' (He abused his two teenage daughters.)

- 'My wife started having major operations and I couldn't have sex with her. There was no one to have sex with.' (He abused his two young teenage daughters.)

- 'My wife was always out at work in the evening when she was needed by the family.' (He abused his three-year-old daughter – and it was he who persuaded her to take the evening job.)

- 'I'd never realised at the time, I'd always felt trapped by my marriage to my ex-wife.' (He abused girls outside the family.)

- 'Me and my partner rowed, she accused me of not taking an interest in them…so I went completely the other way.' (He sexually abused his partner's eight-year-old daughter.)

- 'My relationship (with my wife) had been very rocky…on and off through twelve years of marriage. She still wanted to go out with her friends.' (He abused his niece.)

- 'I was trying to make our marriage work. I was in the army on training abroad but my wife couldn't cope on her own. My colonel came out to get me when I was on manoeuvres and he said to me "go home and sort out your wife" – it was so embarrassing.' (He abused his daughter.)

- 'I don't feel I'm getting any cooperation from my partner…I feel I'm doing all the work.' (He abused girls outside the home.)

- 'It started after my wife had a child.' (He abused his nieces.)

- 'She was abused as a child herself so she should have known what I was doing.' (He abused nephews and nieces.)

Such thinking on the part of an offender creates a sense of 'poor me', which is used to reinforce the sense that he is owed something to compensate for the woman's failings and make him feel better, in other words, sexual abuse of a child. The woman is not aware of it at the time but the seeds of the message are sown. This in itself is debilitating and disempowering to her: tell someone often enough she is useless, stupid or selfish and she may just begin to believe it.

This need for an excuse to offend is again the equivalent of Finkelhor's precondition two, the need to overcome internal inhibitors.

Stage two: related issues for the mother/partner
'I feel so guilty'

- Many mothers and partners experience a considerable and profound sense of guilt, blame and responsibility for the abuse. In assessment this can lead us to question the basis of such feelings. Is it an understandable parental response to her failure to protect her child? Is it because she feels stupid that she did not recognise any sign of a problem in her partner/father/ family friend/other? Or does she feel so guilty because she was suspicious or knew about the abuse and did nothing to stop it or report it? Maybe she was even collusive or involved?

- Turn it around and look to the offender. A helpful question to ask when assessing a mother or partner is: 'looking back at the time when he was committing the abuse, what did the offender do or say to you, or how did he behave toward you, to make you feel that way?'

- If a child has been sexually abused then a mother or carer has failed to protect and that is her responsibility. However, that does not make her responsible for the child's abuse. A sense of guilt and self-blame is natural but needs to be proportionate: she did not do it, he did.

- If left unaddressed, inappropriate levels of guilt and self-blame are likely to have a debilitating effect on her self-belief and self-esteem which can further disempower her. This is the opposite of what the child needs from her. A helpful approach for us can be 'yes, you were responsible for this bit (failure to protect) but he was responsible for all of this (targeting, grooming you, grooming the child, sexually abusive thoughts and behaviour, i.e. the abuse, the impact on the child, you and your family'.)

- In the minority of cases where the woman had knowledge of or colluded in the abuse and did not report it, asking the question above can provide us with valuable information as to how the offender silenced her. None of this should be seen to excuse her behaviour but it helps us to understand more fully and informs our assessment and any intervention plan.

Stage three: sexual fantasy/sexual thinking

Sex offenders are aware of the dangers of speaking about their abusive fantasy life and are adept at cover-up. Any admission is often prefaced with the comment that it 'just happened'. However, sexual abuse of a child does not 'just happen'. The offender thinks about it first. The following are examples from some sex offenders during their in-depth assessment and treatment.

Alan sexually abused his ten-year-old daughter Emma.

Q. When did you start having sexual thoughts about Emma?

A. It just happened.

Q. I know from working with men who have this problem that they usually have some kind of thought or fantasy about doing something beforehand. When did that begin for you?

A. When I saw her coming out the bathroom.

Brian sexually abused his partner's daughter, Chrissie, from the age of seven to ten years.

Q. When did you start having sexual thoughts about Chrissie?

A. I wasn't aware of any sexual attraction to children. I fantasised about other things. I moved in with my partner when Chrissie was five. But then I'd think about how she'd be when she was older. I thought it was normal.

Brian thought about it so often that by the time Chrissie was seven it felt normal to him.

Ahmed sexually abused his 14-year-old daughter Sheena.

Q. When did you start having sexual thoughts about Sheena?

A. Sheena looked just like my wife. It unnerved me. I found myself thinking of Sheena instead of my wife. I knew it was a sin but I couldn't get Sheena out of my head.

Matt sexually abused his partner's daughter, Kate, when she was 14.

Q. When did you start having sexual thoughts about Kate?

A. I didn't.

Q. So it just happened?

A. Yes.

Q. Are you really that dangerous that you do things without thinking? Are you that impulsive?

A. No. Of course not.

Q. So when did you first have sexual thoughts about Kate?

A. When I first saw her. When she was 12.

Pete sexually abused his nephew Robert from the age of 8 to 18 years.

Q. When did you start having sexual thoughts about Robert?

A. I always knew I was attracted to boys since I was 11 and I was sexually abused. I've been attracted to boys since day one.

Q. So when did you first know you were attracted to Robert?

A. I was attracted to Robert when he was born but I didn't touch him till he was eight.

Ralph was arrested for having indecent images of pre-pubescent children on his laptop.

Q. When did you start having sexual thoughts about children?

A. I don't. I only looked at them out of curiosity.

Q. Were you curious also the second and third time you downloaded stuff?

A. Yes. But I didn't think about it in between times.

Q. So why did you go back into that website if you weren't thinking about it?

Rob and his wife had been reliable foster carers for many years and were approached to take children who had been sexually abused. Rob then sexually abused the first such victim placed in their care. In interview:

Q. Had you ever sexually abused any other child or young person?

A. Never, I'd never do that.

Q. When did you start to think about it?

A. It was when the social worker came and talked to us about the kind of experiences these kids had had, with the abuse. Unfortunately instead of making me care it went the other way, and put ideas in my head.

Further assessment suggested Rob had not sexually abused any child before and that his description was accurate. However, it was apparent that he had previously fantasised about sex with young teenage girls but that he had powerful internal inhibitors operating until they were overcome by detailed images followed by ready opportunity within his own home – plus someone else to blame, that is the social workers.

Why do they indulge in these fantasies if they know it's wrong?

The 'why?' question is complex and has propelled much of the research into historic factors that can contribute to the development of deviant and abusive sexuality. In the previous chapter we looked at the research into routes or pathways into sex offending which has highlighted issues such as negative developmental experiences in childhood and factors relating to loneliness, problems with intimacy, attachment, low self-esteem, poor social skills and poor emotional control mechanisms. Even for someone who has adult sexual arousal and an emotional need for an adult partner and a family life, there can still be issues relating to intimacy and performance anxiety, which in turn can lead to a less threatening over-identification with children. Some individuals can mask these difficulties through performance in other life arenas such as a successful career, acquired status in the local community and/or a large group of more superficial social relationships. These complexities of intimacy and attachment in relation to sexual offending were considered in some detail, for example, by Hudson and Ward (1997). Fantasy may be seen as a means of managing these issues and the individual's subsequent unmet needs (Ward, Mann and Gannon 2007).

How fantasy works in the offending cycle

Sexual fantasy is a normal part of healthy adult life. However, sex offending does not just happen and here we are talking about sexual thoughts relating to children or young people that are the precursor to abuse.

We have looked at the type of longer term historic factors that can contribute to sexual offending. Within the offending cycle sexual thinking becomes more specific about a type of child or young person according to age, gender and social circumstance or about a particular child known to the offender or seen on an internet website.

- The sexual thoughts may consist of brief images or an action sequence running in his head.

- They may be occasional, intermittent, intrusive and even unwanted or they may be regular, often and actively sought and pursued in his imagination or on the internet.

- Some offenders can spend long periods in their fantasy world whereas for others it can be a brief build-up to abuse.

In simple terms, in an offending cycle fantasy provides:

- an escape from the negative thoughts and feelings engendered in stage two

- a comfort

- a rehearsal for what he would like to do in practice

- a disinhibitor – in fantasy you can do anything: children like it, want it; children do not get hurt (unless he is sadistic and enjoys inflicting pain, which most offenders do not)

- normalisation: think about something often enough and it becomes familiar and normal.

However, some offenders have powerful internal inhibitors creating a sense of guilt and wrongdoing and so may try to get rid of the thoughts. In treatment we hear some offenders speak of having a profound sense of guilt at having such abusive thoughts, which they knew would be illegal if put into practice, so they masturbated to the fantasy in the hope that this would satisfy their arousal and nullify their need to put it in to practice. Unfortunately such behaviour can have the opposite effect by increasing rather than decreasing their sexual arousal and so making it more likely they will offend.

Fantasy and internet offenders

There are those who argue that they do not have a sexual interest in children per se but were introduced to indecent images of children either 'by accident' or out of curiosity when viewing adult pornography. Some argue, for example, that they did not realise the images were of a minor, or that it was not a real child and therefore not abuse. Some relate it to their own childhood abuse and a curiosity about what makes an abuser 'tick'. Similarly some argue that they were researching sexual abuse of children and paedophilia to understand it more. These can all seem like credible explanations to an offender's partner and infinitely preferable to the alternative belief that he has a genuine sexual interest in children. Whilst in some instances some of these explanations can be genuine, in many others they are not.

Fantasy is a powerful factor for internet offenders, who use indecent images and other material for masturbatory purposes. Furthermore, if the needs of the offender are being met in this virtual world it can lead to more and more time being spent online which may in time become compulsive and out of control (Quayle and Taylor 2003). For some this can lead to direct victimisation of a child. This may be done in the real world on a one-to-one basis or involve the use of web cams. In some situations this will entail one participant sexually abusing a child at the request of an invited audience. It may or may not progress to an offender creating and trading indecent images.

Whilst such possibilities must be considered seriously we should remember also that for others, the cycle does not progress beyond fantasy because the thought of actually meeting a child is a sexual turn-off. When viewing indecent images, reading pornographic stories or talking to a child online he is in control of the content of his fantasy, which an actual meeting would jeopardise. A meeting would also be seen as threatening his anonymity and safety.

Stage three: issues related to work with mothers and partners
'How did I not know?'

It is not uncommon to hear a mother or partner ask 'how did I not know?' and 'I know him, he's interested in adults not children'. There are no fixed answers to questions like this because every situation is different. For example, clinical experience tells us the following:

- Some men who sexually abuse children and/or young people also have genuine adult heterosexual interest as well as an emotional need for an adult life partner and family life. One such offender described himself when in offending mode as 'like living in a bubble, separate from reality'; another described himself as having 'two me's, the abuser and the loving husband and father'.

- For other offenders their main sexual interest is in children and the adult consenting sexual relationship is only secondary, which from a child protection viewpoint may be seen also as a means for him to allay unwanted suspicions.

- Some offenders do fantasise about a child during adult sex but others do not.

- A paedophile is less likely to have a long-term consenting adult partner because, by definition, he has an intensive and recurrent sexual interest in children and/or young people.

Making sense of 'did she know?'

Intimacy problems in adult sexual relationships have featured highly in the research into illegal sexual fantasy, so how come she did not see it? However, such problems on his part may be well disguised, as seen in the many convicted sex offenders who have achieved considerable success in their work, their position in the local community and in their social relationships with family and friends. For some offenders intimacy-related problems can be internalised and hidden from their adult sexual partner or they may be recognised but attributed to other generic reasons, such as the popular assumption in our society that 'men don't do intimacy like women do' or he 'has a low sex drive'.

Acceptance, belief, disbelief, denial

Many sex offenders are aware that the very suggestion of having sexual thoughts about a child/children could end their relationship with their partner. As we saw in Chapter 2, for many women, all considered it is not surprising that they would find his denials and cover-up more reasonable than any suggestion that he should have such sexual thoughts, especially if there is nothing else to validate an allegation or suspicion of wrongdoing and especially if she is not related to the child or young person who is alleging the abuse.

For some women, the notion of her partner fantasising about child sexual abuse can provoke as much outrage as the actual abuse of a child, not least because it strikes at the heart of her sense of emotional and/or sexual self. For some women it is one of the key motivators for believing an allegation and ending a relationship. However, it is not uncommon for a mother or partner to have difficulty believing any allegation of child sexual abuse because of her own adult, consenting sexual relationship with the offender or because he is a relative or friend who is in an adult relationship. This disbelief can persist even in those relatively rare situations where there is physical evidence of abuse: 'I believe someone has done it but I don't believe it was him'; or 'if he was sexually aroused to children why would he have a sexual relationship with me?' For some women there is the question: 'was he thinking of a child when he was having sex with me?' The discovery of abusive child images on a computer can be disturbing but lead to the justification that 'it is not real and he would never actually do that to a child'. In an assessment such responses are troubling but also warrant further consideration.

Making allowances for human nature

With the pressures on us to complete an assessment within a limited time frame any worrying response from a mother or partner can create major concerns about her ability to protect. If a woman voices any of these questions on issues that affect her, this can be perceived as her being too preoccupied with her own worries when she should be focusing on the child, especially if she is the mother, carer or relative of the child who has been abused. But how can she not ask herself these questions? The whole issue of sexual fantasy raises difficult questions for any woman to face and at the time of assessment her emotions are likely to be raw. It is of particular poignancy to a woman who is the sexual partner of a known or alleged offender as it impacts intimately on her sense of self, in addition to what she may be feeling about her failure to recognise a problem in him and/or to protect her child.

Understanding whilst maintaining objectivity

None of this is offered to excuse unhelpful or inappropriate responses by the partner or mother. However, if the aim is to empower her to support and protect in the future, one could argue that it is better to recognise and to acknowledge these natural difficulties for her and to identify how she may best be helped and supported.

Informing assessment and intervention

As we shall see in Chapters 13 and 14, a general awareness on the part of child protection practitioners of how abusive fantasy works can help us with an informed and reasonable approach to the woman's anxiety about such matters or any other worrying responses. Provided such knowledge and specific information is used sensitively it can be used later as part of an intervention plan by helping her understand 'how did he do that to me?' However, an inability on her part to respond to any such help would reasonably raise more concern.

Informing risk assessment: avoiding stereotyping

In Chapter 10 we look at the importance of obtaining a skilled specialist assessment of the known or suspected offender and of the child protection practitioner having a basic understanding of that assessment process. However, one of the main problems for those working in child protection is that specific information about an individual's abusive fantasy life may not be available at the time of the child and family assessments. Risk assessments therefore require a consideration of any other factors in combination. When it comes to questions of contact or residence, with the welfare of the child being paramount, the safest rule may be 'if in doubt, don't'. However, in situations where there are strong counter-arguments in favour of an alleged offender remaining in contact with the child(ren), there is the dilemma of balancing the needs of the child(ren) with the perceived risk, when it becomes too easy to resort to stereotyping. For example: 'if he's done this he must have done that'; 'if he's thought about this he will be fantasising about that'; 'if he has sexually abused one daughter he has probably thought about abusing the other' and so on, none of which may be true. This is a fault in the system and could be rectified by seeking a specialist opinion on the presenting factors.

Stage four: targeting

Sex offenders target their victims by age and gender according to their sexual arousal pattern, by their ability to gain access to the child and by the possible opportunity to commit the abuse and not get caught. The question commonly asked is 'did he target the mother/his partner as well?'

'Why me? Did he target me?'

It is not uncommon to hear reference to 'vulnerable women' being targeted by sex offenders, either to be his partner or by him identifying her as a weak mother who can be manipulated or bypassed to gain access to the child. To some extent this is often true given Finkelhor's precondition three, which is the need to 'overcome external inhibitors'. It also makes sense when we hear so many offenders identifying the woman as the person most dangerous to him in terms of risk of suspicion or discovery. However, again it is not that simple: strong, competent and intelligent women can also find themselves in this position.

There are a number of possibilities. For example:

- An individual may be aware he has general sexual opinions about how children or young people are today, but at the time of meeting his partner he has not yet progressed beyond the point where there are strong internal inhibitors in place that is a strong sense of 'no, I must not' and he has a genuine belief at that time that he would never do so.

- Someone who knows he has sexual arousal to children, who has already sexually abused a child and who knows he wants to continue to offend but not get caught, is likely to select a partner on the grounds that he can see how he could manipulate her into not suspecting or believing he is an offender.

- Others who have already committed sexual abuse, or who have sexual thoughts about children and are worried they might go on to offend, sometimes tell themselves that now they have met such wonderful woman: 'if I'm with this woman I would never do anything to jeopardise the relationship. I'll never be interested in a child again.' For some this may be a genuine wish and belief. However, it is dangerous to place a woman on such a high pedestal. Sexual arousal patterns do not change so easily and when abusive sexual thoughts return it is all too easy for him (in his head) to blame the woman who could not have been so perfect after all.

- Sexual offending is also about the abuse of power. Some offenders exert only the amount of power necessary to commit the abuse and avoid discovery. However, for others the exertion of power can be gratuitous because it is part of their arousal pattern.

Case example: Ian

Quiet, passive, not-very-bright Ian subjected his 14-year-old stepdaughter to a number of his sexual fetishes over a period of 18 months. His wife was a strong competent woman. In assessment he described how he used what he called his 'little boy' approach to make his wife 'want to mother me' and so be likely to disbelieve any accusations that might arise. When I met his wife one of the first things she said was 'I always felt I had three children, two and Ian' and she could not believe her daughter's allegations not only because they were so bizarre but because 'Ian does not have it in him (to behave like that)'.

Case example: Mike

Mike was attending a community social event where he met Trish and her three teenage children. Trish was a single mother and enjoyed a close relationship with all three daughters. Mike presented as a charming, caring person whilst at the same time thinking, 'I wonder if I can get in there and bust that up?' He went on to move in with the family and rape the middle daughter on multiple occasions. He continued to present himself as Mr Nice Guy both to mother and daughter whilst also establishing himself as the powerful, all-dominant-but-caring male.

Stage four: issues relating to work with mothers and partners

- A more helpful way to look at it is not how weak and vulnerable the women are but how cleverly manipulative and persuasive offenders are. We all have our areas of vulnerability and all an offender has to do is to identify it and exploit it for his own ends. For example, if the woman has had a previous partner who was violent he will be the Mr Nice Guy who would never hurt her or anyone else; if she has struggled financially he can show willingness to be a good provider; if her children have been hurt in any way he can promise to be their protector; if she is quiet and unassertive he will see how he can dominate the relationship. Such combinations are not uncommon in ordinary, non-abusive relationships, without the manipulation for an abusive ulterior motive. In assessment we can look for these patterns and formulate a plan of intervention to help address them.

- Where a woman has a history of partners who are known or suspected sex offenders it usually raises the question 'why does she keep choosing offenders?' A more useful question may be 'why do they keep choosing her?' Whilst this does not excuse what may be a repeated failure on her part to protect, it does suggest that if she is an otherwise good parent, we can help her identify what particular area of vulnerability these offenders see in her. By applying this information we can perhaps enable her to be a more protective parent in the home or, if it is decided mother and child should no longer live together, it can be used where appropriate to help a mother maintain a helpful and supportive relationship with her child(ren), albeit from a distance through contact.

Stage five: grooming the mother/partner

Comments often heard from mothers and partners include: 'how did he do that to me?', 'I should have known', 'did I know and do nothing?', 'I can't believe it.' However, at this stage of the cycle the offending is moving from thinking about something to preparing to do something about it. There are three aspects to grooming if he wishes to commit the abuse and avoid discovery:

- He must achieve some distancing of the child from would-be protectors so as to gain access to the child for abuse (Finkelhor precondition three).

- He must manipulate the child into compliance (Finkelhor precondition four) and not telling.

- He must manipulate the child's mother and/or his partner and/or any other carer into not seeing the abuse, not hearing a child's disclosure and if she does hear it, not reporting it.

All three components are important in terms of the impact on the child, the mother/partner/carer and the overall family dynamics, which we will look at in the following chapters.

There is a danger of making over-simplified assumptions about the nature of grooming, which can often be complex, and so limiting our understanding of the mother's or partner's responses. The following are examples of how some sex offenders have talked in assessment or treatment about how they disempowered the child's mother so as to gain secret access to the child for abuse, and how they persuaded the child's mother and/or their partner that they were not a sex offender. These examples are typical of what can be heard from offenders in specialist assessments and/or treatment. For some of these offenders the manipulation was based solely on the desire to silence the mother/partner. For others there was also a genuine desire not to lose their relationships with their partners or their families. For all of them, their behaviour was deliberately manipulative, although some would not have admitted it to themselves at the time. These examples are offered not to excuse women's sometimes inappropriate responses but to enable us to understand them more.

Case example: Alec and Paul

Alec: 'I encouraged her when she said she wanted to get a job.'

Paul: 'I encouraged her to go to bingo with her friends' (which could as easily have been any other social or cultural activity).

Both Alec and Paul sexually abused their own child in their family home. Both men's wives perceived their partners to be kind and sensitive to their needs, as did friends and family: Alec understood his wife's wish for some stimulating activity away from the home and to have an independent income; Paul understood his wife's need for personal time with friends. Both were happy to stay in and look after the children, give them their supper and in the case of younger children put them to bed. A reframe of this, however, is that whilst some sex offenders are risk takers whereby fear of discovery heightens sexual excitement that was not true for Alec or Paul, for whom such fear would have had the opposite effect. Both also had high levels of sexual arousal and a relatively quick offending cycle, which meant they needed to sexually assault their chosen child on a regular basis once a week and with confidence that their wives were out of the home for a set amount of time. This allowed them also to stay in cycle throughout the week, anticipating the next session of abuse in fantasy and reliving it in fantasy until the next time.

Case example: Steve

'I'd encourage her to drink – and have another.'

Steve sexually abused his son from the age of eight in the family home. He and his wife 'enjoyed a drink at home', except on some occasions he would stop drinking whilst encouraging his wife to have more until she became drunk and sleepy and so was unaware of what was going on. When concerns arose about his stepson's behaviour Steve manipulated the investigation away from suspicions of sexual abuse to focus on the mother's 'drink problem', whilst continuing to sexually abuse his stepson.

Case example: Andy

'I make love to her.'

Andy sexually abused his partner's 14-year-old daughter but on each occasion he 'made love to' his wife Angie on the same day. Further discussion indicated that his sex with Angie was not marital rape, as one might have thought, but considerate, equal and consenting. When his daughter told her mother about the rapes Angie's response was to believe her daughter and to say she would throw Andy out of the house and report him. However, among the many questions Angie asked was 'when did he do it?' Belief turned to doubt with the realisation that the dates coincided with the times when she and Andy made love, further encouraged by Andy's insistence of his innocence and that the daughter's allegation was based on jealousy of his close relationship with Angie and resentment of him because he was not her father.

Case example: Dawud

'I just never talked to her…about anything.'

Dawud was aroused to young teenage girls, two of whom he sexually abused away from the family home. He was afraid his partner, whom he described as not being very bright, would become suspicious so he treated her as if she were stupid, deliberately questioning her opinions about everything and undermining her confidence. If she ever expressed any worry about him he would then accuse her of being stupid and 'always getting things wrong'. He succeeded in lowering her self-esteem to the point where she accepted this, including when she became concerned that something was wrong.

Case example: Mac

'I told her she should be careful with the girl – there are a lot of funny men out there.'

Mac sexually abused his maternal niece from the age of four to six. He played the role of 'nice Uncle Mac' in a family of ultra-dominant males. He persuaded his sister of his good intention by constantly expressing a protective attitude toward his nephews and nieces. He cited this as one example, which he said to his sister when they were at a bus stop with the niece he was abusing and a man pushed his way into the queue. Making protective comments such as this would make his sister unlikely to suspect it was him that was the worry: perpetual grooming like the slow drip of a tap.

Case example: Tony

'I'll kill myself.'

Tony committed sex offences outside the family home. His partner Penny worried the authorities because even while he was on remand in prison she remained reluctant to end their relationship and continued to visit him. Tony maintained control of Penny from prison, both during visits and by letter, by telling her how much he loved her and that he would be nothing without her. He repeatedly threatened to kill himself if she left him and that, furthermore, she would have to explain to their children that it was she who was responsible for their father's death.

Case example: Amos

'I intimidated her.'

Amos sexually abused his two young teenage daughters. He never hit his wife because that might leave bruises that would lead to questions from other people, but he was dominant, controlling and intimidating. His 'hobby' was collecting weaponry such as knives and a crossbow that hung on the wall, never used but ever present. When he lost his temper he shouted loudly and aggressively. His wife learned never to cross him. He was confident that if she became suspicious (which she did not) she would never ask too many questions because she would be afraid of what he was capable of.

Threats of violence should not be underestimated. As with any domestic violence, whilst some offenders stop at intimidation others do not and there are situations where women pay a price for making appropriate decisions for their children. For example, in one situation the offender threw acid in his partner's face when she finally believed he presented a risk to her children and ended the relationship. In another situation, the woman attended A&E with serious multiple bruising as a result of challenging her husband over her suspicions.

Case example: John

'He's told me everything.'

Sex offenders can be helped not to reoffend and in treatment they are encouraged to be honest with any possible future partner. However, 'he's told me everything' can also be a powerful grooming tactic. For example, on their second meeting John told Maria he had prior convictions for sexual offences against children. He said he told her this because he liked and respected her so much and before their relationship went any further he wanted to be honest with her. However, he was now a reformed character. Maria confirmed this and said he was a lovely man, she believed he deserved a second chance and that 'he would never do anything like that to my children'. John told her that, and at the time he said it, he meant it, even though he went on to sexually abuse Maria's daughter. Following disclosure Maria confirmed that she never suspected him precisely because he had told her about his past. His apparent honesty led her to believe:

- he's told me everything (which he had not)
- so he's changed, reformed (which without treatment he had not)
- so he won't do it again
- 'I'll know if he does' (which she did not because this was the grooming).

Grooming and internet offenders

Case example: Marcus

Marcus was a happily married man with three children. He was arrested after a colleague borrowed his work laptop in Marcus's absence and found indecent images of children. Marcus's wife Jakki had to accept the images were there but could not believe they were put there by Marcus because she had never seen any indication of a sexual interest in children. Furthermore, her husband's job was in law enforcement and as such his job was to catch those who broke the law in this way. The only logical conclusion for her was that someone else had used her husband's computer, either to avoid detection or as an act of malice. Forensic examination of the laptop found thousands of indecent images and evidence of electronic contact with a 13-year-old girl. Marcus eventually admitted the offences. In assessment he acknowledged having had abusive sexual fantasies for some time, though not about his own children because to him that would be abuse. He did his internet searches during quiet times at work when he was bored, first out of curiosity and then it became addictive. He progressed to contacting one girl and exchanging sexually explicit messages. The fear of being caught, particularly given the nature of his job, gave him an increased sexual 'buzz'. However, he also experienced strong feelings of guilt and became scared that it could progress to a face-to-face meeting. Marcus used his role as a family man and law enforcement officer to groom Jakki into believing that he could not possibly have a sexual interest in children. For Jakki the extent of Marcus's betrayal was difficult to comprehend and so at odds with the home-loving husband she knew, she could only accept the truth when faced with incontrovertible evidence.

Other types of manipulation by internet offenders

Many partners of internet offenders experience similar disbelief to Jakki even when the computer used is in the home. Given the potentially addictive nature of this type of activity offenders have to be particularly adept at cover-up and excuse making. Explanations from partners can include, for example, that their partner or boyfriend was a poor sleeper and they thought that when he was up at night he was watching ordinary films or playing video games; some thought the computer activity was work related and if it was at night time it was due to pressure of work or the need to communicate with customers in different time zones. Conversely, some said they could not believe he was engaged in sexual activity because he did not do it in a clandestine manner: the laptop was in open family living space, they assumed the password protection was for ordinary material and to safeguard the children and if he was going to do that kind of thing he would surely hide it away somewhere.

Other women acknowledged with varying degrees of acceptance that they knew he was 'looking at porn' because he was quite open about it and it was 'what men do'. However, the pornography was known or assumed to be adult and legal. Sometimes pornography was shared as a sexual aid to their own relationship. In some situations, where the woman suspects or is aware that the images being viewed are of children, she may be fearful of the consequences for her and her children of intervening or report the offending and so rationalise that at least it was not real abuse of real children.

The misuse of religion, culture and disability in grooming

Individuals who want something badly enough will often use anything they can find to use to their advantage, including manipulation of faith and cultural mores. For example:

Case example: Mark

'I knew I was her cross to bear.'

Mark was a man in his seventies, whose two daughters disclosed his abuse of them as children when they were in their forties and had teenage girls of their own. Mark's wife Amy was of a similar age but caused social workers considerable concern when she supported her husband at the expense of losing contact with her daughters and grandchildren. Mark explained that he always knew his wife would support him because of her Christian faith. Amy had been a lay preacher in her local church since she was a young woman and believed she was tied to Mark by her wedding vows, made before God, which it would be a sin to break. He also knew she would have to consider it her Christian duty to try to help him reform and he encouraged her belief that God had given him to her as her cross to bear.

Case example: Rafi

'I made her look like a bad Muslim woman.'

Jasmina's first husband was by an arranged marriage. When he knew he was dying he expressed the wish that she marry his business partner Rafi, to provide her and their child with financial security. They lived within the relatively enclosed confines of the extended family and the local Muslim community. Rafi went on to sexually abuse his stepdaughter Aysha from the age of 11 to 13. Jasmina was a devout Muslim but Rafi disempowered her as a protector by making her out to be a bad Muslim, thus isolating her and ostracising her from that confined community with nowhere to turn for support.

Case example: Jim

'He was the perfect man.'

Debbie and Jim had an eight-year-old daughter with a disability that required a great deal of physical care by her parents. Jim was arrested following allegations of abuse by a number of boys and girls within the local neighbourhood. Debbie could not believe the allegations because Jim was so patient and caring with their daughter. She saw him as the perfect family man: he was 'a fun, loving, generous father and husband, a good provider' and when there were problems 'he was always there for us'. Jim was able to separate off his family life from his abuse of other children and he was confident that his behaviour within the family would prevent Debbie seeing him as a sexual risk to children, which even after his arrest she could not. In addition, whilst his feelings toward and care for his daughter were genuine and he had no sexual interest in her, he used the knowledge of doing good for his wife and daughter to help assuage any sense of guilt about the abuse of other children.

Mothers and partners who are survivors of child sexual abuse

Many women who were sexually abused as a child have dealt with issues arising from that experience and are able to live the family life they choose. However, for others it is more difficult and parenthood can reawaken memories and feelings. Clinical experience shows how efficient some sex offenders can be in spotting such situations, even at first meeting.

Case example: Joe

Joe met Kyley at a pub when she was out with a two female friends. He learned that she was a single parent with two girls in the age range in which he was sexually interested. He presented as amiable and interested in her. He encouraged her to talk about herself and asked where her husband/boyfriend was. She said she would never trust another man because she had been sexually abused by an uncle in her teens and she had left the children's father because when he drank he was aggressive. Joe was sympathetic and understanding and said he could never understand why a man would treat a woman that way and that anyone who 'touched' a child should be locked away for good. Because of her own experience of abuse Kyley thought she knew what a sex offender looked like and Joe was not it. However, she did not recognise his seductive charms as grooming. The relationship developed and after a while she introduced her children to Joe hoping he might provide her children with an appropriate father figure.

Collusive partners and co-offenders

In Chapter 2 when considering the issue of 'did she know?' we looked at the spectrum of knowing, ranging from point 1 where the woman knew nothing at all about the abuse and point 2, knowing something was wrong but having no idea it was sexual abuse through to point 4 where the woman knew about the abuse but failed to act and point 5 where she was an active co-offender to point 6 where the woman became an offender in her own right. In Chapter 2 we also argued that most mothers and partners place themselves at points 1, 2 or 3, which is to entertain the possibility that whatever problems may be presenting could be related to child sexual abuse, but to dismiss it in the absence of nothing to support that view. This becomes more credible when put in the context of offenders' meticulous grooming.

However, there are a minority of women who fall into categories 4, 5 or 6 and it is important for us to recognise these individual situations in terms of assessing:

- the decisions she makes about her relationship with the known or suspected offender

- her future ability or willingness to protect

- the therapy of the child or young person or child who has been abused.

Conversely, as we shall see in the next chapter, it is important to differentiate between situations where the woman did know and/or participate and where the child thought she knew but she did not.

The importance of finding out the individual circumstances of a case
With the child's safety and well-being paramount, identifying a woman who was collusive or an active co-offender is likely to result in the removal of the child from her care to a safer place. However, even in such situations decisions must be made as to what happens next and that still requires an investigation of the woman's situation.

Clinical experience in working with such cases suggests a correlation between collusive and co-offending women and their having violent relationships with the sex offender. This is supported by research by Saradjian (1996) who found also that male-coerced women co-offenders are often in an abusive relationship with their sex offender partner. This does not excuse or minimise the woman's behaviour but it should be investigated so as to inform how to proceed in the best interests of the child. Every situation is different. For example, consider the following two cases.

Case example: Yvonne

Yvonne's boyfriend raped her 12-year-old daughter on multiple occasions. He had a potential for violence and kept weapons openly displayed in the house. He enjoyed a gratuitous sense of power over others and their humiliation. Voyeurism was part of his sexual arousal. He did not hide the abuse from Yvonne and it reached a point where he told Yvonne to be present while he raped her daughter. Yvonne did so several times although it was clear from her daughter's eventual statement that her mother did not enjoy the experience. During the investigation Yvonne denied co-offending. However, in the subsequent assessment Yvonne said she complied with her partner because she was concerned that if she did not, he would not love her any more.

Case example: Liz

Liz knew that her husband indecently assaulted their two young daughters and that he was sadistically violent, especially to their son who was ten. They lived in an isolated rural area. Liz was of low IQ. Her husband had driven away family and friends. Liz wanted to leave with the children but had no independent income or transport and had never heard of women's refuges. She tried to protect her son from the physical violence by distracting her husband when he was in a temper or, failing that, by placing herself between him and her son to take the blows. Eventually her husband's voyeuristic tendencies extended to sexual humiliation of her and her son together and he told her to have intercourse with the boy. Liz was nauseated at the prospect but complied because from past experience of his violence she believed that, if she did not, her husband would become so angry he would take it out on their son. She feared genuinely for her son's life. She was physically sick afterwards. Liz never reported it because her husband told her no one would believe her and that she and the children would have to face more punishment. The daughters were young and afraid. The son never told because he knew his mother was forced to do it and he did not want her to get into trouble. The truth came out only when Liz was further assessed after suspicions were raised much later when the son was in care and in therapy. In interview Liz became distraught and physically sick when recounting the truth.

Is there any difference in these two cases?

Neither woman's behaviour is acceptable; both cases consisted of abuse. However, with Yvonne her motivation as a co-offender was to protect and maintain her own relationship with her partner. With Liz, whilst what she did was rape, her motivation was to protect her son from what she feared would be even worse for him.

Why does this matter?

Neither of these stories were discovered until a belated assessment and so the treatment plans for each case was made based on general assumptions.

When Yvonne's partner was convicted her daughter remained in her care; the daughter's allegation against her mother was dismissed as being vindictive payback for mother's failure to protect and intervention focused on helping to improve the mother–daughter relationship. In this instance the daughter wanted to be removed from her mother and the family home and did not want to talk to her mother.

Liz's son was removed from her care on the grounds of her inability to protect and placed in a residential establishment far from the family home. Liz was allowed twice-yearly access, which was supervised under instruction not to discuss the abuse, whereas what Liz's son needed was to have a relationship with his mother and to be able to talk to her about what happened to them both within a safe therapeutic environment, even though they could no longer live together.

Stage five: issues relating to work with mothers and partners

- In cases of child sexual abuse within a family-related context grooming of the mother/partner is as crucial to the offender's own safety as grooming the child.

- Grooming tactics are often complex and multi-faceted.

- We may be tempted to look at the examples quoted and wonder why the mother/partner did not see it for what it was. However, unless or until there is reasonable suspicion, allegation or disclosure of child sexual abuse the behaviour becomes what is seen in many relationships and/or can be linked to other ordinary familial problems.

- Gaining insight into the grooming tactics used by offenders to manipulate the mother/partner is crucial to our understanding of her responses to suspicion, disclosure and in some cases knowledge of abuse: the nature, the style, how long it has been going on for and when it started. Is it a recent phenomenon or has the offender made it an entrenched part of their relationship?

- The concept of grooming the woman helps child protection professionals understand more fully the question 'did she know?' because it puts into the appropriate context. For many women it can help address their debilitating sense of guilt at failing to protect which can lead to self-questioning, re-running in their heads 'did I know?', 'was it when…?', 'where was I…?'

- The fact that the woman has been manipulated in this way does not make her weak or stupid. It can happen to any of us.

- The grooming of the mother/partner has an impact on her relationship with the child who has been abused, on other family members, on her perception of herself and on her social relationships, as described in Chapter 2.

- An understanding of the concept of mother/partner grooming can be built into an intervention plan to help empower the woman for the future if she is receptive to such intervention.

Stage six: grooming the child

This will be addressed in the next chapter together with the impact on the relationship between mother and child. Grooming is in itself a criminal offence in the UK.

Stage seven: committing the abuse

The offender may engage in non-penetrative inappropriate touching or in penetrative acts of rape, buggery or oral sex. He may view images acquired on the internet. He may involve a child(ren) in looking at or in the production of sexual online images, watching sexual activities or encouraging the child to behave in an inappropriately sexual way. He may do this for his own arousal purposes or, in some cases, as a commercial transaction with others.

Stage seven: issues related to work with mothers and partners

A woman's responses can only be meaningfully considered in the light of what she thinks the offender has done. However, there is the danger that we may assume the mother or partner knows what the offender did when she does not. Children and young people often assume she knows because she is Mum and she is an adult; children and young people are also groomed not to tell and/or do not have the language to describe it and/or may be too traumatised to say; sex offenders say as little as possible; practitioners and managers from different agencies may think someone else has told her when they have not.

Stage eight: reinforcing the grooming

Whatever grooming the offender did before he must continue now and, if necessary, increase, so as to prevent or allay suspicion or in the event of disclosure, to make the mother/partner disbelieve any allegations.

Stage eight: related issues for work with mothers and partners

In situations where the woman fails to accept or believe the abuse but where it is accepted by others, including the authorities, the question should be 'what is the offender still doing to persuade her to that effect?'

In many instances it is at this point where the success or otherwise of his grooming tactics become apparent. For example, if his tactics were those of Mr Nasty Guy the mother/partner may be fearful of worse consequences, perhaps not just for herself but also for her child(ren); if his tactics were to undermine her confidence and self-belief it would not be surprising that her response may now be 'how will I manage without him?'

Whatever the woman's response, if it causes us concern we should explore what it is that makes her think and feel that way, including the likelihood that the offender is still manipulating the situation. Where her response is a positive one of acceptance, belief and a determination to protect, we should not underestimate an offender's manipulative ability to reassert his influence. In assessment we can evaluate the best means of helping her to understand and counter that influence.

Stage nine: reliving the abuse in fantasy

Sexual thoughts are difficult to turn off like a light switch especially when so much effort has gone into the sexual act. Therefore it is likely that the offender will relive the abuse in fantasy which in turn runs the risk of reinforcing the arousal.

Stage ten: guilt and/or fear

An offender/child molester who knows what he has done was wrong will experience a sense of guilt. He is likely also to experience fear of discovery: did he manipulate the situation well enough for his own safety? A paedophile who has no sense of wrongdoing is unlikely to experience guilt but he could still experience fear of discovery. Either can slow down the need to re-offend, whether it is for a short while or for weeks, months or years. In some cases guilt and fear may deter further offending although empirical evidence from working with child sex offenders suggests that for many this is unlikely without the help of treatment.

Stage eleven: pushing the guilt and/or fear away

For many offenders time erodes any sense of guilt or fear when weighed against the more powerful sexual interest and so it is pushed away enabling him to re-enter the offending cycle and to re-offend.

Multi-stage: distorted thinking

There has been much debate among those doing research into sex offending about the finer points of offenders' cognitive distortions/ distorted thinking/thinking errors. For the purpose of using offender knowledge when working with mothers and partners it is important to keep matters simple and practicable.

At the beginning of the cycle we looked at the presence of general pro-offending thinking and the presence of over-arching attitudes and beliefs that could support sex offending. Progress through the cycle is accompanied also by more immediate distorted thinking that allows the offender to continue to overcome any sense of 'no, I must not' and change it to 'yes, it's OK'. In practical terms, these include any thoughts that enable the offender to justify, minimise, legitimise or excuse his behaviour to himself. The type of thinking will be geared to the particular behaviour he wants to do. For example:

- It's OK so long as I only do it with my own child.

- It's OK so long as I keep it in the family.

- It would be wrong if I did it with my own child but it's OK to do it with any other child.

- It would be wrong with any other child but it's OK with this particular child.

Each offender will have his own distorted rationalisation. For example:

- It's because I love her/him.

- It's about being close.

- I want her first experiences to be with me, as someone who is sexually experienced, and not with some clumsy adolescent.

- I just meant to comfort her.

- She/he wants it.

- She's asking for it, the way she dresses.

- She was nearly 16 anyway.

- She/he needs to learn a lesson.

- She/he isn't saying no.

- She came out of the bathroom with only a towel round her.

- It's my right.

- She already has a boyfriend so what's the harm.

- It won't hurt her/him.

- It won't do any harm.

- I wouldn't have done it if my wife/partner/boss/someone else hadn't done or said that/behaved that way.

- It was on the internet, it wasn't a real child.

- It was on the internet so it wasn't me that was doing it.

- It won't do any harm just to chat.

Many such thoughts place the responsibility for the abuse on the child, or anywhere other than himself. As can be seen, such thoughts commonly reflect also the elements of the core schema or beliefs (Ward and Keenan 1999) we previously discussed: seeing children as sexual beings, the notion of sexual entitlement, finding comfort from a dangerous world, seeing sex as uncontrollable and the nature of harm. The difference is that now they are put to practical use in enabling the move from fantasy to action.

Offending 'styles'

The type of thinking reflects also the likely *style of the offender*. Whilst all sexual offending is illegal and abusive we can see the different styles of offender approach both in the distorted thinking patterns as well as in the style of grooming. For example, 'it's love' suggests a seductive style of Mr Nice Guy, whereas 'she needs to be taught a lesson' is the more angry and punitive style of Mr Nasty Guy. There is a whole range of other styles, such as the Super Seducer, the Sulker, the Intimidator, and so on. All are abusive.

Post-abuse: managing feelings of guilt

Such distorted thinking continues throughout the cycle. Clinical evidence from working with sex offenders in treatment suggests that when you ask what would happen if they allowed themselves to see that their behaviour was causing pain, harm or distress to the child the most likely response would be that they would have to stop, which at that point they did not want to do.

If an offender knows what he is doing is wrong and has had to overcome any such 'internal inhibitors' he is likely to feel guilty following the behaviour. A retreat into the same type of excuse making – 'it did no harm', 'she/he liked it', 'she/he deserved it', 'it wasn't my fault' – helps alleviate the guilt, which in turn makes it easier to go back into the cycle and repeat the behaviour.

Distorted thinking: related issues for work with mothers and partners

- For some offenders such distorted thinking is as secret and private as the rest of his cycle of offending, masked in an aura of respectability. For others it is more obvious. In assessing the mother or partner we can explore which.

- When assessing a mother or partner we may find similarly inappropriate attitudes and excuses as to why she either does not believe it or why she does not consider the allegation to be serious. For example, 'that child has always been trouble', 'the way young girls dress these days what do they expect?' or 'he wouldn't have done it if he/she hadn't provoked it'. Some of the language used may be similar to that of the known or suspected offender, such as slag, slut, whore, rent boy. This is true also for women whose partners have abused via the internet, who support the offender's view that it is less serious than if he had directly sexually assaulted a child. Such presentation must be of concern in terms of her perception of risk and safety and her ability to protect. However, assessment allows us also to explore the roots of such opinions. For some women such views may be as long-term entrenched as those of the offender and independently held. However, for others, simple questions as to what makes her think that often reveals manipulation by the offender to encourage her to think that way as part of his grooming of her. In the latter situation, as part of an intervention plan many women can be helped to take an alternative view, not only by being given information about, for example, victims of abuse but also information about sex offenders and how they operate.

- Insight into the style of an individual's offending cycle can inform our understanding not only of the nature of the child's victim experience but also of the mother/partner's response to suspicion or disclosure and to the known or alleged offender. For example, a woman may have difficulty in believing an allegation where the offender or alleged offender's style is that of a seductive Mr Nice Guy, or she may be fearful of believing and/or reporting it if he is a Mr Nasty or Angry Guy. We will see more of this later in grooming.

Note: The timing of each stage of the cycle varies from offender to offender, as does the time spent in each stage.

Conclusions

Sexual abuse is not an act or an incident but the corruption of the relationship not only with the child but the child's mother/the offender's partner. Getting inside the head of a known or suspected offender can be emotionally demanding for those working with the child, mother and family. However, understanding the basic concept of patterns of offending is crucial to our understanding of the mother/partner's situation and her responses to allegation, suspicion or disclosure. It provides the all-important context in any assessment of the mother/partner in terms of risk, safety and her ability to protect as well as the content of any subsequent intervention programme.

In particular, the concept of grooming the woman helps us as child protection professionals to understand more fully the question 'did she know?' because it puts it into the appropriate context, without which any such assessment would be relatively limited. The worst scenario is that this could possibly lead to decision making that is not in the interests of the child.

In the next chapter we will take the concept of grooming one step further, to look at how the grooming of the child, in addition to the grooming of the mother or carer, impacts on their relationship together.

References

Blumenthal, S., Gudjonsson, G. and Burns, J. (1999) 'Cognitive distortions and blame attribution in sex offenders against adults and children.' *Child Abuse and Neglect 23*, 2, 129–143.

Eldridge, H.E. (1998) *A Therapist Guide for Maintaining Change: Relapse Prevention for Adult Male Perpetrators of Child Sexual Abuse.* Thousand Oaks, CA: Sage.

Finkelhor, D. (1984) *Child Sexual Abuse: New Theory and Research.* New York: Free Press.

Hudson, S.M. and Ward, T. (1997) 'Intimacy, loneliness, and attachment style in sexual offenders.' *Journal of Interpersonal Violence 12*, 3, 323–339.

Maletzky, B.M. (1991) *Treating the Sexual Offender.* Newbury Park, CA: Sage.

Quayle, E. and Taylor, M. (2003) 'Model of problematic internet use in people with a sexual interest in children.' *CyberPsychology and Behavior 6*, 1, 93–106.

Saradjian, J. (1996) *Women who Sexually Abuse Children: From Research to Clinical Practice.* Chichester: Wiley.

Ward, T. and Keenan, T. (1999) 'Child molesters' implicit theories.' *Journal of Interpersonal Violence 14*, 821–838.

Ward, T., Mann, R. and Gannon, T.A. (2007) 'The good lives model of rehabilitation of offenders: Clinical implications.' *Aggression and Violent Behavior 12*, 2, 87–107.

CHAPTER 7

THE IMPACT OF THE OFFENDER ON THE RELATIONSHIP BETWEEN THE MOTHER/PARTNER AND THE CHILD

Much has been written elsewhere about the effects of sexual abuse on children and young people and therapeutic intervention with them. In this chapter we introduce the offender perspective to further our understanding of the impact of his behaviour:

- on the child
- on the relationship between mother/carer and child, both in the past and present
- on the extended family.

This is crucial to risk assessment, to assessment of the mother/partner's ability to protect and to her ability to help the child and family's healing process. It is important also in terms of providing knowledge and information that can be used to devise a subsequent intervention plan according to the needs of the individual situation.

There are two options to ensuring the child's future safety. The first is to remove the child to a different carer, who may be a member of the extended family, a friend of the family or a foster carer who is not a family member or friend. In some instances there is no alternative. However, in Chapter 1 we looked at the importance of the relationship between the child and the non-abusing mother/carer. Furthermore, the law requires separation to be used only as a last resort. This leaves the second option, which is through a programme of intervention aimed at empowering the mother/carer to protect, which can be done partly by helping to strengthen the mother–child relationship.

Some examples of common problems that can arise in the mother–child relationship during and post-abuse

'I used to have a good relationship with my child but we haven't been as close for some time now.' It is not uncommon to hear comments like this when working with a mother or partner, nor is it surprising. Children and young people know that if they have been abused there is an adult who has failed to protect them, which is bound to have a negative impact on that relationship. For the child it raises questions about their mother or carer such as: did she know? How could she not have known? Why didn't she do something? How can I trust her? How can I feel safe?

Did she know? The child's perspective

The child may believe he or she told their mother or carer about the abuse but that she failed to act. Whilst that is true in some cases, for the most part it is not that simple: in the all-too-frequent absence of clear disclosure or physical evidence of sexual abuse, parents and carers often attribute problems to other everyday factors such as the demands of small children or adolescence, sibling arguments, peer group pressures or difficulties at school. Sexual abuse is not the first thing that comes to mind, particularly as many mothers have encouraged children in their care to tell them if there is ever anything worrying them.

Case example: Family B – Alex, Annie and Suzy

In Chapter 3 we looked at the lengthy example of how Alex raped his daughter Suzy for two years in the family home without his wife Annie knowing about the abuse, and the negative impact not only on Suzy and Annie but also on their mother–daughter relationship. After Alex left the family home, social work intervention focused on rebuilding the previously good relationship between mother and daughter but with little success. Why?

- When asked whether she thought her mother knew about the abuse Suzy said she did: how could she not have known?

- When asked if she ever told her mother about the abuse she said no.

- When asked what made her think her mother knew, if she (Suzy) never told her, Suzy expressed bewilderment at such an apparently stupid question: 'because she's Mum and married to Dad'.

- On consideration, this is a natural perception by children of their parents who are a) adults and b) apparently close and c) work as a team in everyday family life.

- When asked what effect this had on her relationship with her mother during the two years of abuse Suzy explained: 'Mum went up in my head as being responsible for the abuse – I could get her to stop it if only she wasn't so weak and stupid and if I didn't have to protect her, as Dad said – and down in terms of my respect for her.'

- What Suzy did not know at that time was how Alex manipulated her into thinking her mother was weak and would be unable to cope even though Annie was clearly a strong woman, but if you are a child and your father tells you your mother is weak and vulnerable you believe him. Neither did Suzy know how her father ensured her mother did not know.

Dealing with a child's anger at failure to protect

For many children and young people the anger or even rage they can feel at their non-abusing parent for failing to protect them can be as great as their anger toward their abuser. For some, it is easier to displace their anger toward their abuser onto their non-abusing parent as a safer target. For Suzy, her mother became as culpable for her abuse as her father was. Once information became available about his grooming of both mother and daughter when Alex was in treatment, it was used in a positive way to facilitate more effective work in helping Suzy and her mother understand one another and move on in their relationship.

Other possible effects of sexual abuse on the child or young person

As we have seen (Chapter 1), research has highlighted the negative effects the discovery of child sexual abuse can have on mothers/parents/carers. When assessing the woman's ability to cope and to protect we need to take into account the fact that she is not dealing with an ordinary situation: the victim is also dealing with the fall-out from the abuse on themselves, on their relationships and on their perception of the world. Other children in the family will also be affected.

The possible effects of sexual abuse on the child have been well documented over the years and have provided a focus for work with victims. This section is not intended to duplicate that work in detail but to highlight some key issues before adding the context of how offender knowledge can contribute to our understanding of why this particular child is reacting in this particular way.

Early research

The foundation for working with children and families took place primarily in the 1980s and continues to influence our work today. For example Browne and Finkelhor (1986), in a review of the empirical evidence available at that time, highlighted a range of victim reactions to sexual abuse. These included fear, anxiety, aggression and sexually inappropriate behaviour, with frequent long-term effects including depression and self-destructive behaviour, anxiety, poor self-esteem, difficulty with issues of trust, feelings of social isolation and stigma, possible substance abuse and sexual difficulties.

Particularly helpful was Finkelhor's (1988) identification of 'traumagenic dynamic responses' in children where there is repeated abuse over a period of time which he linked to:

- *a sense of powerlessness*: associated with the sense of personal and physical discomfort

- *stigmatisation*: linked to issues of contempt, blame and denigration within the abuse

- *betrayal*: through the manipulation of trust, violation of care and lack of protection

- *sexualisation*: through premature and distressing arousal of sexual responses or through induction to a sexual partner role.

Possible physical and emotional signs of abuse

Early research tended to focus on behavioural effects and manifestations of abuse. To summarise, these included: sleep disturbance including poor sleep patterns and nightmares, bedwetting, eating problems such as loss of appetite, unusual fussiness, over-eating or more serious eating disorders, alcohol or drug misuse, aggression, withdrawal, unusual fears and phobias, clinging behaviour, sexually inappropriate behaviour, self-harm and/or running away, pregnancy and sexually transmitted diseases. In some cases children acted out problems through cruelty to other children or to animals. Symptoms of post-traumatic stress were found to include re-experiencing the abuse through flashbacks, emotional flatness, memory impairment, anxiety and hyper-alertness, irritability, mood swings and/or poor concentration.

Many of these early findings have been substantiated through subsequent research (e.g. Goodyear-Brown 2012) and represented in the literature and in UK government documents and guidelines for professionals.

Possible emotional and psychological effects

More recent research has looked more closely at some of the emotional and psychological effects. For example, Allnock *et al.* (2009) highlighted issues relating to depression, eating disorders, difficulties in emotional and stress management and post-traumatic stress. Similarly, Whitehead (2011) identified issues for some victims relating to memory impairment and dissociation.

No apparent effects

Every child is different. In terms of suspecting sexual abuse, the most difficult of all is the child who displays no apparent sign of any of these adverse effects. For example, school problems are often seen as being truancy or under-performing but less obvious is the child who is seen to perform normally but is perhaps overly committed to doing well.

Case example: Lisa

No one suspected that Lisa, aged 14, was being sexually abused by her father. She presented as being a bright, intelligent, vivacious and popular girl, much admired by her teachers for her academic abilities and her enthusiasm for sports and music. Eventually Lisa told a friend about her abuse, asking her friend not to tell anyone else. Such was her friend's concern that she reported it to a teacher. Both her mother and the staff at school found it hard to believe because Lisa did not 'act like a victim'. In interview Lisa described how the only way she could cope with her abusive home life, where she had no sense of control over her situation, was to make school her 'happy place' and where she could be herself.

The nature and longevity of effects of child sexual abuse

The negative impact of abuse can be acute, prolonged, delayed and/or long term. Finkelhor and Berliner (1995) found that up to 40 per cent of sexual abuse victims experienced no significant long-term negative experiences relating to their abuse. However, where the abuse is not disclosed or where there is inadequate understanding or support, the negative effects can become lifelong (Goodyear-Brown 2012). Such behavioural and/or emotional problems can alert other sex offenders and paedophiles, who then target and manipulate the child or young person for further abuse, which in some cases can include prostitution, whether online or in the real world.

Research also suggests that suicide is twice as likely as the norm in later life for victims of child sexual abuse (Calder, McVean and Lang 2010).

Why is this particular child reacting in this particular way?

It is important to use knowledge of the offender's cycle to increase our existing understanding of victims of sexual abuse. Research-based checklists are helpful in understanding how a child might respond to abuse but they can also lead to an overgeneralised approach and incorrect assumptions.

- How is it, for example, that two children who have experienced the same sexual assault by the same offender can be affected so differently?

- How is it that a child who is sexually 'touched' can be as traumatised as a child who is raped?

- Whilst sex offenders have many things in common every offender is different, therefore every child's experience is unique to them. Why is *this particular child* reacting in *this particular way?*

- Why won't this child talk to me?

There are a number of factors that can contribute to a child or young person's reactions to abuse: the physical nature, frequency and longevity of the abuse; the relationship between the offender and the child (whether parent, close relative, friend or stranger); the child's age at the onset of abuse; the stages of development through which the abuse continues; the effect on the child's developing patterns of attachment; the support (or otherwise) of the non-offending parent(s) and family. However, to understand these additional issues we can look again to the offender: not only what he did but how he did it, that is, to the cycle of offending. Whilst sex offenders have many things in common, every offender is different, therefore every child's experience is unique.

Stage six of the cycle: grooming the child and implanting thinking errors through the offender's distorted thinking

When we ask the question 'when did the abuse start?' this should relate not to when the acts of abuse began but when the grooming began. Child sexual abuse is not an act or an incident but also the corruption of a relationship. Most sex offenders do not go straight into assault as that would be too risky. Power and control are crucial to the offender's success. An offender must trap the child into a) compliance and b) not telling. The low conviction rate suggests they are adept at doing so. Research suggests that one in three children do not report abuse at the time (Radford *et al.* 2011). Clinical experience also suggests that if and when children do disclose, it is rarely in the form of a complete and clear disclosure, even when mothers or carers have taught the child they should tell if ever anything bad happens to them. Victims of abuse may drop verbal hints, or present worrying behaviour or emotions which provoke suspicion, or make partial disclosure but be reluctant to say more. Such is the power of grooming.

The complexity of grooming

This is a concept that has received much publicity and is now a criminal offence in the UK. However, it presents potential difficulties for mothers, partners and child protection practitioners alike. For example, grooming often consists of ordinary, commonly seen behaviour or acts of affection or kindness by an adult to a child and only becomes grooming when it is linked to a subsequent act of sexual abuse. So given how adept most sex offenders are at manipulation and cover-up, how to tell the difference?

There is a danger also that the concept of grooming can be oversimplified. Even the most obvious types of grooming such as bribery with gifts and treats can have a powerful cognitive as well as emotional impact on the child, and the process of grooming is often more subtle and complex as we have seen from the various examples quoted in previous chapters.

Grooming through his distorted thinking

Offenders not only engage in distorted thinking for their own needs but can also create thinking errors in the child. For example, if the offender convinces himself this is not abuse then it is equal and consenting. There are two ways he can do that. In his head the offender can either:

- upgrade the child to adult

- downgrade himself to child and sell the abuse as joint play.

Case example: Michael

Michael is an example of upgrading the child to adult, which he did by showing his seven-year-old niece a film of adult pornography, telling her 'that girl (i.e. woman) is beautiful, you're just like her' and treating her accordingly by having her copy the sexual acts that were on screen with him. He treated his niece like an adult cognitively, physically, socially and emotionally even though the child did not have any of the necessary sexual development or life experience to deal with it.

Case example: Ben

Ben, on the other hand, was a paedophile who sexually abused young boys. His grooming was to downgrade himself to child, providing the boys with games and activities he knew they would love. In Ben's case he was more comfortable with children than with adults and his pleasure in their play was genuine, which the boys recognised; they welcomed what they perceived to be his love, care and attention and had no reason to suspect where it would lead.

The following is a summary of comments by three sex offenders on how they groomed their victims:

- Offender one: tell them you're a friend.

- Offender two: tell them you love them.

- Offender three: tell them they love you.

Which is the most powerful? All these victims would find it hard to report someone whom they believed loved them but all three knew the message to the child was that of offender three. How can a child who 'loves' you willingly want to get you into trouble?

Tables 7.1 and 7.2 give further examples of relatively simple grooming techniques used with children and the powerful messages that are conveyed. The messages given do not happen by osmosis: they can be heavily implied by the offender or actually spoken, including during the act of abuse, further reinforcing the negative message to the child. Every child needs love, affection and an attachment to significant others. The offender will use the type of message to which his target child is most susceptible and which he thinks meets the particular wants or needs of the child, as well as meeting his own needs for power, control and, with many offenders, to convince himself that what he is doing is acceptable.

TABLE 7.1 BLAME MESSAGES

THE OFFENDER SAYS	THE CHILD THINKS
You're my friend I'm special	I'm his friend
I love you	This is love
You love me	I do, I can't live without you
You're so pretty	It's because I'm pretty
You like it	I must have asked for it
This is a game	We're just playing
You began the game	I did, it's my fault
Here's some money	I took the money, I'm a prostitute
You did it for free	I must have done it because I enjoyed it
You could have said no	I could have said no and I didn't
I've seen you with boys – you're a slut	I'm a slut
You haven't got a girlfriend	I must be gay because he likes me
If you don't like this you're a lesbian	I'm not a lesbian so I must have liked it – or am I gay?
This is natural, this is how men/dads are	This is how men/dads are
Your vagina is wet/penis is erect	I must have wanted it
I won't do it again	And he does – don't believe or trust men/adults
I love you because you're different	He's doing this because I'm black and black is bad
You're a good Muslim boy	Is this what my faith is about?

Adapted from Still *et al.* (2001)

TABLE 7.2 CONSEQUENCES OF TELLING

THE OFFENDER SAYS	THE CHILD THINKS
If you tell it will kill your mother	It will kill my mother
Your mother won't be able to cope without me	My mother is weak/stupid
If you tell you'll be sent away	I'll be sent away
If you tell your brothers and sisters	My family will split up, my mother will will be sent away hate me
If you tell we'll get into trouble	So I'm as responsible as he is

Adapted from Still, Faux and Wilson (2001)

As one particularly controlling offender summed up his goal in grooming his daughter for sexual assault: 'get her to think what I think, do what I do'.

The message from practitioner to child: 'it's not your fault'

One of the key messages given to victims of abuse, by child protection professionals and mothers alike, is to tell the child 'it was not your fault and you are not to blame'. Whilst this is correct, on its own it fails to take into account the actions of the offender in giving the child the opposite message. Offenders do this because they know that a child who thinks they are culpable or collusive in their own abuse is a child who is less likely to tell.

The abuse of culture and faith in grooming

As we saw when we looked at grooming of mothers and partners, a sex offender will use what is available to manipulate the young person or child, which can include issues of faith and/or culture. Consider the following case examples:

Case example: Matt

When Matt married Rose he became the only white member of an African Caribbean extended family. For Matt this encouraged him to consider himself to be something exceptional. Did this impact on his sexual arousal to his six-year-old niece? Issues relating to race and ethnicity can be seen as too sensitive to approach but in cases of child sexual abuse they can be important. For Matt, work on his offending cycle showed a clear association of white adult power over a black child, which in turn fed into his sexual arousal. For his six-year-old niece there was the message: 'is it because I'm black?' and/or 'this is what white men do'.

Case example: Imran

Imran was considered to be the head of his Muslim extended family in the UK. He sexually abused his eight-year-old nephew who was on a visit from other family in Pakistan. Imran had promised the boy's family that he would ensure the boy's continuation with the faith. Part of Imran's grooming of the boy was to tell him during the assaults that he was a good little Muslim boy. Later on when Imran was in assessment and doing an exercise on victim awareness he said he would like to ask his nephew's forgiveness because only then could he (Imran) receive God's forgiveness. What confusion does that create for this boy about his faith and his God? What if he does not want to forgive his uncle? Where does that leave him with his God?

Such issues can arise for children within any faith or ethnicity.

Different grooming styles

As with grooming of mothers and partners, an offender may present to the child as, for example, Mr Nice Guy, Mr Seductive, Mr Scary Guy and/or Mr Nasty Guy. Different grooming styles are likely to have a different impact on the child's cognitive learning, sexual development and attachment styles according to messages given to the child and the different ways the child has to find to survive.

For example, a seductive Mr Nice Guy can make himself emotionally indispensable to the child, especially if there are emotional deficits in the child's life such as an absent father. For one boy who was sexually abused by his mother's partner from the age of eight this emotional bond was so powerful that it led to him seeking out his abuser for love and attention (i.e. sex). When the abuser eventually lost interest because the boy was no longer in his age range of sexual interest, the boy threatened to disclose their relationship if he was abandoned.

A Mr Nasty Guy can rule by fear and intimidation, which may be just enough to silence the child or involve gratuitous power and control because it is part of the offender's sexual arousal.

Consistency and inconsistency in grooming style and behaviour

Some offenders are consistent in their style of grooming. Other offenders find it better to be unpredictable, presenting as Mr Nasty

Guy to the child one minute and Mr Nice Guy the next. They know the child must try to appease Mr Nasty Guy in order to maintain his or her special relationship with Mr Nice Guy. The offender is in control and the child is left guessing, reacting and trying to cope. This accounted for one daughter becoming withdrawn and self-harming as the only way she could deal with the stress not only of the abuse but the unpredictability of her situation: 'is this the day he will love me? Or reject me?'

Some offenders may behave one way with the child and completely differently with friends and family. This may seem obvious but it is nonetheless a powerful way to make the child think he or she will not be believed without the offender even telling them that. For example, Jim raped his niece Angie from the age of eight to 11, during family get-togethers. Hers was a close family but she never told anyone because: 'they all thought he was lovely, funny and kind. But when he was with me he was a different person. He threatened me, hurt me, terrified me...said he'd hurt me even more if I told anyone. I knew none of them [my family] would ever believe he was like that.'

Some offenders may commit similar assaults on several children but have different grooming styles with each child. This can lead to children being disbelieved because of what are perceived to be inconsistencies and conflicting statements. For example, one offender committed the same sexual assaults on his two seven-year-old nieces who were cousins. His sexual arousal was to one of the children with whom he became obsessed. He was not sexually interested in the other niece but because they were close friends he could not separate them: whenever he persuaded his 'target' to come to the house (when his wife was at work) the other child came too. As they were inseparable he could only abuse the child to whom he was aroused if he abused them both, but his style of grooming differed with each child. His style of grooming the child in whom he was sexually interested was seductive, like a 'love affair', whereas his style with the other child whose presence he resented was one of anger, impatience and irritation.

The same grooming tactic can be used for different grooming styles. We can hear words used by offenders to describe their grooming but words can have different meanings.

One of the most common grooming tactics is to encroach gradually on the child's physical and emotional space through play. This can be effective with any age group, whether in ordinary games, digital games or rough-and-tumble horseplay. However, there can be different styles of play.

EXERCISE
COMPARE RICK AND JAZ

Rick

Rick abused sons of friends aged eight and nine. He felt more comfortable with the boys than with their adult parents. He was affectionate, loving and fun. He took them to air shows and played games with them that any boy would love and which Rick genuinely enjoyed as much as they did. For the boys the message was 'this is play, love, warmth, affection, friendship', of which the sexual abuse became a part.

Jaz

Jaz also said he groomed his victims through play but his kind of play was the coercion and intimidation of the bully: 'I choose the games and I set the rules'. He set up some of the children to win and others to lose, for whom there was the humiliating message that 'you're no good and this is your forfeit/punishment which you deserve', that is, sexual abuse, but 'it's just a game'.

Again, the mixture of cognitive, emotional and sexual impacts will differ whilst the grooming tactic of 'play' is the same.

Sadistic offenders versus non-sadistic offenders

Most sex offenders who abuse children engage in distorted thinking to persuade themselves that they are not causing harm to the child. However, it is important to remember that for a minority of sex offenders who abuse children the opposite is true. Sadistic offenders are different from Mr Nasty Guys because their motivation is to inflict pain, which is a part of their sexual arousal.

Non-sadistic offenders and the invisible child

Salter (1995) highlighted the difference between sadistic and other offenders and the consequences for how children adapt and survive. The non-sadistic Mr Nice Guy offender commonly projects onto his victim his own sexual arousal and reinterprets the child's responses to suit his own needs. So distress in the child is read as their being sexually aroused and cooperation in the abuse to avoid hurt and pain is seen as the child liking and wanting it. For him the real child becomes invisible. Ask such an offender what would happen if he allowed himself to see what was truly happening with the child and he is likely to say that he would have to stop – which at the time he did not want to do.

For the invisible child whose responses are misread there is cognitive confusion and emotional dissonance in terms of what is right or wrong in human interaction and sexual behaviour. The message from the offender that he or she must have liked it and wanted it can contribute to the child's sense of blame and responsibility for their own abuse. However, such a child's response to treatment can often be positive in terms of welcoming recognition of themselves as a valid individual after having been treated as a sexual object throughout the abuse.

Sadistic offenders and the visible child

However, for the sadistic offender the child remains highly visible because registering their fear and pain feeds into his sexual arousal. Salter notes how 'sadistic offenders know the child's reactions and use them as a guide to increase suffering' (1995, p.129). For example, the offender sees the child loves a particular toy or a pet and something nasty happens to that toy or pet. Such a child soon sees it is dangerous to show their true thoughts and feelings and learns not to do it. Salter observes that victims and adult survivors of sadistic sexual abuse typically 'resist intimacy – not because they fear betrayal, as the survivor of non-sadistic abuse does – but because they fear that their vulnerability will be used to hurt them' (1995, p.129). Furthermore, a child who has been abused by a sadistic offender is likely to have a fearful response to any adult who tries to encourage them to 'open up', whether it is a police officer, a social worker, or a mother or carer.

The sadistic offender can be sadistic in grooming as well as in the nature of the assault.

Differences in timings in the offending cycle

Children and young people who are sexually abused do not know about the theory of cycles or pathways to sex offending but many who are subjected to repeated abuse will instinctively recognise the offender's pattern and then find ways to cope and to survive. Important factors will be not only the nature of the act of abuse but also the timing of it and the style of grooming, for example, predictable and unpredictable timing.

Predictable timing

Some offenders are the same all the time and have predictable timing to their cycle so the victim begins to know when it will happen, which in turn will produce emotions and behaviours and coping mechanisms accordingly. This accounted, for example, for one stepdaughter hiding under the bed at night to sleep when she knew it was 'that time'.

Unpredictable timing

Some offenders are unpredictable in their timing. One teenage daughter found the only way to cope with this was to go to her father and say 'let's do it' because that was the only way she knew she could sleep safely for the next few nights and take back some control of her life. Needless to say, in therapy the offender said 'I did it because she asked me to', which was true, except he was omitting his actions that placed her in that position.

Believing and disbelieving children: difference in the child and offender perspectives

It takes considerable courage for victims to disclose, but before action can be taken they have to be believed. It is not uncommon for children's stories to be considered unreliable, not least because the offender challenges the veracity or accuracy of the child's statement. Whilst this is often based on the offender's blatant lies, sometimes it reflects a difference in perception of the same events.

Case example: Joe

Joe, who had abused his partner's seven-year-old daughter, threw doubt on the veracity of the child's statement by insisting that her claim that he sexually abused her in the bathroom was a lie. Further investigation led to an admission by Joe of 'fondling' her in the bedroom but an insistence that the child was still exaggerating and that he did nothing to her in the bathroom, which discredited the rest of her statement. During an extended specialist assessment the following was elicited. Joe acknowledged letting the child come into the bathroom to use the toilet when he was undressing to have a bath. He admitted to already having fantasised about her sexually, that he was aroused by her presence (i.e. his penis was erect) and that he was wearing only a T-shirt. When asked to describe the scene he acknowledged that his height compared to the child's meant his erect penis was at the level of the child's face and that the bathroom was so small that the child's face was in close proximity to his penis. He was not able to progress to the abuse of his fantasy because he was interrupted by someone else wanting the bathroom.

The difference was in the perceptions of the offender and the victim: to the offender the sexual touching in the bedroom was most arousing and most memorable because his fantasy reached fruition but the incident in the bathroom was most frightening and more memorable to the child.

Grooming can be as traumatising as assault

When all these types and styles of grooming tactics are considered, it is not difficult to see how for some children the grooming tactics of the offender can be as traumatising as the sexual assault.

Placing the child's experience into a developmental model

This understanding can be further enhanced by placing the child's experience into a developmental model: at what age and stage of development was the child exposed to the offender and through what stages of development did it continue?

Some implications for work with the child

An awareness of how sex offenders function informs our therapeutic approach to the child because it can help us:

- to convey to the child a truer sense that we know about men who sexually abuse children – how they do what they do – and therefore we have an understanding of what they have experienced

- to find answers to questions such as 'why is this particular child or young person reacting in this particular way?' and 'why might a child who is indecently assault be as traumatised as a child who is raped?' and many others

- to gain a greater understanding of the emotional, cognitive and psychological impact on the individual child or young person, taking into account his or her whole abusive experience being caught up with each stage of the offender's cycle

- to avoid inadvertently duplicating the offender's grooming style in the therapeutic relationship

- to address the thinking errors in the child that contribute to an inappropriate sense of guilt and self-blame

- to understand that a child who has been abused by a sadistic offender will have special needs and a different perception of the therapeutic process from other children.

Knowledge of sex offenders in general, and of a particular offender where possible, is vital to decision making as to what is and is not in the child's best interests in terms of risk and safety as well as decisions about residence, contact and any conditions that may be laid down in child protection plans.

Seeking an apology from the offender: a good or bad idea?

It is vital also if we are to know when something is a good or bad idea. For example, sometimes victims and survivors express a wish to confront their abuser and seek an apology from him as part of their own therapeutic process. However, their right or need to do so needs to be balanced with an awareness of the degree to which the offender is likely to abuse such a meeting by using words, gestures or other trigger mechanisms relating to earlier grooming which we as the supervising practitioner may fail to recognise, as explained by Eldridge and Still (1995): 'Although some offenders can change and do have genuinely positive agendas, some do not and will inadvertently or even wilfully reabuse under the guise of an apology' (p.158).

Where issues relate to the abuse of culture or faith, a child protection worker may need some specialist guidance as to how to help the child unravel those particular implanted thinking errors.

Conclusions

As we have seen, preconditions three and four to sex offending (Finkelhor 1986) require the sex offender to disempower any protective carer who may get in his way and ensure the child does not tell; within the offending cycle, grooming refers not only to his grooming of the child but also his grooming of the mother/carer to ensure that if the child does tell, the mother will not hear or believe the disclosure or act on it. The application of knowledge about sex offenders in general, and where possible specific information about a known or suspected offender, is therefore invaluable in terms of working out how this was achieved.

In Chapter 13 we look at how we can use this knowledge to inform the questions we ask a mother/partner in assessment. In Chapter 14 we look also at how this knowledge can be put to good use in direct work with her. However, whilst the primary focus of this book is on mothers and partners, this section also demonstrates the potential value in applying knowledge of sex offenders to our work with victims of abuse.

References

Allnock, D., Bunting, L., Price, A., Morgan-Klein. N. *et al.* (2009) *Sexual Abuse and Therapeutic Services for Children and Young People: The Gap Between Provision and Need: Full Report.* London: NSPCC.

Browne, A. and Finkelhor, D. (1986) 'Impact of sexual abuse: A review of the research.' *Psychological Bulletin 99*, 1, 66–77.

Calder, J., McVean, A. and Yang, W. (2010) 'History of abuse and current suicidal ideation: Results from a population based survey.' *Journal of Family Violence 25*, 2, 205–214.

Eldridge, H. and Still, J. (1995) 'Apology and Forgiveness in the Context of the Cycles of Adult Male Sex Offenders Who Abuse Children.' In A.C. Salter (ed.) *Transforming Trauma.* Thousand Oaks, CA: Sage.

Finkelhor, D. (1986*) A Sourcebook on Child Sexual Abuse.* Beverley Hills, CA: Sage.

Finkelhor, D. and Berliner, L. (1995) 'Research on the treatment of sexually abused children: A review and recommendations.' *Child Adolescent Psychiatry 34*, 11, 1408–1423.

Finkelhor, D., Williams, L.M. and Burns, N. (1988) *Nursery Crimes.* Thousand Oaks, CA: Sage.

Goodyear-Brown, P. (ed.) (2012) *Handbook of Child Sexual Abuse: Identification, Assessment and Treatment.* Hoboken, NJ: Wiley.

Radford, L., Corral, S., Bradley, C., Fisher, H. *et al.* (2011) *Child Abuse and Neglect in the UK Today.* London: NSPCC.

Salter, A.C. (1995) *Transforming Trauma: A Guide to Understanding and Treating Adult Survivors of Child Sexual Abuse.* Thousand Oaks, CA: Sage.

Still, J., Faux, M. and Wilson, C. (2001) *The Thames Valley Partner's Programme.* The Home Office, London. Crown Copyright 2001.

Whitehead, J. (2011) 'How do children cope with sexual abuse?' Protecting Children Update 84, 9–10.

CHAPTER 8

THE EFFECT OF THE OFFENDER ON FAMILY DYNAMICS

We have seen the various ways in which sex offenders manipulate mothers and partners into a position of ineffectiveness as a protective carer, marginalising her from the child they intend to abuse. Post-disclosure, this inevitably affects the perception of other children in the family, for whom her position as the primary protector and carer will have also been undermined. In this chapter we consider what she has to manage in terms of the impact of the abuse on the family.

All family members are affected by the abuse, by the disclosure and by the intervention of outside agencies and whether the family has lost the victim or the perpetrator or both, creating problems such as anger, blame, rivalry and scapegoating. Even if the offender is no longer present the family pattern of communication persists. This not only creates family dysfunction but it leaves the family vulnerable to further sexual abuse.

Further worries for the mother/partner

As we saw in Chapter 2, she is likely to have a range of concerns about other children in the family: did he abuse them too? Might he in future? Will I lose them too? Will they blame me? If they say they weren't abused does that mean it didn't happen or are they just covering it up? Am I the only one who didn't know? Are there any more secrets? How do they feel about me? If I choose to end my relationship with the known or suspected offender will they blame me for the loss of father/stepfather/grandfather/friend from their lives? For many women the natural response is to promise themselves never to let abuse happen again. Whilst this is a laudable goal and one of which the child protection authorities would approve, it carries the risk of being over-protective and stifling the child or young person's natural need for social and sexual discovery, expression and development.

The impact on the victim's relationships with other family members

For children and young people who have been sexually abused the impact on their relationships with other family members can vary according to the nature of the offender's grooming tactics. For example, they may have been groomed:

- to be protective of their mother ('it will kill her if you tell')

- to protect their siblings ('they'll be taken away and put into care')

- to sacrifice themselves to protect siblings ('if I let him do this to me he won't do it to my sister/brother' – but maybe he did)

- to think they are special, only to discover they were not special because he has abused ('loved') other children.

Some consequences for siblings

- When an offender treats his victim as special this will mean other siblings are not special and so don't receive the love, gifts or treats. This in turn creates jealousy, resentment, tensions and conflict.

- Favouritism can be subtle but as we have seen there are those offenders who enjoy a gratuitous sense of power and control or who may enjoy inflicting hurt on others. Their favouritism may be more obvious, as with the offender who said to his victim 'you get the good stuff, the others get the trash', or the offender who said 'I only want you. I don't want your brother because he's too ugly', when all the brother knows is that he is not special because he is ugly.

- An offender who is scary, intimidating, strict, aggressive and sometimes violent, but not with his victim, provokes resentment: why is it he/she never gets punished?

- The offender who scapegoats his victim whilst making his or her siblings feel special conveys the message to the other children not to rock the boat because they too could fall out of favour.

Post-disclosure

It would be good to think that when a child discloses sexual abuse the family is kind, supportive and understanding but sadly that is often not the case. Siblings can be angry with the victim:

- for being responsible for the abuse

- for reporting it

- for causing the problems in the family

- for hurting their mother

- for causing them to lose their father, stepfather, relative or family friend and for causing him hurt, pain, embarrassment, loss of job and/or to going to prison

- for loss of their provider.

Siblings can experience a sense of guilt, for example, for not knowing, for knowing or suspecting but not reporting, for having bad feelings towards others. Post-discovery the 'favoured' victim still may not see the offender's treatment of them as abuse and so defend him from the criticism and vilification of other family members, thus prolonging conflicts.

Removing the offender does not make it all go away

The offender has manipulated the whole situation, which often means playing off family members against one another. If he is removed from the family home children may be protected from further sexual risk but the dysfunctional family relationships which he created remain. Furthermore, family members will often have no idea how things got so bad. This happens not only in cases of incest but also in cases of abuse by family friends and associates where the connection with the family is a close one.

EXERCISE
THE M FAMILY

The nuclear family consists of:

- Ian Stepfather to all three children
- Jean Mother to all three children
- Jim Son, age 15 years
- Carol Daughter, age 13 years
- Emma Daughter, age nine years

Background

When Ian met Jean six years ago he saw a close-knit single parent family with warm relationships between mother and children. When he and Jean married Jean saw him as being a good husband and stepfather. He was a nice man, not violent, had a good sense of humour and provided for his family. He raped Carol regularly from the age of 11. He told Carol it was because she was so special and he was in love with her; that one day he would marry her and she could have his baby. At first he made Carol feel very special. He was always generous with all three children but Carol always received more than her brother and sister – which they noticed and didn't like. Ian got Carol on her own when his wife went to do the regular weekly supermarket shop. It was at a time when Carol's brother Jim regularly went to a friend's house to play video games but her younger sister Emma would be home. He would always make a game with Emma that she should do something special for her mother for when she returned, for example, draw her a picture or make her something, which Emma would then get absorbed in doing. He would also sit Emma at the table by the window and tell her to watch out for her mother's return, to make sure her surprise for her mother was always ready – and he always told Emma to shout out to him that her mother was on her way, so that he could welcome her back too. Everyone thought Ian was lovely. No one knew about the abuse. Carol was confused; there was a part of Ian she loved but she hated the rape. She could not tell because she knew how much the rest of her family loved him.

Consider the following

- How would these family members feel about one another before disclosure, when only Ian and Carol know about the abuse?

  (Possibilities include sibling jealousy of Ian's favouritism and Carol's extra treats; sibling rivalry; offender's divide and rule, distancing of victim from mum because of the secret – and mother in the middle of it all.)

- What do you think would happen to these family relationships if Carol were to disclose the abuse and Ian denied it?

  (Would the family automatically believe Carol? Or Ian? Would they all think the same thing? Are there vested individual and family interests to be protected?)

- What if Ian were then made to leave home by the authorities?

  (Remember Ian presented as Mr Nice Guy. Likely associated issues for other family members would be denial; blame the victim – 'she took the extra treats, she told' – seeing it as less serious than it is; anger at outside agencies; blame mother for letting them send stepfather away; be angry about their own loss of their nice stepfather – 'he's Dad'; 'he was nice; he looked after us, we had money'; grief and loss; isolate and scapegoat the victim and/or feel guilty that they did not know what was going on; sense of guilt and betrayal by youngest daughter if she has any suspicion that she was set up as a look out.)

- What if brother Jim knew but did nothing to protect?

- What if Carol complied with ongoing rape because she thought by doing so she was protecting her little sister, and then discovers that Ian was also sexually abusing Emma? What effect might that have on Carol? On Emma? On their relationship?

- What if Ian had not been a Mr Nice Guy but a Mr Angry – intimidating and creating fear by threatening physical punishment?

  (Possibilities include relief that he's gone; protective of one another; feel guilty that they weren't able to stand up to him; embarrassed and unable to face one another; avoidant of one another; angry that it has messed up their lives; displace their anger on to others and not the abuser; angry at mother for not telling him to go earlier; they just want it to go away; worry that it could happen again; distrustful that mother will bring someone else like that into the family.)

- What if he was always nice to Carol and Jean but angry and intimidating to Jim and Emma?

- What if he was Mr Nice Guy who did not abuse anyone inside the family but he sexually assaulted one of Carol's friends?

- Might Jean be worried about all these possibilities?

Implications for work with mothers/partners, children and families

The goal in assessing mothers and partners in cases of known or suspected child sexual abuse is to understand the circumstances of her failure to protect and to devise an intervention plan, where appropriate, to consider what assistance may be needed to empower her for the future to keep her child(ren) safe and to help the child who has been abused in their recovery. This requires an understanding not only of her responses to abuse, as considered in previous chapters, but also what she now has to manage in terms of the impact of the abuse on the child and on other family members and relationships.

Conclusions

In assessing and working effectively with mothers and partners in cases of child sexual abuse we do so in the context of the impact of the abuse not only on the mother/partner but also on the victim and on wider family relationships. When we see dysfunctional and problematic family dynamics we need to ask the question 'how did they get this way?' Or, more precisely, 'what did the offender do to make them that way?' Or if they were a problem before, 'how did he use that to his advantage in manipulating the situation for abuse?' This in turn needs to be put into the context not only of the nature of the abuse (what did he do, when, for how long?) but also the type of offender: how did he do it? The question as to when the abuse started is more helpful when it looks at when grooming started. To repeat the mantra of this book, whilst sex offenders have many things in common every sex offender is different so every child, mother/partner and family's experience is unique to them.

In cases of suspected or alleged abuse where there is no prosecution or conviction, general knowledge of how sex offenders operate can be used to help us understand the family tensions and conflicts caused and/or encouraged by an offender during abuse and post-abuse. In cases where there is a known and convicted offender, detailed information should be sought from his past or present supervising officer and any sex offender treatment programme he may have attended. By using this information in our assessment of the mother/partner we gain a more detailed understanding of her situation within the family.

Dysfunctional family dynamics do not just disappear if and when an offender is removed. By applying this knowledge as part of an intervention programme of work with the mother/partner any residual family conflicts and tensions can be addressed to inform work on helping to repair damaged relationships and to help the family move into a more united front, with all parties considering the question of 'how did he do that to me, to us?'

The practical application of this knowledge to assessment and intervention is addressed in Chapters 13 and 14.

CHAPTER 9

WHAT CAN HINDER A GOOD ASSESSMENT?
THE MOTHER'S OR PARTNER'S PERSPECTIVE

Any human interaction is open to positive or negative influences, perceptions, interpretations, understandings and misunderstandings. In Chapter 1 we looked at issues related to denial and disbelief. We looked at how such responses are worrying in terms of the mother's or partner's ability to protect but how they may also represent normal reactions in terms of human nature. In assessment we may see women who are ready and willing to cooperate in order to understand what is happening. However, few of us would choose to be in this situation and research suggests that non-offending parents experience overwhelming emotions and conflicts with child protection investigations which they find difficult and intrusive (Tuttle *et al.* 2007). The following are some more of the issues mothers and partners have fed back over the years relating to their worries, hopes and fears about their assessment.

'Why are you spending all this time asking me all these questions? I didn't do it – he did'

When the mother or partner is being assessed the spotlight is on her. In Chapter 2 we looked at how we pursue the question of 'did she know?' Where there is no prosecution or prior conviction and no viable assessment of the known or suspected offender the onus falls on her as a source of information and as the protective parent or carer. This means that our assessment of her is often longer and more intense than our interviews with him, increasing her sense of guilt, blame and responsibility and that it is she who is being punished. So whilst our goal may be to help and empower her, for many women the assessment process can feel hostile and accusatory.

'You think I'm a bad mother?'

Some women in this situation may already be known to various agencies for other parenting problems, such as neglect, and the issue of sexual abuse needs to be considered in that context. However, for many other women that is not the case. From the woman's viewpoint, the sense of being blamed may be compounded by the fact that our duty to protect the child may require short-term protection measures, such as the removal of the alleged perpetrator from the family home or removal of the child or strict conditions on contact and/or the establishment of rules on what is and is not allowed in the family home, all of which will add to the existing negative impact on the mother, child and family of any abuse and its disclosure to the authorities, as described in Chapter 1.

Any such action, whilst being deemed necessary, has the further effect of demonstrating to children that their mother/carer is not trusted by the authorities, who appear to have taken over decision making from her, even if efforts have been made to include her in that process. If the authorities do not trust her why should the child(ren)? This can further exacerbate the problems we saw in the last chapter on the negative impact of the offender on family relationships and weaken the mother's position further.

'Do they know what they're doing?'

Assessment outcome can have a huge impact not only on the woman and the child who has been abused but also the whole family. Therefore it is important for her to have faith in the expertise of the person assessing her. So any inability to answer simple questions about offenders will not inspire confidence. For example, one common and reasonable question for the woman to ask any child protection worker when she is given a known or suspected offender's risk evaluation (low, medium or high) is 'how do you know?' A common response to this is 'because the probation officer/police officer/psychologist says so' without being able to explain how or why. In those cases where there is no specialist offender assessment of the known or suspected offender there is often bewilderment: 'if you are so worried how come you haven't done that?' Limited resources will seem like a poor reason when she and her family have so much at stake.

'Why should I believe you?': mixed messages

At a time when her life has been turned upside down it is natural for the woman to look for something to hold on to for clarity and guidance. Mixed messages do the opposite.

For example, it is possible to see in one case file conflicting references to an individual being all of low, medium and high risk (see the next main section of this chapter), so the mother or partner who receives this information receives conflicting messages. This will not inspire confidence.

'Low risk equals no risk'

Specialist offender assessments are commonly framed in terms of high, medium and low risk (see the next section). When asking a mother or offender's partner her thoughts as to what, for example, 'low risk' means it is not uncommon for her to say it means 'no risk', not because she is stupid but because that is what the offender has told her. Needless to say, a sex offender who has been found out and knows he is still a risk and does not want to stop offending will choose to quote the low version to anyone who may need to hear it, especially if he wants to persuade his partner and/or the child's mother that he is safe to stay in the family or retain contact, or if he wants to move in with a new family.

It is not uncommon for the woman never to meet the person who did the assessment. If she has not had an adequate explanation as to why professionals are concerned then we should not be surprised if the offender's version prevails.

'What is "child sexual abuse"?'

This may seem a ridiculous question and women are not stupid. However, sometimes a mother or partner can present as not seeing a situation as being as serious as we do. We saw in the previous chapter how not only mothers and partners but also professionals can have different perceptions of what does and does not constitute abuse.

Furthermore, a sex offender who is already distorting his own thinking to justify, minimise or deny the seriousness of his actions will tap into any misconceptions the woman may have. So when she asks him 'did you sexually abuse him/her?' the abuser can say convincingly that they did not, even though they did. She may believe him and not us because:

- she has heard different versions of 'the truth' from different agencies and practitioners

- the offender is so convincing

- she shares popular misconceptions of what constitutes abuse

- the offender's influence has been so powerful that she now shares his definitions of abuse.

'I'm a survivor of childhood sexual abuse and I know more about this than you do'

This raises several issues. For example:

Reliving her own abuse

We must be sensitive to the fact that in such cases the woman is dealing not only with the current situation but also that she is also likely to be reliving her own past through flashbacks with varying degrees of related trauma. This is likely to be especially difficult for women who received no help or counselling at the time of their abuse.

At an advantage? Or a double disadvantage?

It is not unreasonable for a woman who has experienced sexual abuse to consider that she knows what sex offenders are like, perhaps better than child protection professionals. The problem is that whilst sex offenders have many things in common they are all different. This is likely to distort her perception of risk because although she may know her individual offender well, the current known or suspected offender may bear no similarity to him. Worse, some sex offenders will see this as a vulnerability they can employ in grooming: 'it was terrible what he did to you and I'm not like that'. Therefore although she may believe her evaluation of the situation is more accurate than ours, it is not. However, this is not a message a woman will want to hear as it can feel like she is being re-victimised.

Similarly, as someone who has been abused herself she may consider she knows what it is like and that therefore this would provide her with the advantage of additional insight into the experience and needs of the child. Whilst that may be true for some women, for others the opposite can be true. No two sex offenders are the same, no two acts of abuse are the same and no two responses to abuse are the same. Furthermore, if she has unresolved emotional and/or cognitive issues of her own relating to her own abuse it can be doubly hard for her to understand the child.

The danger is that in child protection terms this can be seen as a lack of victim awareness and/or empathy, which in assessment can go against her, whereas it is simply that no one has helped her unravel her confusion. Clinical experience suggests that once a situation has been identified many women can move forward with appropriate help.

'I'm not the kind of person who can be manipulated!'

It may be helpful to us to know that sex offenders manipulate and groom their partners and/or the child's mother but this too is not a message any woman would want to hear.

As one woman said following assessment: 'you mean in addition to what he did to my daughter he manipulated me as well? Was it all manipulation? Was any of it real?', to which the answer might be yes, no, some of it, most of it. None are good news and responses of fight or flight would be understandable.

'Will this assessment never end?'

It is often assumed that to be thorough an assessment must take many hours spread over months. By the time the assessment begins the mother or partner will have already gone through hearing about the suspicions, allegations or disclosures plus the investigation process, so it may be safe to assume that she is feeling emotionally raw and would rather not have to go through this further experience with us. We have seen that research suggests the discovery of child sexual abuse has a negative impact on non-offending parents. Prolonged exposure to the doubts, suspicions and questioning that have to be dealt with in assessment is unlikely to help and may account for some of the research findings that non-offending parents experience overwhelming emotions and conflicts with child protection investigations which they find difficult and intrusive (see Chapter 1).

For the mother or partner, the unavoidably intrusive assessment can lead to a loss of confidence in the decision making process and a depressing sense that it will never end.

'What about me?': the forbidden question

We have established the many difficulties mothers and partners can face following child sexual abuse and the prospect of being assessed is unlikely to make her situation easier. She may have little support because the offender manipulated her into a situation of isolation because that was safer for him; where there are family and friends it is a subject that women commonly do not wish to discuss with them for fear of being questioned, blamed, stigmatised or gossiped about. Yet feedback from many women suggests they are reluctant to share this in assessment for the following reasons:

- They were afraid of being perceived as weak and therefore not able to care for and/or protect their child(ren).

- They believed they had to present as being strong even if they were struggling and needed help.

- If they did anything to relieve their own unhappiness it was seen as being uncaring and insensitive about the child (for example, a mother received a bad assessment because she was seen out having a drink in a pub with a friend, whereas the friend knew she was depressed, knew that would not help her or her child and had spent weeks persuading her to leave the house).

- If they have mentioned their own problems they were assessed as being self-centred at a time when they should only be concerned about the child.

Implications for work with mothers and partners

- When we as professionals are under pressure and have limited time it is easy to forget the human perspective of the woman's situation. However, this carries the risk of misunderstanding responses and inappropriate conclusions.

- It is important to safeguard against giving mothers and partners mixed messages. If she cannot make sense of or trust what we are saying, she will be more susceptible to the persuasive arguments of an offender and more likely to go behind the back of the authorities by, for example, breaking any conditions of residence or contact that may be set.

- We need to understand any additional factors relating to the mother's/partner's history. If a woman is a survivor of abuse that does not make her a bad person or a bad mother. However, it can raise issues with which she may need additional assistance to enable her to meet the needs of the child(ren).

- We have seen the extent of the difficulties many mothers and partners have to face. Their situation will not be helped by the offender who is likely to feel threatened at the prospect of her spending individual time with any professional worker who may try to tell her otherwise, especially if he is not present to counter their arguments. We have seen the extent to which sex offenders need to manipulate and groom their partner/ the child's mother into not suspecting abuse or believing a disclosure. If the offender is still on the scene it is likely that he will need to prime her to think favourably of him.

- How long should an assessment take? We need to strike a balance between an assessment not being so short as to impinge on its accuracy and not so long as to lose its focus. And we need an assessment approach that is specific to the issues related to child sexual abuse.

References

Tuttle, A.R., Kundson-Martin, C., Lewis, S., Taylor, B. and Andrews, J. (2007) 'Parents' experiences in child protective services: Analysis of a dialogical group process.' *Family Process 46*, 3, 367–380.

CHAPTER 10

ARE WE ALL SPEAKING THE SAME LANGUAGE?
IMPROVING INTER-AGENCY UNDERSTANDING

Cases of child sexual abuse can cover a wide range of scenarios, which draw in professionals from statutory and voluntary child protection agencies, health, education, police, probation, psychology and potentially two legal systems: the criminal courts and the family courts. Decision making is therefore a multi-agency task but as Salter observed (1995) there is a divide between those working with offenders and those working with victims and families, and little has changed. Whilst we all talk of child sexual abuse we use different language, we apply different meanings to key words, we assess safety and danger in different ways and we use different clinical approaches. This can cause bewilderment and misunderstanding to mothers and partners for whom the stakes are high. If someone is considered a sexual risk, who says so? How was that conclusion reached? To whom does he present a sexual risk? How and when? If there has not been a prosecution or conviction why should she believe it? Or, if she is more worried about him than we are why is there not more being done? What if there are several assessments that differ in opinion, for example, between one saying low risk and another saying high risk? This is exacerbated by the fact that it is often the social worker or another child protection practitioner who is left to answer these questions, often with insufficient information to do so. This in turn creates loopholes which sex offenders can and do use to manipulate situations to their own advantage.

In Chapter 2 we looked at issues relating to denial and disbelief. If we as child protection practitioners are asking a woman to believe her partner or someone close to her presents a low, medium or high sexual risk to children it is not unreasonable for her to ask us how we know that. That is not an easy question to answer but given that what is at stake for her is, for example, the possible removal of her partner and/or child(ren) from the home and/or restricted contact it is incumbent on us to be equipped as best we can, to give her some idea as to how and why, even when it is someone else who has conducted that assessment. We should be able to respond also to any legal challenges. We do not need to be experts but we should have enough background information to understand key issues. For example, there are a number of ways in which sexual risk can be assessed. Some assessments are based on models derived from research into 'lower risk' sample populations from community-based sex offender treatment programmes and others are based on 'high risk' sample groups from prison populations, which can therefore skew the research results; some can only be used in certain types of situation; some of them are more accurate and/or more thorough than others.

In the previous chapter we considered the assessment process from the mother's/partner's perspective. In this chapter we consider some of the pitfalls of inter-agency working and how they may be remedied not only through good communication and cooperation but also through a greater understanding of each other's perspective during multi-agency assessment, discussion and decision making.

We will consider the following issues:

- different uses of terminology

- a simple explanation of five different approaches to risk assessment, including their strengths and limitations, to illustrate the differences between how risk is evaluated by different people in different ways in different agencies

- an explanation of how these issues can create problems in our assessment of mothers and partners

- by way of solution, we will provide child protection practitioners and managers with questions to ask about any particular risk assessment or use of language, so as to inform answers to questions we can be asked by mothers and partners.

Our use of terminology

The simple answer to this question is that there is a fair chance we are not. In child sexual abuse the absence of clear evidence and information makes the need for good communication essential, yet the scope for getting our wires crossed not only between us and the non-offending parent, but also between us and other professionals and agencies is considerable. This problem would be greatly diminished if everyone involved used the same correct language and terminology. Consider the following.

What is sexual risk?

The cornerstone to any assessment in cases of child sexual abuse is the concept of present and future risk. When there are other factors that argue in favour of continuing contact and/or residence in the family home, a risk assessment informs the question 'what would be safe enough?' But the term risk means different things to people in different professions and different agencies. This is a complex area but the following explains some basic principles relevant to everyday practice.

Civil versus criminal justice concepts

When discussing risk of further abuse by the same offender, in child protection we commonly talk about the likelihood of him *re-offending* meaning 'if he has done it to a child once will he do it again?' In the criminal justice system, however, risk assessment commonly uses research-based models where the term 're-offending' refers to the likelihood of their being reconvicted (Craig *et al.* 2008, p.34). In such assessments the concept of risk refers to *recidivism*, that is, 'will he do it again, be caught and be convicted?' Furthermore, in child protection risk is also perceived in terms of *likely significant harm*, a concept that does not feature in criminal assessments. In family courts there can be a *Finding of Fact*, which also does not feature in criminal courts and is not the same as a *conviction*. A Finding of Fact means the family court Judge has considered allegations to be valid, which informs his or her decision as to whether or not the case warrants any legal Order to protect the child, but there is no capacity for criminal punishment. For some professionals this is their everyday work, but not so for others. So in multi-agency discussions are we sure we are all talking about the same thing?

Low, medium and high risk: divided by a common language

There is no such thing as zero risk. In child protection what we look for is:

- what is in the best interests of the child

- what is safe enough

- how that can best be managed.

Sex offender assessments within the criminal justice system use protocols that categorise risk in terms of *low, medium* and *high risk* and this has become the formal language of risk assessment across the inter-agency board. However, whilst a social worker may consider any risk to be high out of motivation to play safe and protect the child, the police or probation officer may, or even should, evaluate the same case as low risk. It is possible therefore to see in one case file conflicting references to an individual being all of low, medium and high risk. This is one reason why women can receive conflicting messages, and also sometimes the child or young person. We as practitioners and managers need to be able to explain what is meant and how it was assessed.

What is 'child sexual abuse'?

Whilst those working in child protection know this term covers a wide range of scenarios, if you ask a lay person the range is likely to shrink considerably simply because it is outside their experience and/or imagination. For example, some people connote it only to rape whilst others think of rape only in terms of vaginal penetrative sex. Some do not consider online activity as abuse if it does not involve direct sexual contact with a child or young person. Similarly, the belief that young people can present as being overly mature for their age and sexually precocious is not restricted to sex offenders but can often be heard being expressed, albeit erroneously, among the general population.

Professionals from all agencies need clarity on this issue otherwise mothers and partners receive mixed messages. This can undermine the woman's trust and confidence in us, which in turn can be used by a sex offender to his advantage. For example: 'they said it was indecent assault but I only touched her'; 'they said I raped her but it was oral sex'. In 2010 HM Government provided the following definition:

> Sexual abuse involves forcing or enticing a child or young person to take part in sexual activities, not necessarily involving a high level of violence, whether or not the child is aware of what is happening. The activities may involve physical contact, including

assault by penetration (e.g. rape, or oral sex) or non-penetrative acts such as masturbation, kissing, rubbing and touching outside of clothing. They may also include non-contact activities, such as involving children in looking at, or in the production of, sexual images, watching sexual activities, encouraging children to behave in sexually inappropriate ways, or grooming a child in preparation for abuse (including via the internet). Sexual abuse is not solely perpetrated by adult males. Women can also commit acts of sexual abuse, as can other children. (HM Government 2010, p.38)

Grooming was made a criminal offence in England and Wales in the Sex Offences Act 2003.

Paedophiles and monsters

In Chapter 4 we saw that the word 'paedophile' is often used excessively and inaccurately outside the criminal justice system and that most individuals who abuse within a family context do not fit the definition of a paedophile. We looked at other correct terminology such as 'child molester' or 'sex offender'. To recap, it is not uncommon for the word paedophile to be used incorrectly because it conjures up a popular image of a predatory monster, which can make it harder for a woman to hear concerns about her partner or a close friend or relative. If she says she cannot believe the person in question is a 'paedophile' we can help her make sense of what we mean by using the correct terminology. Also, if she says 'that's not what the police or probation officer said' we can identify the source of her confusion.

It matters also because a lot of sex offenders *do* know what paedophile means, from the internet and/or from probation officers and others. If we use that word inaccurately it has the potential to give any sex offender the message that we are uninformed, which in turn can encourage him in his confidence that he can manipulate and groom us. It can give him also a sense of the moral high ground because if we call him a paedophile and he is not, then he is right and we are wrong. Also, if we use the wrong terminology in court we devalue our credibility further.

Differences in the way different agencies determine risk

Risk assessment is determined by a number of factors. However, the ability of the mother or partner to protect is crucial and this can only be assessed in the context of the perceived risk presented by the known or alleged offender. For example, whilst all decisions must be made in the interests of the child:

- a low risk known or suspected offender combined with a highly protective mother/partner may be acceptable

- a high risk known or suspected offender combined with a poor protective mother/partner would not be acceptable

- but more commonly, there is a variety of difficult combinations in between.

Five common types of assessment models

To help us in providing such explanation, let us consider a brief description of five types of assessment models in common usage:

1. assessments by child and family agencies

2. structured clinical risk assessment of alleged and suspected offenders and known sex offenders with historic convictions used by probation officers, psychologists and other specialists involving:

3. actuarial risk assessments of known and convicted sex offenders used by probation officers, psychologists and other specialists

4. assessment of sex offenders attending recognised treatment programmes

5. a research-based model for assessment for use with adult males who are alleged to have sexually abused a related child, and/ or who have convictions for sexual offences against a related child, for use by child protection professions.

This is not intended to provide a complete analysis of sexual risk assessment methodology but to provide a simple overall guide, highlighting strengths and limitations and questions for child protection practitioners to ask, examples of which are then provided. *Note:* No assessment can determine guilt or innocence.

Model one: assessment of risk by child and family agencies

Given the low conviction rate for sex offenders, most assessment of alleged or suspected offenders or those with ancient convictions are undertaken by social workers or other child protection professionals with the possibility of referral to the family court. However, with sex offenders staying in silence or denial we are left working in an information vacuum and having to rely on other sources. Given that most sexual abuse happens in secret the only other person who can give an account of the abuse is the child. This is likely to be limited by factors such as the child's age, cognitive and linguistic development and the social and cultural influences on the child – as well as by the impact of the offender's grooming to maintain their silence and any trauma caused by the abuse. We supplement this information through interviews with the mother and/or partner or carer and other family members, as appropriate, as well as by information drawn from various agencies on issues such as family and other social relationships, criminal records, education, employment, health and housing. Readers of this book will be familiar with this use of generic formulaic assessment frameworks.

Reasons why such assessment frameworks are useful

Clarity and continuity of practice are important and historically this has led to the development of government-approved assessments protocols based on obtaining the above information, of which the assessment of mothers and partners is a part. Such protocols provide a common framework:

- to ensure evidence-based best practice

- to ensure continuity of practice

- to identify proscribed time lines to give guidance as to what should be accomplished and by when, to avoid unnecessary delay.

There is the additional benefit for busy professionals in that set protocols provide a checklist for both practitioners and managers: have all the bases been covered?

Whilst these aims are admirable and present a considerable improvement on any previously more ad hoc approach, frameworks of this kind also have their limitations when applied to child sexual abuse.

Reasons to be cautious
Child and family-based generic assessments do not assess sexual risk

Such standard assessment models are designed to meet the generic needs of a wide range of situations in terms of safeguarding children including child abuse, which in itself includes physical abuse, emotional abuse, neglect and failure to thrive as well the even wider field of 'children in need'. Whilst cases of sexual abuse can contain elements of all the above, generic assessment protocols do not assess sexual risk. A generic assessment approach can provide a wealth of information about individual responses and family functioning and this is invaluable when it is combined with knowledge of sex offenders to analyse what happened, how it happened, why individuals and the family are responding this way and what can be done to help their recovery. Such analysis can also provide further insight into the known or suspected offender and throw more light on the nature of risk he may present. However, hundreds of excellent social work reports of this type can be read but when the page is turned to find analysis specific to sexual risk it is not there. If opinion is not available from another reliable source the assessment becomes overly subjective and can be prone to stereotyping and false assumptions.

As one social worker said during a training course on sex offenders: 'now I know why it's been so hard; it's like working with your eyes shut and your hands tied behind your back'. Others have described applying offender knowledge as being 'like a light bulb going on in my head'.

Restricting the use of appropriate professional skills

Given the complexity of child sexual abuse, practitioners are often in a no-win situation because of having to meet the conflicting demands of gathering thorough information within tight recommended time limits. Whilst a formulaic approach can help a busy professional identify key issues to address there is the risk of it becoming assessment-by-tick-box, which in turn can have the inadvertent effect of closing down the assessor's thinking and devaluing the individual approach by failing to encourage the pursuit of other relevant lines of questioning. This problem is recognised in the Munro Report (Munro 2010, p.21), which reviewed a succession of such approved assessment protocols:

> A key question for the review is why the well-intentioned reforms of the past haven't worked. Piecemeal changes have resulted in a system where social workers are more focused on complying with procedures. This is taking them away from spending time with children and families and limiting their ability to make informed judgements.

Child protection professionals at a disadvantage in interview

Any such assessment must include interviews with the alleged or suspected offender. Only he knows the true extent of what he has done and how he did it. He knows what information he must hide, what is safe to give away and how to divert the conversation from dangerous ground. Most sex offenders have a battery of defence mechanisms to deal with risky topics: playing Mr Nice Guy, exuding charm, being very cooperative; playing Mr Nasty Guy through anger, indignation and/or threats, bewilderment; playing dumb, citing their abhorrence of paedophiles and sex offenders and citing other well-rehearsed explanations as to why everyone is wrong, to name but a few.

Sex offenders are adept manipulators and will look also for the vulnerability in their interviewer in order to groom and to manipulate them. Most social workers know this but with insufficient information about sex offenders it can be difficult to identify manipulation as opposed to genuine responses. Because sex offenders are such expert manipulators and good at closing down an interview they may only be seen once, because nothing helpful is forthcoming. This is not uncommon for a number of reasons. For example, social workers and others can feel intimidated by him, they can be aware of their lack of knowledge and skills in interviewing him and they can feel they are getting nowhere – so what's the point?

What do sex offenders think of this type of assessment?

It is depressing to hear how often sex offenders say they like this type of generic assessment because they hold all the cards. Their interviews are only part of the overall family interviews. With the probability of limited information coming from the child or other sources sex offenders know all they have to do is to maintain their denial and/or give away as little relevant information as possible. They can talk about their job, their income, their family relationships and their social life with impunity. As one sex offender said during his own assessment: 'I love the way they [social workers] work. They know about kids and families but they don't know about people like me. I can answer their questions all day and they'll never get close.' It also reinforces the offender's distorted thinking: 'they're interviewing all these other people so it must be at least partly their fault'. This can be made worse if the offender sees the mother or partner is spending more time being assessed than he is.

The need to keep an open mind: maybe he is telling the truth

A further major difficulty for those who work with children and families is the possibility that when someone is accused of sexual abuse and he says he did not do it, in a minority of cases he is telling the truth. But that goes against the grain because of our need to believe and to protect children. If we do not have and apply knowledge of sex offenders that task becomes even more difficult.

Implications for work with mothers and partners

- Information gained through a generic child- and family-based assessment is invaluable to our understanding of the situation but on its own it does not assess *sexual* risk.

- To do that we need to augment our existing skills by applying knowledge of sex offenders to gain some idea of the kind of profile of the particular alleged, suspected or known offender in question: what kind of an offender might he be? If he did sexually abuse a child how did he do it? What kind of a risk might he present and how should that be managed?

- In Chapters 13 and 14 we look at how this can assist in assessment and intervention with the mother/partner.

- Alleged or suspected sex offenders need to be interviewed. Child protection professionals are trained in interviewing children in both clinical and legal situations but the rules for interviewing sex offenders are different, as are the skills required. Sex offenders can take advantage of this. The difficulties faced by social workers and others, as have been described, need to be recognised. This is a systemic problem that needs to be addressed through training otherwise even the most skilled and experienced social worker or child care practitioner will remain at a disadvantage.

- The situation would be helped also by child care practitioners having greater access to specialist opinion in risk assessment as described below and therefore more inter-agency cooperation.

Models two and three: assessments of known and suspected sex offenders

The most important difference here is that the risk assessment focuses on the person of concern. As with assessing children and families, standardised formulae have been devised in the search for continuity and best practice based on an ever increasing body of research and empirical evidence (see Chapter 4). However, no assessment system can be 100 per cent perfect and each has its strengths and limitations. There have been two main approaches to risk assessment as summarised by Craig *et al.* (2008, pp.69–87):

- structured clinical risk assessments for use in alleged or suspected sexual abuse and cases of historical sexual convictions

- actuarial risk assessments for use with convicted sex offenders.

Note: Each of these types of assessment has their critics. In recent years efforts have been made to bring these two approaches together (for example, Beech *et al.* 2002).

Model two: specialist structured clinical risk assessment of alleged and suspected offenders and known sex offenders with historic convictions

There is no statistically predictive formula for use when abuse is suspected but when there is no prior sexual conviction because research is only available from those convicted of sex offences. Therefore this type of model is based on the assessor's interviewing skills and his or her ability to draw on research and theoretical models into sex offending to consider the extent to which there may or may not be combinations of factors that cause concern.

Information is obtained from existing background information gained from the child, mother and family and from any agency that has had contact with the family – for which a social work type assessment can provide valuable information as described above – combined with multiple interviews with the alleged offender. Knowledge of how sex offenders operate is employed to inform the nature of the questions asked. Also, because interviewers are not bound by the restrictive rules of evidence that apply to questioning children, a range of techniques can be used to pursue questions, query responses and counter any perceived manipulation or grooming.

Whilst there is no one set profile of a sex offender, such information combined with a solid knowledge of the nature of offending can be employed to identify whether or not there are sufficient factors in combination to believe there is good and reasonable cause for concern. Structured clinical risk assessments are valuable when working with alleged or suspected abuse or where there is an ancient conviction with no subsequent history of problems.

Reasons to be cautious

- Of necessity this requires particular skills in interviewing sex offenders and knowledge of sex offenders to interpret responses.

- This approach on its own is open to a degree of subjective opinion and assessors must be prepared to be challenged. It works best when it takes into account all the information gained by a generic child and family assessment as previously described, like filling in the pieces of a puzzle.

Model three: actuarial risk assessments for use with convicted sex offenders

To counter the limitations of structured clinical assessments researchers have developed a range of assessment formulae based on statistical probability. These actuarial formulae have become a staple within the criminal justice system and have been devised to assess the risk of recidivism – the risk of re-offending and being reconvicted, in terms of low, medium and high risk. They work on the same principle as is used in the insurance industry, for example in evaluating premiums for car and home insurance, whereby certain agreed factors are taken into consideration to assess the statistical probability of something bad happening and the likelihood of a claim. There has been a plethora of measures devised in the psychology community for use with adult male sex offenders with much debate as to which is the most useful with what type of sex offender. Some also relate to risk of violence. This is why child protection workers should ask which clinical tool was used. For anyone who is not a psychologist who enjoys being steeped in research and statistics the number of such measures can be bewildering, for example, the Structured Anchored Clinical Judgement Scale (Thornton 1997), the Rapid Risk Assessment for Sexual Offence Recidivism (Hanson 1997), MnSOST-R (Epperson, Kaul and Hesselton 1998), Static-99 (Hanson and Thornton 2000), Risk Matrix 2000 (Thornton, *et al.* 2003) to name but a few. Each has their strengths and their limitations as described, for example, in Craig *et al.* (2008).

Some employ two stages of assessment entailing consideration of a further set of factors, which research suggests can either heighten or decrease the original risk calculation. For example RM2000 has two stages: stage one is based on *static factors* (historical facts that cannot change such as current age, age at first conviction, number of convictions, etc.); stage two is based on *dynamic factors* (factors that can change in time through positive life experiences and/or therapy which in turn can increase or diminish risk). Risk is then calculated in terms of low, medium, high or very high balanced on statistical probability. Assessments using stage one are tick-box paper evaluations based on factors that research has identified as being correlated to raised risk. The second stage provides a more individualised in-depth assessment undertaken in face-to-face interviews by psychologists, probation officers or other trained specialists, identifying research-validated factors that have been identified as increasing or lowering risk.

As with the other forms of assessment, such protocols provide a much improved evidence-based approach, which is aimed at producing efficiency, continuity and best practice. However, as their authors would caution, each has its limitations.

Reasons to be cautious

- Actuarial assessment protocols cannot be used with alleged or suspected abuse because the type of information required is not available.

- They cannot be used with men of whom there has been a Finding of Fact in a family court.

- Any actuarial approach identifies trends rather than individuals. Therefore, if a known offender is assessed as having a 40 per cent chance of recidivism there is a 60 per cent chance he will not, which is sometimes forgotten – unless there is a more detailed face-to-face assessment that says otherwise.

- There is the possibility of under-estimating risk level of offenders abusing within the family. These actuarial formulae are designed for use with the full range of offenders who have sexually abused adults and/or children. Because they are being compared with those who have abused inside and/ or outside the family, with career (i.e. long-term, multiple victims) paedophiles and with child murderers, men who have been convicted of sexual offences within the family invariably come out as low risk. For some this low risk assessment may be accurate. However it can also mask the fact that sex offenders in the family can abuse over long periods without detection because they are in an environment they can control. Also, children commonly do not report abuse within the family and if they report it once the consequences can be so dire that it can deter that child or any other child within the family from reporting further abuse. Therefore such factors should also be taken into consideration.

- Levels of thoroughness vary. For example, whilst RM2000 has two stages it is not uncommon for only stage one to be used and as a paper tick-box assessment, with either no use of stage two or only limited application.

- Not all assessment formulae of this kind translate well for use with internet offenders. For example, RM2000 was found to overestimate levels of risk posed by internet offenders who download child pornography and a revised version was created to reflect this (Thornton 2009).

- We should be aware that strictly speaking, measures of this kind do not answer 'will he do it again?': they assess risk of recidivism, that is, doing it again, being caught and being convicted.

Model four: assessments of men attending sex offender treatment programmes

These present yet another form of assessment, based on a carefully devised battery of psychometric tests which evaluate areas of progress and prognosis.

Sex offender group treatment programmes (SOTPs) have been run since the early 1990s in up to 28 prisons in England and Wales, throughout the probation service, and by the Lucy Faithfull Foundation's residential Wolvercote Clinic. Common structured programmes were first introduced in prisons based on a framework devised by Mann (1999) and Mann and Thornton (1998), combining assessment and treatment. This was later revised by Beech and Fisher (2004) to produce the 'CORE' 2000 programme. Since 2001, community based treatment programmes run by the probation service have been based on one of three programmes based on research and best practice and accredited by the Joint Prison and Probation Services Accreditation Panel for England and Wales. These are the Thames Valley Programme Sex Offender Group Programme (TV-SOGP), the West Midlands Programme and the Northumbria Programme. The TV-SOGP has a parallel approved programme for non-offending mothers and partners (Still, Faux and Wilson 2001). Programmes are based primarily on a cognitive behavioural approach, addressing underlying attitudes, beliefs and behaviours that support sexual offending. Progress and prognosis evaluation is based on a carefully devised battery of psychometric tests, which evaluate the key remedial areas of functioning identified in the research (see Chapter 4). These psychometric tests have a built-in mechanism for testing 'faking'. Programmes in the prison service and in the community differ because they are designed in length and content according to the need of the sex offender population and the location. Overall, a broad range of research has found treatment programmes to be effective in reducing sexual recidivism (Craig 2008, pp.160–162). For example, an evaluation of sex offenders who completed the community based programme in the West Midlands found that treated offenders (including child sexual offenders and rapists) were half as likely to offend as untreated offenders (Allam 2000, 2001). Similarly, an evaluation of the national prison-based programme (Friendship, Mann and Beech 2003) identified significantly lower rates of sexual and/or violent recidivism among those who had attended treatment.

Model five: the Faithfull Assessment Classification System (FACS-4) by child protection workers with alleged or suspected sexual abuse within a family context

To counter the difficulty of there being no research-based protocol for use by child protection workers with alleged or suspected sexual abuse within a family context, Consultant Psychologist David Thornton, author of RM2000, worked with the team of therapists from the Lucy Faithfull Foundation to rectify this. The Lucy Faithfull Foundation is an organisation working throughout the UK specialising in child sexual abuse and providing an expert witness service to family courts and child care agencies. The Foundation employs professionals with expertise in working with sex offenders, with children and with families. By providing such collective joint expertise and working closely together this enables a fully integrated approach, making maximum use of information available from all parties.

The FACS-4 (Thornton 2000) is designed for use by social workers and other child protection professionals and is intended for use with adult males who are alleged to have sexually abused a related child, and/or who have convictions for sexual offences against a related child. It is based on factors that research has associated with repeated offending by familial sexual offenders.

Reasons to be cautious

- FACS-4 is designed to give additional guidance when combined with findings from the generic protocol for assessing the child and family where other factors may raise or diminish concern.

- It is not a psychometric test.

- It is not an actuarial tool based on statistically probability and therefore is not statistically predictive.

- Many alleged offenders do not meet the criteria within the model. However, where these criteria are met should raise concern and further questions.

- It cannot be used with convicted offenders or for purposes for which it was not designed.

Answering mothers' and partners' questions about sexual risk

A mother or partner is entitled to know how the sexual risk level was decided and what it means: but who is to tell her? When an individual has been charged and/or convicted there should be an assessment by a police officer, a probation officer, a psychologist or some other specialist practitioner as to the nature and severity of the sexual risk he does or does not present. However, it is not uncommon for the mother or partner never to meet the person who did the offender assessment so it is left to the social worker or some other child care practitioner to explain things and to answer her questions. How are we meant to do that? It is not good enough for us simply to say 'because someone else says so'.

To maximise the chances of clarity in a way that is consistent across the inter-agency board the following are suggestions of the type of questions that can be asked about any sexual risk assessment:

- The context of the assessment and how it was conducted:

    » By whom? (by someone trained in working with sex offenders?)

    » When and where? (in prison, on remand, in a police station, in a probation office, on a sex offender treatment programme?)

    » Using what assessment model? (was it relevant to the situation?)

    » How were the conclusions reached?

    » How thorough was the assessment? (tick box only or based on interviews with a trained practitioner?)

- Is everyone agreed on the meaning of the terminology used?

- If the terms low, medium or high risk are used what does it mean for this particular individual offender? (Clinical tools vary; statistical tools measure trends, not individuals.)

- How long ago was the assessment? (Ancient risk assessments may no longer be accurate or reliable: has anything changed? If so, what and how? Is an update needed?)

- Is/was he put on the Sex Offender Register? Has he had treatment? What is/was the outcome and prognosis?

- Did the assessment highlight what factors in this particular case are deemed to raise or lower risk?

- Are there any other factors coming from other sources (e.g. the child and family assessment) now that could raise or lower risk?

- If agencies or individuals are not in agreement as to the level of risk can we explain the reason for our difference of opinion in a sensible, logical way?

- Has anyone explained any of this to the mother or partner?

- Are we able to explain this to the mother or partner in a way that we would wish if we were in her situation?

- Are we using correct terminology and are we being consistent with other agencies in its usage?

- If there has been a Finding of Fact but no charge or conviction do we know why? (In the event of a prior conviction or Finding of Fact, we should hang on to that as an indisputable fact and seek information about risk level, along with explanations as to how that was calculated.)

- If in doubt, ask for clarification.

- If we cannot deal with this can we arrange for the mother or partner to meet the person who did the assessment? Or someone with similar expertise?

- Is the risk assessment we have sufficient in this case or does it still need to be referred elsewhere, for example to a specialist?

Conclusions

When we are sitting in a multi-agency case conference or reading other people's reports we can all think we are speaking the same language and interpreting it in the same way when we are not. Furthermore, we need to remain alert to the fact that when a non-offending parent or partner joins the proceedings she too can be thinking and interpreting what is said in a different way.

A mother and/or partner has a right to know how we assess risk and safety, how we draw the conclusions we do and the decisions we make. We should anticipate the kind of questions she may have, some of which we discussed in the previous chapter, and we should be ready to answer them. If she is unable to ask the questions we should tell her anyway.

If the child protection practitioner cannot answer her questions about how the sexual risk level of her partner, relative or friend was assessed then it is only reasonable that the person who conducted that assessment should do so.

Child protection workers need information also if we are to counter the manipulative skills of a sex offender. Yet it is surprising how often there is a resistance from other agencies or individuals to sharing detailed information from any specialist risk assessment and/or treatment programme, sharing only the conclusions instead. Sometimes this is because those working with children and families do not ask for the detail because they do not want to hear it. Sometimes information is refused on the grounds of confidentiality. Either way, this gives the advantage to the sex offender. This is an issue for training of child protection workers. Such information should be available to all child protection professionals who are involved in undertaking assessments in cases of child sexual abuse, not only of the mother/partner/carer but also of the child and family, as well as when required to assess known or suspected offenders.

References

Allam, J. (2000) 'Community Based Treatment for Child Sexual Offenders: An Evaluation.' Unpublished doctoral thesis, University of Birmingham.

Allam, J. (2001) 'Effective Practice in Work with Sex Offenders: A Reconviction Study Comparing Treated and Non-treated Offenders.' Report to the West Midlands Probation Service. Birmingham: West Midlands Probation.

Beech, A.R., Friendship, C., Erikson, M. and Hanson, R.K. (2002) 'The relationship between static and dynamic risk factors and reconviction in a sample of UK child abusers.' *Sexual Abuse: A Journal of Research and Treatment 14*, 2, 155–167.

Craig, L.A., Browne, K.D. and Beech, A.R. (2008) *Assessing Risk in Sex Offenders: A Practitioner's Guide*. Chichester: Wiley.

Epperson, D.L., Kaul, J.D. and Hesselton, D. (1998) 'Final Report on the Development of the Minnesota Sex Offender Screening Tool-Revised (MnSOST-R).' 17th Annual Conference of the Association for the Treatment of Sexual Abusers, Vancouver, Canada, October 1998.

Friendship, C., Mann, R.E. and Beech A.R. (2003) 'Evaluation of a national prison-based treatment programme for sexual offenders in England & Wales.' *Journal of Interpersonal Violence 18*, 7, 744–759.

Hanson, R.K. (1997) *The Development of a Brief Actuarial Risk Scale for Sexual Offence Recidivism*. (User Report No. 1997–04). Ottawa: Department of the Solicitor General of Canada.

Hanson, R.K. and Thornton, D. (2000) 'Improving risk assessment for sex offenders: A comparison of three actuarial scales.' *Law and Human Behaviour* *24*, 1, 119–136.

HM Government (2010) *Working Together to Safeguard Children.* London: The Stationery Office.

Mann, R.E. (1999) 'The Sex Offender Treatment Programme: HM Prison Service England and Wales.' In S. Hofling, D. Drew and I. Epple-Waigel (eds). *Auftrag prevention: Offensive gegen sexuellen kindesmibbrauch.* Munich: Atwerb-verlag KG Publikation.

Mann, R.E. and Thornton, D. (1998) 'The Evolution of a Multisite Sex Offender Treatment Program.' In W.L. Marshall, Y.M. Fernandez, S.M Hudson and T. Ward (eds) *Source Book of Treatment Programs for Sexual Offenders.* New York, NY: Plenum Press.

Munro, E. (2010) *The Munro Review of Child Protection: Part One: A Systems Analysis.* Sections 143 and 144. London: Stationery Office.

Salter, A.C. (1995) *Transforming Trauma: A Guide to Understanding and Treating Adult Survivors of Child Sexual Abuse.* Thousand Oaks, CA: Sage.

Still, J., Faux, M. and Wilson, C. (2001) *The Thames Valley Partner's Programme.* The Home Office, London. Crown Copyright 2001.

Thornton, D. (1997) *Structured Anchored Clinical Judgement Risk Assessment (SACJ): Proceedings of the NOTA Conference.* Brighton, September.

Thornton, D. (2000) 'The Faithfull Assessment Classification System.' Lucy Faithfull Foundation National Conference, Birmingham, October 2000.

Thornton, D. (2002) 'Constructing and testing a framework for dynamic risk assessment.' *Sexual Abuse: A Journal of Research and Treatment 14*, 2, 139–155.

Thornton, D. (2009) *Scoring Guide for Risk Matrix 2000.9/SVC.* Available at www.birmingham.ac.uk/Documents/college-les/psych/RM2000scoringinstructions.pdf, accessed on 3 February 2016.

Thornton, D., Mann, R., Blud, L., Travers, R. et al (2003) 'Distinguishing and combining risks for sexual and violent recidivism.' *Understanding and Managing Sexually Coercive Behavior. Annals of the New York Academy of Sciences 989*, 225–235.

CHAPTER 11

ASSESSMENT OF THE MOTHER/PARTNER
PRE-ASSESSMENT PLANNING

The purpose of this book is to look at an approach to assessment specifically in relation to child sexual abuse in a way that can either build on information provided by the generic type of framework previously discussed or that can stand alone.

When child protection professionals are under pressure and facing time limits set by our agency, by protocol and/or the by courts it can be too easy not to spend enough thinking time beforehand. This chapter aims to act as an easily referenced reminder of some of those important issues to consider and do before making face-to-face contact with the person we are assessing. It is not intended to be comprehensive but to address some of the particular issues relating to child sexual abuse and those discussed in Chapter 9 on the woman's perspective of assessment, which if not dealt with appropriately can cause problems later. There are three main sections:

- practical issues to consider
- building offender knowledge into the assessment process
- preliminary thoughts about other issues that might arise.

This leads on to the next chapter, which focuses on the importance of engagement and motivation and interviewing style.

Practical issues to consider

The basic function of assessment: why am I doing this?

'Why am I doing this?' may seem a ridiculous question but it is important to ask it every time if we are to apply a more individualistic approach that enables us to escape the limitations of overly rigid and generic formulae.

Aims

In cases of known or alleged sexual abuse of a child or young person by an adult male the basic function of an assessment of the mother or partner is:

- to assess the potential risk of any further sexual abuse to this child or any other child in her care and/or any related significant harm

- to understand her previous failure to protect

- to assess her present and future ability to protect and to meet the healing needs of the child

- to consider what needs to change

- to evaluate her capacity *to hear* new information, which could help her understand what she is to protect against and *to apply* any such information to become more empowered to protect

- to make recommendations for any appropriate intervention of a clinical, practical and/or legal nature

- to convey our conclusions and recommendations in a written report in a way that enables everyone (other child protection professionals and agencies, the court and her) to understand, including our references to sex offenders with which they may not be familiar.

This remit can be widened according to the specific needs of the case.

What we do not want to do

We want to avoid:

- making it feel to her that we are creating hoops through which we judge how well she jumps

- making it go on too long

- having no clear goals

- giving mixed messages
- letting our own personal feelings about sex offenders and failure to protect get in the way of objectivity.

Some baseline rules

We need to bear in mind at all times:

- that unless the allegations or evidence suggest otherwise, it was not the mother or partner who committed the known or suspected abuse
- the need to work with her in a way that places responsibility for the abuse where it belongs that is, with the offender, whilst not minimising the seriousness of her failure to protect and her responsibility to do so
- that the welfare of the child is paramount but that does not preclude us from recognising her difficult situation
- the potential importance of the mother/carer to the child who has been abused and/or to other children in her care.

Assessment of the mother or partner is only part of the whole: gathering background information

Any assessment requires us to gather as much information from as many sources as possible before we interview the mother/partner. Because information is so often lacking in cases of child sexual abuse, the assessment of risk, safety and therapeutic need cannot be done in isolation and must take into consideration the impact of the abuse on the child and family, the child's developmental needs, the mother's parenting capacity and other relevant social factors. This is familiar territory to child protection practitioners and is often achieved along the lines of a generic assessment approach, but any information about the known or suspected also needs to be incorporated. It is like putting together pieces of a jigsaw without knowing what the final picture looks like: at the outset we have a large number of disparate pieces that individually do not make sense, or we think make sense but later turn out differently from what we expected.

Every situation is different

Whilst a victim should not be placed with his or her abuser if it is legally possible to avoid doing so, there can be complex other circumstances that suggest it is in a child's best interests to live with or stay in contact with a suspected or even known sex offender. In any such situation our assessment of the mother or partner is particularly crucial in terms of risk management.

Some scenarios where we need to balance risk and the welfare needs of the child include:

- where separation might do the child(ren) in the current situation more harm than good

- in cases of historical abuse where there has been no known offending for years, perhaps not since adolescence

- where the abuse was not against a child within the immediate family

- where the known or alleged offender has been assessed as low risk

- where the current situation does not appear to fit any past known or alleged pattern, for example, where previous abuse was outside the family, against a much older/younger child or against a child of a different gender

- where there may be valid concerns but no legal means of removing him or the child

A further major difficulty for those working in the civil child protection system is the possibility that when someone is accused of sexual abuse and he says he did not do it, he is telling the truth. But that goes against the grain of our need to believe and protect the child.

In any such situation, whilst it is the mother's or partner's responsibility to protect it is primarily the offender's responsibility not to offend.

Protecting children: what would be safe enough?

Any assessment of the ability of the mother or partner to protect can only be made in the context of the relative risk level of the known or suspected offender in this particular situation, taking into account the various definitions of 'risk' as described in Chapter 9.

It is understandable that we might take the view that the only acceptable risk is 'no risk' but there is no such thing and as child protection professionals we are often in the difficult situation of assessing what is safe enough. As Munro (2010, p.20) observed: 'Risk management cannot eradicate risk; it can only try to reduce the probability of harm'. The mother or partner's role is central to this. For example:

- A situation may be considered *safe enough* where there is an alleged or known offender deemed to be a low level risk paired with a highly protective mother or partner if that is in children's best interests.

- A high risk offender paired with someone who is considered a poor protector with little capacity for change would be *unacceptable*.

There are any number of *variations* in between.

Balancing sexual risk and safety with other needs of the child(ren)

It is helpful to consider in advance the possibility that further action may be required. In some situations removing a child or known/suspected offender from a family home may remove the child from sexual risk and provide them with the best opportunity to begin their recovery. Similarly, a child may be presenting such a worrying response to the abuse and/or as having developed such a level of mistrust of a mother who failed to protect that it is necessary to remove the child to somewhere he or she can feel safe, at least as a temporary measure.

However, it is easy to become so preoccupied with assessing sexual risk and safety that we become blind to other possible needs of the child or young person. For example, there may be a close bond between a known or alleged offender and a child who is not his victim, which combined with an assessment of him as being a low sexual risk may lead us to conclude that to break that bond would cause even greater trauma to that child. The nature of that close bond would need to be assessed to ensure it is genuine and not a result of grooming and manipulation. For this, the related assessment of the child would consider issues relating to attachment.

Attachment behaviour has been defined as: 'any behaviour designed to get children in a close, protective relationship with their attachment figures whenever they experience anxiety' (Howe *et al.*1999, p.14). This is of particular but not exclusive importance when the abuser is in the role of carer who should be the child's protector. Given the potential complexity of the grooming of the child (see Chapter 7), a child's response can vary depending on the nature and style of their abuser's grooming, and the assessment of the child should consider issues relating to the possibility of adaptive responses, defensive strategies and/or avoidant and ambivalent attachments. For example, a seductive style of child grooming can lead to the creation of the child's emotional dependency on his or her abuser. So we hear the child say 'I love him, he's nice to me, he's kind to me, just tell him to stop and things will be fine'. Whilst this may present as close attachment it is really trauma bonding, that is, a self-protective but dysfunctional way of their dealing with the abuse, where the fear of losing that close relationship can be experienced by the child as being as bad as or even worse than the sexual abuse itself. Similarly, a child who is abused by a scary and/or sadistic offender will have developed adaptive responses to avoid displeasing his or her abuser. Both can skew the child's view of him or herself and of the world. which can cause problems elsewhere in their lives (see Chapter 7).

The need for caution

However, that does not apply in all situations, and any decision to remove the child(ren) or the known/suspected can have other negative and perhaps unnecessary consequences such as grief and separation trauma, family conflicts caused by blame and recrimination as well as financial hardship. In some situations such consequences are unavoidable but in others they are not. It is the mother who must cope with and manage these problems as well as keeping children safe. She has to do this whilst dealing with her own often complex difficulties.

Where should the assessment take place?

This is important. Much consideration has been given over the years to providing a suitable environment for interviewing children and the same consideration should be given to the mother/partner. If there is one basic rule it should be that assessments of the mother/partner should not be conducted in the family home.

Why not? The following are important reasons:

- In previous chapters we have looked at research that highlights the likely negative impact of child sexual abuse on a non-abusing parent and how stressful the assessment process can be for her, yet we still expect her to continue to function as a normal, competent, appropriate and caring adult throughout this process. It is unreasonable for us to expect any woman to do this if she has no personal space to which she can retreat following her interviews with us, where she can think, recover and try to bring back some sense of normality to the rest of her family.

- The interviewer should have control over the environment and there are too many distractions in the home.

- We have seen the manipulative power of sex offenders and their need to control the situation. Any sex offender will be worried about what the mother/partner may say or hear and it is not uncommon for an offender to try to crash in on the interview and insist on being present. This is unacceptable. The interviewer cannot control this situation in the home, which may or may not be his home also.

- We can sometimes have the notion that it will be more comfortable for the woman to be interviewed in her own home, or maybe we choose to do it there simply because it is the easiest option or because there is nowhere else available. However, interviews in the home should more appropriately be seen as an unacceptable intrusion into her personal space. One mother, for example, whose partner left home after he was arrested and then convicted for online sexual offences against children, described how it was bad enough that he committed the abuse in what had been the family home for 20 years, but having her assessment interviews there compounded her sense of its 'contamination' even further, to the extent that she no longer wished to live there and was seeking to move house. Other women do not have that luxury.

The type of interview environment can either reduce or exacerbate these problems. Consideration needs to be given to providing an interview environment that is comfortable and safe. The mother/partner may already have experienced being interviewed in a police environment and it is not appropriate for that to be repeated here.

How long should an assessment take?

As practitioners we have to juggle any such assessment with the other demands on our time. However, planning the timing and content of interview sessions in advance is crucial. With good background information and clear aims and objectives in interview an assessment can be completed in a reasonable time frame. Assessments that are too short and hurried leave inadequate time to consider the complexities of the presenting situation, perhaps reducing preordained assessment formats to a tick-box approach or making over-generalised assumptions. A more common problem is that assessments drag on too long.

The following can cause unnecessary delays, which lead to the mother/partner asking 'will it never end?'

- a lack of a clear agenda and subsequent loss of focus

- too many long gaps between each assessment interview, which in turn reduces continuity and risks both interviewer and interviewee losing the plot

- unclear boundaries between assessment and intervention.

The longer the process drags on the more unnecessarily debilitating it is likely to become for the woman we are interviewing and the more opportunity the sex offender has to counter-manipulate the woman's thinking and responses to his own advantage.

The most productive approach

Efficiency has to be balanced with flexibility. Reliability on the part of the assessor is crucial not only in terms of treating with respect the person we are assessing but also because it enables her to make the necessary child care and/or workplace arrangements.

The most productive approach is to arrange with the mother/partner in advance a schedule of interviews relatively close together, interspersed by a few days to allow both interviewer and interviewee thinking time: it gives the woman time to process her thoughts and feelings; it gives the interviewer time to reflect on what has been said and to give consideration to alternative interview approaches if those being used on the first occasion did not really work effectively. It is easy to argue that such an arrangement is impracticable for professionals with a busy work schedule and sometimes unpredictable demands elsewhere. However, the task has to be done some time and careful time planning is usually more efficient. This can be achieved with good organisation by practitioners combined with the necessary support from supervisors and managers.

When more time is needed

If at the end of the designated sessions we need more time we should ask the relevant authority for it, which may be senior managers, a case management team or the family court, but we should be prepared to say why we want it, what we would do with the extra time and how we would do it. We should explain this also to our interviewee. This is discussed further, along with a proposed interview schedule, in Chapter 13.

Avoiding delays between assessment and intervention

Long delays between assessment and putting into action any recommend intervention plan with the mother/partner will undermine the goal of achieving a positive outcome: mother, child and family will be left in limbo with temporary protective arrangements which, as we have seen in previous chapters, can also be detrimental to their well-being and maybe even inappropriate. Furthermore, it gives an offender more time to counter-manipulate the situation for his own ends.

Is an interpreter needed?

In some ethnic minorities there can be instances where other family members speak good English but the mother or partner has maintained a traditional role within the family and community, providing little opportunity to learn a new language beyond simple day-to-day practicalities. In such cases it is particularly important to ensure good communication is possible and if in doubt an interpreter should be sought. This should be someone who is able to deal with the content of the discussion relating to child sexual abuse without contaminating it with inappropriate reactions, opinions or even interpretations. Speaking through an interpreter takes time and allowances should be made for this when planning interviews.

Building offender knowledge into the assessment process

Gathering background information

Social workers and other child protection professionals are already trained in conducting generic assessments. Every situation is different and accurate background information provides context for each assessment. However, as has been argued throughout this book, in cases of child sexual abuse the value of any such background information is greatly enhanced when it is overlaid with the application of information and some understanding about sex offenders.

The starting point is whatever information is forthcoming from the disclosure or allegation of sexual abuse and the subsequent investigation. This can vary from being extremely limited because it is based on suspicion and with no disclosure from the child, to detailed reports of joint police and social worker interviews with the child, with the known or suspected offender and with the mother/partner. At a basic level such reports usually address who said and did what to whom, when and how, the impact of any known or alleged abuse on the child as well as observations on individuals' reactions to questioning. A basic generic type of approach to assessment would include information sourced from any other relevant agency such as health, education, police, the probation service and/or the prison service on issues such as individual family members and significant others, family relationships, children's education and social interests, parents' social history, employment and social issues.

'Profiling' the offender: if he did it, how might he have done it?

What is less customary but equally important is to be proactive in seeking as much detailed information about the alleged or known offender as possible. This is not to suggest formal psychological profiling but to look for clues in all the background information. By combining that information with our knowledge of sex offenders and of the implications for the mother/partner, child and family (as discussed in Chapters 5 to 8) we can ask ourselves the question: 'if he did this, how did he do it?' This can provide us with some insight into the presenting situation and therefore the mother's/partner's and child's experience.

Where the offender is known

An offender may be known because:

- there is a history of sexual allegations made against him but with no criminal charges or conviction

- he has been charged but not convicted

- he has been convicted of sexual offences

- there has been a prior Finding of Fact against him in a family court

- the police have other relevant intelligence they are able to share.

In any such situations information should be sought from the relevant agencies such as the police, the probation service or the prison service as to whether or not he has been (or will be) subject of a specialist assessment and/or attended a sex offender treatment programme. This does not just mean asking 'what did he do?' and 'was he convicted?' or accepting a brief summary of his assessment or progress in treatment, but asking the assessor all the questions suggested in the previous chapter. Information should also be sought about his sexual interests and known target group, his pattern or cycle of offending and his style of offending. We can then combine this offender information with what we know about the child and family, which in turn can provide a more informed context for our understanding of the mother/partner.

Sometimes other agencies or individuals can be reluctant to share such detailed information, for example, on the grounds of clinical confidentiality where an offender is in treatment. It would be reasonable for them to know from us why we want the information, what we intend to do with it and our commitment to any appropriate rules of confidentiality. Good inter-agency understanding and cooperation is vital in this regard.

In cases of alleged or suspected sexual abuse

Where sexual abuse is alleged or suspected but with no clear outcome from the initial investigation, we can use our understanding of sex offenders and how they operate to consider whether there are any factors in combination that could suggest a cycle and style of offending, as described in Chapter 5. For example, is there anything that could be seen to support the notion that he targeted, isolated and groomed a particular child for abuse and/or manipulated the mother/partner and others so they were unable to protect and/or recognise the abuse? Is there any indication of inappropriate sexual attitudes and beliefs and/or pro-offending thinking?

A cautionary note

The purpose of this is not to reinforce any presumption of guilt or stereotypical thinking but to inform the questions we ask the mother/partner in interview and to help us understand the responses of the child, the mother/partner and the family.

No such preliminary thoughts should be cast in stone. This initial process only provides us with a starting point from which to work and should be open to change based on any new evidence or information we may receive. For example, if we thought it likely his style of grooming was that of a seductive Mr Nice Guy but new information in interview suggests he was an aggressive Mr Nasty Guy, we should follow that line of thought.

Some preliminary thoughts about other issues

The manipulation of culture and religion

There is a serious under-reporting of child sexual abuse among ethnic minorities and when it does arise it is important to consider the cultural context in advance of any interviews. It is impossible to cover here all the different aspects of every culture. However, consideration should be given to common themes such as cultural traditions, faith, perceptions of immediate and extended family and of individual behaviour and responsibilities, as well as what is and is not acceptable within different generations and also the perception of the role of women versus men. There may be more practical issues to consider. For example, some women we interview will be more integrated into the wider and predominantly white community, whilst others may live more within the confines of their own ethnic community; some will have perfect command of the English language and others will not, maybe to the extent of needing an interpreter.

One solution would be for all assessments to be undertaken by a practitioner of the same ethnicity as the person we are interviewing but that is often not practicable. Gathering basic information from colleagues who are of the same ethnicity would give the interviewer some advantage and additional insight.

Whilst all these things should be considered these are some baseline rules to remember:

- Pursuing cultural issues does not make the assessor racist. Failure to act for fear of any such accusation has been a common feature of public inquiries in the UK into cases of serious child abuse, to the detriment of the child.

- Sex offenders commonly use their culture as an excuse for offending, as in 'you don't understand, in my culture it is legal to have sex with a 13-year-old'. It is important to recognise this as his attempt to manipulate and groom us but a) careful examination is likely to show it to be untrue and that the offender is relying on our ignorance and our desire not to be seen to be racist and b) the rules of this country apply and not those of his country of origin.

- As we saw in Chapter 5, sex offenders will abuse and distort cultural values for their own ends to groom and manipulate mothers, partners, victims and sometimes whole families, as well as us. For example: telling a child and maybe also his partner that his sexual behaviour is normal and his entitlement; using the knowledge that the woman is isolated from the wider community to guarantee her silence; persuading mothers and partners that disclosure of abuse will ruin the young person's or child's marriage prospects and/or making distorted faith references to make abusive behaviour sound acceptable.

- On a human level the 'impact issues' for the mother/partner as listed in Chapter 2 still apply.

Are there additional concerns other than sexual abuse?

Many families will not be known prior to their referral for child sexual abuse but in some cases they are. For example, there may be existing concerns about a child's presenting behaviour and about physical abuse or neglect. In such cases prior thought should be given as to how any such problems fit in with the known or suspected child sexual abuse in terms of their being used to groom mother/partner and child and as a consequence of sexual abuse.

Contact

What we think is safe needs to be seen and felt by the child to be safe. If contact were to be considered appropriate, the assessment of the mother/partner should include some thoughts about not only where, when and how often but also whether or not she would be the appropriate person to supervise it, either on her own or accompanied by a named official person. It is unreasonable to ask anyone to protect a child if they have no real idea of what they are protecting against. This applies also to other contact supervisors, including paid but untrained staff.

Knowledge of sex offenders generally and especially of the individual in question is crucial not only in deciding what would be and what would not be a safe environment, but also what would be specific warning signs relevant to that particular person in question and what kind of restrictions.

Case examples of ill-informed decisions

The following are examples of where a lack of understanding of sex offenders has led to bad decisions about risk and safety. It must be emphasised that such examples may represent a small proportion of situations, but where such risks are missed they place unfair expectations on any contact supervisor and can have disastrous results for children:

- Sex offenders can use simple but specific code words to send a signal that they are still in control, as with the offender who used the phrase 'I'm not feeling so well' to denote to his girlfriend's daughter 'follow me upstairs for sex'. The girl had not disclosed the abuse and he replicated that during contact with her and her mother to demonstrate 'don't talk, I'm still in control', unbeknown to the girl's mother or the contact supervisor.

- They can use particular behaviours for the same effect, as with the offender who used the signal of putting an unlit cigarette on the edge of the table as an instruction to his victim to go to the top room of the house for sex, which he was able to replicate in contact sessions to tell her 'I'm still in control'.

- They can use gifts and symbols to manipulate partners and children's mothers, as with the offender who was excluded from contact but still tried to manipulate the situation: he met his partner on her way to contact and presented her with a soft toy pig. The social worker in that instance was aware that this was part of the offender's deliberate grooming behaviour: his wife collected toy pigs and after any marital conflict or whenever she suspected abuse he would buy her one to add to her collection to reinforce the message 'I'm a lovely guy, you mean the world to me, I'd never hurt anyone.' Fortunately in this instance the social worker was already aware of this and how the child interpreted this as 'Mum cannot be trusted, she'll never believe me over him because she forgives him everything', and so prevented the mother from taking the toy pig into the contact session.

- Lack of knowledge of offenders can lead to other kinds of bad decisions. For example, in one case where all three young children were removed from the family home following medical evidence to suggest sexual abuse but by an unknown perpetrator(s), the parents were apparently so convincingly loving and distraught the local social services provided transport for the children to have daily contact with their parents at a family centre. Traumatised behaviour continued on the part of the children until contact was terminated following a specialist assessment that identified both the mother and the father not only as the children's abusers but also as being violent and sadistic in their abuse. What looked like a close parent–child relationship was an insecure attachment on the part of the children as a means of survival, combined with continued grooming by the parents to maintain the children's silence which was further solidified by the local authority's inadvertent collusion.

When victims demand to meet with their abuser

Sometimes a young person may express the wish to meet with their abuser face-to-face as a means of managing their own distress, in order to confront him with the harm he has caused. Whilst this can be seen as the young person's right and an acceptable thing to do, such meetings are susceptible to similar manipulation by the offender unbeknown to others present and can have unforeseen negative consequences exacerbating the victim's trauma, as described by Eldridge and Still (1995).

Important paranoia alert

It is acknowledged that such things do not happen in every situation and such examples can create a sense of paranoia. This in turn can tempt us to take a 'better safe than sorry approach' in all situations by imposing draconian measures restricting the type of interactions allowed during contact, which in hindsight are deemed to have been inappropriate and even harmful. However, possibilities must be entertained and the best decisions can only be made by professionals – and mothers/partners – who have an awareness of sex offender behaviour.

Setting conditions and restrictions in the home

Similarly, one possible outcome of any assessment could be for all parties to remain in the family home but under a strict regime of conditions and restrictions. With the benefit of hindsight, in some cases those measures will be deemed appropriate and helpful but in other cases they may come to be regarded as having been harsh and even potentially harmful.

Case example: Family A

Alleged offender A was allowed to stay in the family home but restrictions were placed not only on him as to what he should wear, what he could do and where he could go within the family home, but also on all the children in the family. The girls were not allowed, for example, to go outside their bedroom wearing nightwear and had to stay covered up at all times, giving them the unintended message that girls can be sexually provocative and are 'asking for it' and to blame for any subsequent abuse. The same rules of limited access and behaviour applied to the son, giving him the unintended message that 'boys can't help it and must be controlled' and 'they think my dad's a sex offender and I must be like him'. The result was an even greater sense of tension and mistrust in the family, with the mother/partner tasked to keep an eye on everyone at all times, which was impossible no matter how hard she tried.

Case example: Family B

Four-year-old B loved her father (which may or may not have been linked to sexual grooming) and could not understand his sudden departure from the family home and his continuing absence over many months (during the family's assessment). The only other person to have gone missing in her life was her grandfather, who had died, so she presumed her father was dead. She knew it was linked to something she had said, which led her to believe she had caused his death. This had a serious traumatising effect, which was later deemed to be greater than any sexual abuse that may or may not have taken place.

Case example: Family C

Whilst most sex offenders are not risk takers, some are, and there is no point setting a long list of 'do's and don'ts' for an offender whose pattern is that of a risk taker because he will simply see that as a challenge, which could in turn feed into his arousal.

Stepfather C remained in the family home because all legal attempts to remove him failed. A Care Plan was put in place with restrictions similar to those of family A. The trouble was that no one had conducted a proper assessment of C, whose pattern of arousal was that of a risk taker. That is, the risk of being caught did not deter his offending but fed into his sexual arousal. So the more obstacles that were put in his path the more exciting and sexually challenging it was for him and the more likely that he would reoffend.

Conclusions

When assessing mothers and partners it is a false economy of time and effort to scrimp on preliminary thinking and planning. It is important to entertain possibilities without any such early thoughts being cast in stone. Early thoughts can guide our questions but with child sexual abuse it is important to be open to the unexpected and to be ready to respond accordingly. Other important issues to consider are:

- the style of engagement

- did she know? – the spectrum of knowing

- the mother's or partner's experiences to date

- what to tell the mother/partner and when

- personal feelings about sex offenders generally and this case in particular.

These will be dealt with in the next chapter.

References

Munro, E. (2010) *The Munro Review of Child Protection: Part One: A Systems Analysis.* London: The Stationery Office.

Howe, D., Brandon, M., Hinings, D. and Schofield, G. (1999) *Attachment Theory, Child Maltreatment and Family Support: A Practice and Assessment Model.* Basingstoke: Palgrave Macmillan.

Eldridge, H. and Still, J. (1995) 'Apology and Forgiveness in the Context of the Cycles of Adult Male Sex Offenders Who Abuse Children.' In A.C. Salter (ed.) *Transforming Trauma: A Guide to Understanding and Treating Adult Survivors of Child Sexual Abuse.* Thousand Oaks, CA: Sage.

CHAPTER 12

THE IMPORTANCE OF ENGAGEMENT AND MOTIVATION

In this chapter we consider some of the issues that can get in the way of our ability a) to engage with and motivate a mother/partner and b) to help her move on in a way that is positive for herself and therefore for the child and the family. If there is little or no engagement on her part, which may lead to conclusions that she is unsafe in her ability to protect children, we need to know that was not due to our limitations as an interviewer.

The style of assessment

In all social encounters there are ways in which we relate to others that can make them either want to see us again or to run a mile at the prospect of a further encounter. Engaging with a woman for assessment is no different. No woman would ever choose to be in this situation. Given the importance of the mother to the child or young person who has been abused as well as to any other children in the family, as discussed in Chapter 1, it is incumbent upon us to engage with her in a way that enables us to do our job without pushing her into defensive fight or flight. As we have seen in previous chapters there is no such thing as a simple case of child sexual abuse. So often we are hampered by working with allegation, suspicion and denial. Even when an offender is known, information can be limited. It is in this context that we have to try to understand the mother's or partner's situation before the abuse, at the time of abuse and now. A good assessment requires that we engage with the person we are assessing and the first meeting sets the tone for the rest of the assessment.

Did she know? Is she safe?

As we saw in Chapter 2, experience suggests most women did not know of their child's abuse and/or their partner's or significant other's offending but it is important for us to work out where she was on the 'spectrum of knowing'. However, in isolation this question can sound hostile and accusatory. We need to use an approach that allows us to assess her:

- without being inappropriately judgemental if she did not know about the abuse

- without becoming so soft that we become inadvertently collusive and miss the woman who did know and was further along the spectrum.

We need to adopt a style that is both professional and objective, whilst helping her feel she can face subsequent sessions. To achieve this, 'come down this road with me' will always beat a confrontational approach. We need to convey through verbal and non-verbal communication:

- our wish to be straightforward with her

- no guarantee of outcome – how can we know what we have not yet heard?

- our wish to understand and help her as well as to protect the children involved

- our understanding of the wider context of abuse

- unravelling any inappropriate sense of guilt, blame or responsibility on her part

- hope – and a way through the mess, positively, for the future

- partnership with her – we have knowledge and understanding we can share.

To maximise our chances of achieving a fair and accurate assessment we need:

- to ensure the mother or partner is clear about why she is being assessed, what for and our remit for the assessment

- to listen to and hear what she is saying

- to gather information

- to interpret information in the context of the problem – child sexual abuse (known or alleged)

- to understand any significant cultural context.

Crucially, we need to remember that wherever she was on the spectrum of knowing, this must also be put in the context of the known or alleged offender: we need to work out what the offender did to keep her there and her likely ability to move on from that.

Checking out our own feelings

We need to ask ourselves 'How do I feel about this woman who failed to protect and/or who failed to recognise her partner/relative/friend as being a sex offender? How do I feel about sex offenders?' If we are to have the right approach in interview these are important questions to consider beforehand. It is understandable for anyone who works with victims and families to have strong feelings about sex offenders and also that we might feel angry and hostile to a woman who we perceive to have had a responsibility to protect and failed to do so. However, what is not acceptable is to take those feelings into the interviews or to let those feelings cloud our objective analysis of what we hear. Strong support and supervision are necessary to manage such feelings. If we are unable to remain objective then we should not be doing this work. This should not lead to our being seen as being incompetent. On the contrary: not everyone can do everything and it requires professional self-awareness and confidence to recognise boundaries and limitations, otherwise it is the woman, the child and the family who will pay the price.

Understanding her starting point in the assessment: what is she likely to have been through already?

When assessing the mother or partner we need to take into consideration where she is coming from. Such an empathic approach is not about being soft on failure to protect but an attempt on our part to understand it more.

In addition to the inevitable manipulation by the offender her experiences are likely to include disclosure, investigation, probably a generic assessment, dealing with the impact of the abuse on the child (if hers) and on other siblings, dealing with any reactions from the extended family, local community (if it has become public knowledge) and possibly her workplace – as well as her relationship with the offender and the impact of the abuse on herself. (See the list of possible impact issues list in Chapter 2).

The phrase 'secondary victimisation' of non-offending mothers and partners has been used to describe women's experiences relating to the discovery or suspicion of child sexual abuse and their exposure to the investigative process (e.g. Strand 2000). It is not our job to abuse such women further. If our role is to understand the situation then it is important that we stop and consider what the woman's experience has been so far because that is the baggage she will be bringing to the interview.

What information does she have and how reliable is it?

Whatever responses we see in her an assessment will be based on whatever information she does or does not have.

- She may have anything from no information (if neither the child nor the alleged/known offender has been forthcoming), some information to more than one version – not all of which will be accurate.

- If she has information, what is it and where did she get it from and how reliable is it?

- How recent or long ago was the disclosure, discovery or suspicion of sexual abuse?

- What has happened since?

EXERCISE
FAMILY M

The aim of this exercise is to help us understand where the mother/partner is coming from. It can be done individually or with colleagues. It is set out in two parts:

- Part one: three different assessment scenarios to consider
- Part two: possible answers and responses for each scenario.

Part one: three scenarios
Family M: scenario one

You are about to assess Kayleigh, whose 14-year-old daughter Jasmine told a teacher her stepfather Paul sexually abused her by touching her on her breasts and between her legs on several occasions. There has been a joint police and social services investigation during which Paul consistently denied the allegations. Paul and Kayleigh married many years ago and went on to have three children together; he said he had always treated Jasmine the same as his own children and they had always had a good relationship. Kayleigh agreed with this. Paul said he could only assume that in adolescence Jasmine developed issues about being left by her own father, that she had become jealous that her half-siblings had a real father and that she had made up the allegations in a moment of teenage rebellion. There have been no allegations of any kind of abuse from any of the other children in the family and no history of allegations from elsewhere. There is no prosecution of Paul due to lack of evidence. Kayleigh does not know what to believe but has continued to support Jasmine because she knows there is some kind of serious problem. Paul is much loved by his own children and this has caused friction between Jasmine and her half-siblings, who blame her for the absence of their father. Paul and Kayleigh have cooperated with social services' request for Paul to move out of the family home pending further assessment.

Questions to consider

It is the evening before the first interview. Kayleigh has never met you before.

1. How do you think Kayleigh might be *feeling* about the assessment tomorrow? Why?

2. What do you think Kayleigh might be *thinking* about the assessment? Why?

3. Might Kayleigh have any worries? If so, what might they be about?

4. If you were Paul and you *did* sexually abuse Jasmine and you knew Kayleigh was about to be assessed what might you be thinking? What do you think you (Paul) would do?

5. Do you think it likely that Kayleigh has discussed any of this with anyone: family or friend? If not, what might have stopped her from doing so?

6. Do you think any of this would be different if this family came from a different social background or culture? How?

Family M: scenario two

What if it is accepted by the authorities that Paul did sexually abuse Jasmine but Paul continues to deny it? How might Kayleigh's perspective be different if:

- Paul has been charged but not yet appeared in court?
- Paul has been prosecuted but not convicted?
- Paul has been prosecuted and convicted but still denies it?

How might this have affected Jasmine? How might this have affected relationships within the family?

Family M: scenario three

Whilst we should always remember how hard it is for a child or young person to tell and not be believed, we have seen also that in a minority of cases they might make an allegation that is untrue. Maybe that is what Jasmine has done and now she is horrified at the fall-out of her accusations but can find no way to rescind them for fear of getting into trouble herself. What would be likely to be happening in this family if that were the case?

Part two: some examples of possible answers to the questions in the three scenarios

Scenario one

1. Kayleigh may be feeling anxious, nervous, angry, hostile, defensive.

2. She may think 'why are you interviewing me? I haven't done anything wrong' and/or that it is she who is in the wrong, especially if she is being interviewed more often than Paul.

3. She may worry that 'they think I'm a bad mother', 'they want to take away my other children', 'what if I say the wrong thing?', 'I mustn't say the wrong thing – what do they want to hear?'

4. If Paul did abuse Jasmine he would be thinking 'I need to stay in control even though I won't be there' and so resume grooming of Kayleigh: by phone, text, email, letter, a visit; an offer to take her to the interview; an offer to be there afterwards to comfort her. He would need to maintain grooming style, for example Mr Nice Guy (I love you, it's not fair on you, I'm so sorry, you are the most important person to me, I'll kill myself if I lose you) or Mr Nasty

Guy (threats, physical abuse) and any other variation previously discussed.

5. Kayleigh may have wanted someone to talk to about it but who could she trust? How would they react? Think of the gossip and its effect on her child/family/partner. Would they believe it? Would they blame the child, or her? What would they think of her? If it became public knowledge would she risk reprisals from within the community against her as a 'paedophile lover'? If she is one of the minority of women who had some awareness of any abuse, or who was collusive in the abuse she may worry about being prosecuted.

6. In many ethnic minority communities these issues can become even more pronounced, with the fear of shame, victim blame and loss of future marriage eligibility, plus pressure to keep quiet about any information she may have; she may fear ostracism from her already minority community and/or within her faith.

Scenario two

Remember that whatever Kayleigh's responses may be, Paul's continued grooming to persuade her of his innocence would likely be a major influence, with the relevant knock-on effect on her relationship with Jasmine.

Scenario three

It is accepted that for us as child protection professionals this scenario will be unpalatable because we are taught the importance of believing the child and it is true that our failure to do so can be a double betrayal for that child, with all the negative consequences. However, it is important in assessment to remain objective. We need to be aware that in in such a situation many of Paul's attempts to persuade others of his innocence could still be assumed to be grooming, albeit wrongly. So in assessment we have to use what we know about men who are sex offenders to look for the presence – or absence – of factors in combination. This in turn can help us with the questions we ask when interviewing the mother/partner (see Chapter 13) as well as when working with the child and family.

Our use of language
Avoiding use of the term sex offender or paedophile in relation to alleged or suspected sex offenders

There is nothing more likely to alienate a woman who has a close connection to the person who is suspected or accused than to call him a sex offender or a paedophile. As we saw in Chapter 1 when discussing belief and disbelief, it is a natural human response for a woman to doubt an allegation where there is no physical evidence and limited other information. Even the many women who believe the child can still have trouble believing it of her partner, father or other relative or close friend. She may be torn also by a sense of loyalty to him and so think there must somehow be some mistake. Therefore, to use the term sex offender or paedophile in relation to this individual during assessment is likely to provoke a negative response from her.

Furthermore, in Chapter 10 we looked at the need for accuracy in our use of language. It would be an inaccurate use of the term 'sex offender' in cases of alleged or suspected sexual abuse because technically someone only gains the title of offender if and when they are convicted. Similarly, we should not use the word paedophile without reasonable evidence that that is what he is.

Avoiding clinical and legal jargon

Talking about intimate sexuality can be embarrassing for both the interviewer and interviewee and the use of clinical or legal jargon may provide a safe refuge from any such embarrassment. However, different terminology means different things to different people so we might think we are talking about the same thing when we are not and everything becomes gobbledegook.

Some guidelines

- A question such as 'did you know your husband/friend is a sex offender?' would be inappropriately worded unless there is a prior conviction.

- Neither do we want to duck the issue. A simple solution can be to talk in these early stages about what we know about 'men who have this problem'.

- This is not about being soft or colluding with denial but ensuring accuracy and engaging with the mother/partner.

- Plain, simple language is essential irrespective of what we perceive to be the woman's intelligence, social abilities or social and/or cultural background. Where legal or clinical terms are necessary their meaning should be clarified.

How much should I tell the mother/partner during the assessment?

If I have more information about the offender from another source that the mother/partner does not have, should I tell her?

Obviously we must share enough information to explain why we are concerned. In many situations we too may have minimal information about the known or alleged offender. However, when the offender is known and we have acquired more detailed information about him from his specialist assessment and/or his treatment programme, we are put in a situation where we know a great deal more about the offender than the mother or partner does. This presents us with a dilemma. What do we tell her? When, how and why? This is a complex question and a potential minefield in terms of the relationship between the mother/partner and her assessor.

There is a school of thought that assessments should begin with telling the mother/partner everything we know that she does not. We may be motivated by a wish to be respectful and honest with her: it can feel condescending not to tell her everything we know and many mothers and partners would be angry about being kept in the dark. If, on the other hand, we are angry with her for failing to protect or because she is continuing to support the alleged or known offender, our motivation may be more punitive: we might want to tell her something difficult because she deserves to hear it.

However, if our goal is to engage with her then it could be argued that too much information too soon can be counterproductive. If, for example, we knew from the probation officer or psychologist that a known offender was fantasising about buggering a boy during marital sex, should we share that detail with his partner in assessment? How do we expect her to react? Do we penalise her if she is too calm, too angry, too accepting, too dismissive, too disbelieving? What is the correct response?

If information is too difficult and unexpected she will not be able to take it in and she will stop hearing what we are saying. If she does hear it her response will probably be one of fight or flight, possibly expressed in a hostile manner by 'shooting the messenger'. After all, why should she trust us to know and tell the truth? As a reminder, revisit the exercise of 'imagine you get home and your best friend tells you' in Chapter 2.

Understanding the impact of information

It is up to the interviewer to weigh up the balance between what should be shared now or later. Child sexual abuse is never good news. The closer to home it is, the more difficult it is to hear and absorb difficult information. The following are other useful issues to consider.

Processing painful information

When we hear painful information we go through a process whereby, put simply, we:

- hear content

- interpret content (understand the language, especially if jargon or unfamiliar words are used)

- process content cognitively (what does that mean?)

- feel the impact of content emotionally

- process that impact

- find equilibrium to enable coping

- act on or reject the information.

Therefore it is not unreasonable for us to give any mother or partner time to do that, which means any initial responses such as anger and hostility toward us (shoot the messenger), minimising or denial (I don't believe it, it's not true) may be temporary whilst she is en route to a more balanced conclusion.

Finding the balance

Every situation is different but we may be guided by the following principles:

- her right to know
  (she asks, she is an adult and a mother/partner)

  versus

- her need to know
  (for child protection)

  versus

- her right not to be abused.

Note: When a woman says 'I want to know' we should be aware that she does not know what she is asking for and our information about a sex offender is likely to be beyond anything she expects.

Some guidelines on what to do with information

As we have seen from the above exercise every situation is different and must be decided on its own merits. Whatever type of scenario we are faced with it is always necessary for us to share with her enough information to explain why we are concerned, why this assessment of her is taking place and why any interim protective measure may be necessary, such as the known or suspected offender being asked to leave the family home.

However, a good baseline rule is that the function of the interviewer in assessment is first and foremost to listen to and hear what is being said, which we can then analyse to provide an understanding of the mother/partner's situation both in the past and now. This means finding out about what *she* knows about the known or suspected abuse and not about what we have to tell her.

So whilst it might be sensible to share information about the nature of the abuse, the number of allegations and/or known victims and any convictions, it may not be appropriate during assessment to share any detailed information we may have about his cycle or pattern of offending. Indeed, part of our job during our assessment of her is to draw out information that will add to our profile of the known or alleged offender.

However, it is not fair to women to leave them with unanswered questions, which in turn can cause anxiety and frustration, undermine her future confidence as a parent and leave her insufficiently informed to make good decisions about her partner, relative or friend about whom there are concerns. Therefore it is important that assessment should not be an end in itself but should become part of a carefully devised and informed intervention plan.

Issues relating to sharing and not sharing information are addressed in more detail in Chapters 13 and 14 when we consider an interview format and then an intervention programme.

Conclusions

In the next chapter we look at devising an assessment interview format geared specifically to child sexual abuse. However, our style of interviewing is as important as the questions we ask. No woman wants to be in this situation and if we do not succeed in engaging with her appropriately then she will be less likely to want to participate fully in the assessment.

References

Strand, V.C. (2000) *Treating Secondary Victims: Intervention with the Nonoffending Mother in the Incest Family.* Thousand Oaks, CA: Sage.

CHAPTER 13

THE ASSESSMENT INTERVIEW

WHAT QUESTIONS TO ASK, WHY, HOW AND WHEN

The model used here enables us to move on from a generic assessment format to one that focuses specifically on the problem of sexual abuse. The aim is not to minimise or excuse failure to protect but to understand it more in order to maximise the mother's or partner's her ability to protect in future and to identify those genuinely worrying cases where prognosis is poor and alternate action needs to be taken. It draws on the contents of previous chapters by taking what we know about how sex offenders operate and using it to increase our understanding of the mother/partner. It should only be used in conjunction with that information.

In so doing it also adds to our understanding of the young person or child who has been abused and the whole family, which provides a fuller context for assessment. The model aims also to address some of the problems relating to the woman's perception of her being assessed as discussed in Chapter 9.

The proposed model includes potentially difficult questions, which require tact and sensitivity on the part of the interviewer. Its practical application requires the interviewer to be familiar with the information and preparation discussed in previous chapters. Every situation is different: whilst sex offenders have many things in common every sex offender is different and therefore the experience of every woman, child and family is also unique to them. Particularly important references to previous chapters are flagged up in the context of the assessment interview process.

A guide to method

Child sexual abuse is a potential minefield of complex emotional, practical and legal issues and a mother or partner can be encouraged or discouraged to engage in the assessment by the style adopted by the interviewer. The following is offered as a guide to maximising the chances of positive engagement.

Questions to ask: What? Why? How? When?

We need to think about the following in advance:

- *What* do I want to ask?

- *Why* do I want to ask it?

- *How* do I ask it?

- *When* do I ask it?

It is all too easy to think about the first of these questions and forget the other three. However, if our aim is to engage with and motivate the mother/partner in a positive way they too are important.

Why?

The question 'why' keeps the interviewer on task. Furthermore, given that any particular question may seem exceptionally personal or intrusive to the recipient it can be both helpful and respectful for us to explain why we are asking it. Even for that minority of women who we know to be further down the 'knowing spectrum' we need to know the story behind it.

How?

The question 'how' is important because the way a question is asked can either encourage her active participation or make her not want to attend any more. For example, with regard to questions about the woman's sexual relationship with her partner and about whether or not she has ever been sexually abused – why should we ask these questions when it is not her who is suspected or accused of child sexual abuse? Yet they are crucial questions to ask. When approached at an appropriate time and in an appropriate way they can provide important insight that can then inform decisions about what is needed to help the situation via an intervention plan; asked in the wrong way they will likely cause anger, distress and possible disengagement.

When?

The right question asked at the wrong time can provoke an otherwise unnecessary response of fight or flight or the mother/partner simply freezing up. For example, many practitioners would start with the question 'can you tell me what you know about what has happened?' This is a sensible question to ask at some stage and it may seem sensible to make it the first question. However, it is heavy content to begin with plus the wording carries assumptions that she must have known something, both of which could make her defensive, which could then have an unnecessarily negative impact on her subsequent responses.

The questions laid out in the model below are put in an order that experience suggests is most likely to help the interviewee to become engaged in the assessment process. However, the order of questions is not fixed because whilst there are known patterns of sexual offending there is no set pattern or predictability as to how a mother or partner may or may not react: every situation is different and requires suitable adaptability on the part of the interviewer. The order may therefore need to be changed. Additional follow-up questions will arise depending on the responses given. The proposed format then acts as a checklist to ensure nothing is forgotten, because there is nothing worse than realising after the event that we forgot to ask something important.

The use of open-ended questions

As we never know what we are about to hear it is important to keep an open mind. The use of open-ended questions allows us to do so. In this way we can, for example, strike a balance between not making automatic assumptions about what the mother/partner must or must not have known about the abuse, whilst also allowing us to entertain the statistically small possibility that she was aware of or collusive in the abuse and/or even a co-offender, as discussed in Chapters 2 and 6.

The need for flexibility

The suggested questions are phrased to relate to known or suspected abuse by the woman's partner. However, they can be adapted to relate to other close relationships where the known or suspected offender is a relative or family friend.

Content and process: timing and pacing

It is easy to become so focused on obtaining information that we become insensitive to the mother's/partner's emotional as well as cognitive responses. There is little point in continuing to pursue a particular question at a particular time when her thoughts and feelings have clearly disappeared elsewhere. A simple question or observation such as 'you've disappeared, where have you gone?' or 'that question has clearly caused you distress, can you tell me why?' not only treats her with appropriate respect but can elicit what is often the most important information we need to hear. Timing and pacing are all-important in helping the woman to remain engaged in the process. The most important information can often come as we are about to end the interview. It is not a good idea to let this go.

There is a great deal to remember and there is no harm in taking a checklist into the interview.

Use of language

To recap from Chapter 10, we should be careful in our use of language. We should be particularly careful not to use the terms paedophile or sex offender inaccurately. In cases of alleged or suspected abuse the use of either can reduce interviews to repeated indignation that 'he isn't one', causing frustration to both parties and getting nowhere. In such instances we can use phrases such as 'what we know about men who have this problem'. We should avoid using unnecessary legal or clinical jargon.

Similarly, it is important to understand what the interviewee means when using particular language and to recognise the difference between when she is avoiding an issue and when she is simply having difficulty putting her thoughts and feelings into words.

Listening versus talking

If we have information about the offender from another source are we there to listen or to talk? This is a complex question that we considered in previous chapters. To recap, if we get the questions right, as a general rule assessment is about listening and sharing basic information as to why there are concerns. Ideally, the subsequent intervention plan is where more detailed information can be shared and is dealt with in the next chapter. However, every situation is different and must be considered accordingly.

Interpretation of information

Analysis of information gathered from the mother/partner needs to take into account additional information from the child and family and also from the known or suspected offender. Similarly, information from the mother or partner can inform the assessment of the known or suspected offender, providing clues as to his pattern and cycle of offending.

Cautionary reminder: One worrying observation does not confirm sexual abuse. Any behaviour can be seen as grooming and it is important to look at factors in combination.

Issues of faith and culture

A sex offender is likely to use whatever is available to him to manipulate and groom the child, the mother/partner and even an entire family, including issues relating to faith and ethnicity, and to use it to justify and excuse his abusive behaviour to himself, as discussed in Chapter 6. At the time of writing all UN member states – with the exception of the US, Somalia and South Sudan – have signed up to the 1989 UN Convention on the Rights of the Child, which became law in the UK in 1992. The guiding principle is that it is the law of the home land that applies irrespective of faith, culture or ethnicity.

A good assessment is the basis for devising an intervention plan geared to the needs of the individual case

Assessment is not only about the need for child protection but also about recognising and addressing other related issues that may impede the child(ren)'s well-being. For example, to keep a child safe it is not uncommon for a woman to say she will never trust any male again and never let the child(ren) out of her sight. This is natural and may satisfy the question of child protection but in the real world as a plan it is not only impracticable but it also carries the risk of inadvertent harm through over-protectiveness, stifling the child or young person's other healthy developmental needs as well as robbing the woman of her right to a normal life. We need assessments to identify any such subsidiary issues for her, for her child and her family, to make appropriate recommendations and to propose an appropriate intervention plan accordingly. This is discussed more fully in the next chapter.

The interview

Under each question below there are guidelines as to why the question is important and how information we receive may be understood using knowledge of men who are sex offenders, which can then be applied in our subsequent analysis and report writing. Whilst it is not our job to confirm the guilt or innocence of the known or suspected offender, we can use such an approach to inform and explain our opinion on issues relating to the mother/partner.

The explanations of 'why' we are asking a question are for the benefit of the *interviewer* in terms of focusing on issues relating to child sexual abuse. The explanation of 'how' offers ways of asking a potentially difficult question.

Welcome (and) Can I ask – do you know who I am and why you're here?

Why?

- When meeting a mother or partner for the first time it is easy to assume someone else has told her why she is there. It is astonishing how often that is not the case.

- Asking her the question rather than making a 'why we're here' statement gives the immediate signal that we are interested in her and that we are here to listen.

- It enables us to find out what she has been told about the assessment, by whom and how. Even if she has been told she may not have taken it in. It gives her permission to say 'no I don't know why I'm here' without feeling defensive or stupid, which is never a good start. It enables us to rectify any misconceptions she may have.

Setting the ground rules

Why?

- This ensures fairness, respect and the need for clarity on both sides.

- It avoids the mother/partner saying later 'you didn't tell me that', for example, if we have to report further concerns to the police. If there is a sex offender in her life she will have been manipulated by him, so honesty from us is even more important.

How?

- We can explain who we are, what we do, our professional title and who we are doing the assessment for, for example Social Services, the family courts, and so on.

- We can explain the specific remit we have been given, that is, the issues we have been asked to address.

- We can outline to her what the interview process will be, how long it will take and when it will be completed.

- We cannot give guarantees how it will turn out because we don't know what it is we are about to hear. But we can acknowledge that the situation for the child, for her and for her family is difficult and explain that our assessment will help to move things on.

- It is important to give her confidence in the process: we are there to gain an understanding of her situation and we also have knowledge and experience that can help.

- We can explain that it is important we both understand one another so if anything is said or not heard or not understood each should feel free to say so.

- On confidentiality issues we need to explain:

  » who will receive our report

  » that we will ensure she sees the report and we or someone else will go through it with her (this does not always happen and can cause unnecessary problems later)

  » that what she tells us will be confidential and only shared with the official agencies who receive our report

  » that if we hear of any new offences and/or offenders we are duty bound to report them (this is not a legal requirement in the UK but should be an obligation as our primary consideration is the safety and well-being of children)

  » that she may have issues which she may not want to share so widely (e.g. about sexuality, maybe about her own previously undisclosed survivor issues) but failure to include it in our report may mean the recipients have less understanding of her situation and our recommendations.

- We can explain that she is important and we are there to listen and understand but the law states our primary concern has to be the child(ren)'s safety and well-being.

This has been a difficult time. How are you doing?
Why?

- She is not just someone's mother or partner but a person in her own right and she has the right to have her feelings validated.

- It is natural that she may be feeling anxious, nervous, maybe defensive or angry and that she may worry about telling us that for fear that she will be perceived as unable to cope.

- If she is living with or still in contact with a sex offender we should be aware that he is likely to be continuing grooming: he will probably have done it before the session and he will probably do it afterwards too. We can use this to help us understand her responses throughout.

How would you describe yourself? (or) How do you think other people would describe you?
Why?

- We need to form our own opinion and not rely on quotes from background papers, which may be ill informed or relevant to another time.

- This question focuses on personality, not her background. It provides immediate insight into her present emotional state. Research suggests that the discovery of child sexual abuse can cause non-offending mothers and partners to experience poor self-esteem and loss of personal confidence (see Chapter 1). This can be indicated, for example, by the woman not being able to answer or only being able to think of negative things about herself. Is this usual or only since the discovery or suspicion of child sexual abuse?

- Such a response would be natural and only of longer term concern if it persists, especially if combined with other problems.

How?

- Keep it light. Acknowledge most people would be self-conscious answering this question.

- If she only focuses on negatives, invite her to think of two positives, no matter how simple.

Can you describe your children for me?
Why?

- For many mothers this is an easy question to begin with and helps ease them into the interview.

- It provides insight into her relationship with her children. For example, it may be the only time in interview she smiles; she may speak warmly of one and not of another; she may describe all her children in one lump and not as individuals; it can provide insight as to why a particular child was targeted for abuse; it can indicate estranged relationships before, during and after the abuse.

- It can provide preliminary insight into how the offender operated, or how the suspected offender might have operated: what is there that he might have seen to help him target and abuse a child?; what did he see in the situation as a means of driving a wedge between the mother and his victim? (for example, was this the quiet child who was less close to the mother and/or siblings and who he could therefore isolate and emotionally and sexually 'seduce'? Was there previously a close bond between mother and this child or young person where the offender saw an opportunity for power play? etc.); what did he think he could manipulate to prevent the mother/partner from hearing/seeing/believing abuse – even if she responded appropriately and he therefore got it wrong?; what impact has the abuse had on sibling relationships (how might he have groomed and manipulated the sibling dynamics to isolate the victim?). How do possible issues raised here combine later with other worrying factors?

Can you tell me briefly about your own background?
Why?

- Some women question our need to know this because it is not they who have abused a child: again, we can explain that it helps us to understand the whole situation better.

- It can highlight anything of concern in terms of a particular vulnerability that a sex offender could have used to his advantage in targeting and grooming her. For example: difficulties in childhood such as social isolation, historic low self-esteem, possible physical, sexual or emotional abuse – some of which may be indicated in the offender/alleged offender assessment – or none of the above and a well-grounded, happy childhood.

- *Caution: tread with care.* If she has been abused she may never have disclosed it before. Be aware that this could be difficult for her to talk about, especially in these circumstances.

- If there have been any such problems they do not make her responsible for the abuse in question now.

- We need to understand what effect her own experiences have had on her perception of the present situation, not only to understand that but to inform any subsequent plan for a programme of intervention with her.

How?

- Keep this question brief, especially if it is already covered by others in a generic assessment: too many repeats can feel intrusive and abusive of her.

- It is helpful to ask about the following – even if they have been covered elsewhere – to hear it for ourselves:

  » her family of origin; past and present relationships with her mother, father and siblings; schooling; childhood and adolescent friendships; adult friendships, interests and hobbies

  » has anyone in her family or close friends ever been accused or convicted of sexual abuse?

- If she mentions she has been abused:

  » has she ever told anyone that before?

  » acknowledge what she said – we are interested to hear more – and ask her if we can come back to it later (otherwise we can be side tracked away from the present task in hand, and if she has only just met us why should she trust us?).

Can you tell me about the partners you have had prior to your present situation?
Why?

- Again, the woman may question why we want to know if it was not her who committed the abuse. Explain that it helps put her present relationship in context.

- Is there a pattern that a sex offender could pick up on? For example, is there a history of her having physically/sexually violent or inappropriately controlling and dominant partners?

- If this partner is different from previous partners and nicer than them this can sometimes be used as a grooming tactic on his part: 'I'm not abusive like…was, I'd never do anything to hurt you'.

- Maybe she has found someone who is a good person.

How?

This can be kept brief unless there are reasons to pursue questions further. We can ask the following:

- When she had her first sexual-type relationship with a boyfriend – or girlfriend – as appropriate. (This is not to be judgemental and we do not need to know about every person or detail: we are looking to see if there were any real difficulties in early relationships and/or whether as a young girl she had a 'relationship' with an older man, i.e. abuse. This helps us understand her own views on children and young people's developing sexuality as per next question.)

- Could she describe subsequent relationships with any partners in terms of the following:

  » How did they meet?

  » Were they live-in relationships?

  » Did she or the other party have children?

  » Were they happy relationships for her?

  » Who made the decisions e.g. about finances and day-to-day activities?

  » Was there ever any serious conflicts and/or violence of any kind?

  » Were her sexual relationships equal and consenting?

  » Were any previous partners convicted or accused of sexual offences?

Can you tell me about your relationship with…(her present partner or the known offender/suspected offender in question)?
Why?

- The same question will have been asked of the known/suspected offender and this provides an additional perspective to his answers.

- It gives further insight into the known/suspected offender's possible style and pattern of offending in relation to his possible targeting and grooming of both her and the child.

- It provides insight into day-to-day domestic arrangements, which in turn can provide information on, for example, how an offender could have gained access to the child or young person for abuse.

How?

The following are examples of the kind of questions we can ask:

- How did they meet? Where? What age was she? What age was he? (Was it a peer relationship or was there a big age differential, especially if they met when she was very young? If so, was this illegal and so abuse?)

- Can she describe him? What kind of a person is he?

- Can she describe the nature of their relationship? Do they get on well? Who makes what decisions? How do they resolve arguments?

- Does he work – what is his job?

- What are his interests? (Are they adult or child focused? Are they in the home or elsewhere?)

- What kind of relationship does he have with her/their/his children?

- Who does what in the home and in terms of child care? Is she happy with that?

I know this is very personal but we are talking about sexual concerns about him. So could you tell me about your sexual relationship with him (where he is her partner)?

Why?

- Many practitioners balk at asking this question because it feels too embarrassing and intrusive. However, it is crucial to ask it because it throws light on *his* sexual interests.

- We are looking for issues that would raise concern in this particular case of child sexual abuse. For example: if there is an activity he likes and she dislikes such as, for example, oral sex, and she knows oral sex is reported by the child she may be inappropriately blaming herself for him turning to a child; if their adult sexual relationship is poor that may mean he is less interested in adults and has a greater sexual interest in children, when looked at in combination with other factors; if he has a preoccupation with a particular sexual activity this may resonate with the child's descriptions of abuse.

- In a minority of cases, where there are indications of adult sexual coercion, violence, and/or voyeurism on his part, this also raises the possibility of his coercing the woman into co-offending (see Chapter 6). Is there any information from any other source that would further suggest that, which should be pursued further?

How?

- We can explain that because her sexual partner has been accused of sexual abuse it is important for us to understand *his* sexuality and it is she who can tell us about that.

- We should acknowledge she may find this embarrassing but for us it is our job and we do this all the time. We will not be shocked or surprised by anything we hear. What adults do that is legal and consenting is fine.

- *Important note: It should always be explained that we will only put in our report what is relevant to helping others understand our conclusions and recommendations.*

- We can ask about the following:

  » levels of sexual interests (how often?)

  » who instigates it?

  » preferred sexual practices? We need to think beyond our own sexual experiences and to entertain all possibilities. The best way to do this is to give her a list of sexual practices – as if we were talking about the price of baked beans – to which she can say either yes or no. For example: oral sex; anal sex; use of blue movies/pornography in books, videos, magazines; filming their sex; dressing up (child focused?); use of sex toys; insertion of objects (what/where); use of food; sadomasochism; sexual preoccupations/fetishes; sex power games; computer/access to internet/chat lines on internet or mobile phone; other?

- We can ask if the sexual adult relationship is equal, consenting, non-abusive and enjoyable to her or if there are signs of coercion and/or sexual violence and/or of voyeurism (he likes to watch others)? Does she perceive that as normal or inevitable or 'what men do'?

- The question 'what did he have you do?' should be asked but only when there is good reason to do so, such as indications from the child, the offender or any other sources of threats or violence (see Chapter 6).

Why are people concerned? What do you think has happened? How do you know this?
Why?

- Putting it as a question reaffirms that we are here to listen and not just to tell her what we think.

- We should not assume she knows everything we know or that what she does know is accurate.

- If the offender is still in contact with her he will be telling her what he wants her to believe.

- This will address issues relating to where she is on the 'spectrum of knowing' and why? and issues relating to belief, disbelief and denial.

- If the child is her child and has not told her much about what happened that gives an indication of the power of the offender's grooming, insight into the mother–child relationship and his ability to drive a wedge between mother and child.

What has been your reaction to what has happened? Who do you think is responsible?
Why?

- Again, it gives insight into the extent of the offender's powers of persuasion, manipulation and grooming of which she is likely as yet to be unaware.

- It is important to allow for human responses. Doubt and denial may be worrying but denial is a natural defence mechanism against hurt and pain – it is where she can move on to that counts.

- Even the strongest of mothers/partners who have the perfect child protection response of believing the child unequivocally, totally rejecting the offender and who may appear to be coping, are likely to have times of worry and self-doubt.

- If her responses are inappropriate and entrenched it may suggest a poor ability to protect, at least in the short term, and the need for action to be taken to protect the young person or child.

What is your understanding of the term child sexual abuse?
Why?

- As we saw in Chapters 4 and 10 it means different things to different people.

- Confusion does not make her stupid.

- We need to make sure we are both talking about the same thing.

Children and young people have to start learning about sex at some point: what in your view would be OK and what would not be OK?
Why?

- It tells us her general views on children's developing sexuality and on issues of consent and responsibility.

- How does she apply these views in this particular case?

- Are there signs of grooming and contamination by her exposure to any distorted thinking learned from the offender? Do her views resonate with his views? Are they more extreme than those that may be heard among the general public, even if we may not agree with them?

- Does she raise issues relating to a different faith or culture, which may have been distorted by the offender?

How?

- This is not something the average person thinks about every day. To make it easier, we can give some examples of scenarios. The following are suggestions from which to choose, to address whatever issues are most concerning:

» What would she think about two five-year-olds playing by showing one another their different 'bits'?

» At what age would it be OK to have a boyfriend/girlfriend?

» What does she think would be OK for them to do sexually together? What would not be OK and why?

» When does full sexual intercourse become OK?

» Would it be OK between, say, a 17-year-old boy and a 16-year-old girl and if so, why?

» Would it be OK if her son had full sex at 15? Would it be OK if her daughter did the same? Is there a gender difference?

» What about any sexual behaviour between a 20-year-old man and a 14-year-old girl?

» What if it were between a 30-year-old man and a 19-year-old female? What would the difference be?

- What makes her have those opinions: where do they come from (e.g. her own family, the media, the known/suspected offender)?

- Has she always held these opinions? If not, what has changed?

What might the effects of sexual abuse be on a child or young person a) generally? b) specifically for the child(ren) in question? Why?

- We should not expect a detailed answer because this is likely to be outside her experience, unless she is an adult survivor of childhood abuse, but it offers an indication of victim awareness and victim empathy.

- If there is none, what is preventing that? Is her understanding of children generally poor? Is this situation too scary and/or painful to think about? Is it a temporary defence mechanism or more deep seated?

- If she is a survivor of sexual abuse could her responses be more of a reflection of her own experiences? (See Chapters 2 and 6.)

How?

- Starting with the general question is less threatening and allows the mother/partner to think about the relevant issues before homing in on 'what about in this specific situation?'

What do you know about sex offenders who abuse children or young people a) generally? b) specifically about this known or alleged offender?

Why?

- We should not assume she knows anything about sex offenders or paedophiles: why should she? Has anyone ever told her? Most people's source of information is the mass media.

- That does not make her stupid. However, whilst her belief in her own ability to protect is likely to be genuine it is likely also to be based on this limited and probably inaccurate information and knowledge.

How?

- The priority in assessment is to listen to the mother's/partner's views.

- However, it can also be appropriate to share brief, simple and basic information as to what we know about men who are sex offenders and how they operate (it doesn't just happen, cycles/steps to offending). This may produce a response of 'yes, but he's not like that'. However, it may give her food for thought, which may produce other thoughts she can bring to subsequent sessions.

- The sharing of more detailed information about sex offenders and paedophiles can form part of a later intervention programme whereby, if it is believed there was sexual abuse, she can be helped to profile the known or alleged offender. This helps to answer the question 'how did he do that to the child and to me?' and informs the child protection plan. This is dealt with in more detail in the next chapter.

Have you ever known any other person who has been convicted of sexual offences or who has had allegations of sexual abuse made against them? If so, do they know one another?
Why?

- If there is a pattern we need to know.

How?
If the answer is yes we should pursue it further:

- Has he/they had access to the known or suspected current victim or any other children in the family?

- If those others know one another is there an extended family network of sexual perpetrators?

- Or are they in a ring of unrelated paedophiles? (Such situations may be less common in a family-related situation but signs should not be missed.)

- If the mother/partner is leaving her child(ren) with such people why does she think they will be safe?

- If she was aware of any such connections, to what extent did she feel (or not feel) able to escape involvement? (As previously described, women co-offenders can become equal offenders or reluctant co-offenders under threat. This can happen within an extended family or community network.)

(If she has previously said she had been sexually abused): Can we talk more about your own abuse?
Why?

- In talking about the current child sexual abuse, if the mother/partner has herself been abused she will most likely be reliving it through flashbacks and any associated trauma. We need to be sensitive to her emotional state.

- Her own experience will colour her perception of the current situation (see Chapters 2 and 6).

How?

- Assessment is not therapy but sensitivity is crucial.

- Some women fear they will be labelled as weak, stupid, gullible. It is important to make clear that is not our intention but it will help us to understand her responses and to respond appropriately if she gets into emotional difficulty.

- *Note: It should always be explained that we will not include details of her abuse in our report unless they are relevant to the present case.* This requires her consent. If she does not give it that is fine, but she needs to understand that without that information others reading our report may not understand some of our recommendations.

- We can ask the following:

  » Is this the first time she has ever talked about it?

  » Has she ever had counselling?

  » How is she coping now, for example with flashbacks to her own abuse?

  » What does she need?

The discovery of child sexual abuse can make a woman feel and think things about herself. Has that happened to you?
Why?

- To recap, research and experience suggests mothers/partners can experience a profound sense of guilt and personal failure, which is unlikely to empower her to protect if that were to become a long term issue.

- Again, this does not make her stupid (which is how she might be feeling) but highlights the manipulative abilities of the offender.

- This can be worse for a woman survivor who has told herself she would never let it happen to her child, and/or ever to be caught up with a sex offender again.

- A subsequent intervention plan should address any issues specific to her, which in turn could enhance her ability to protect.

If the mother/partner is in denial or minimising the child's abuse/her partner's behaviour, we can ask: what would it mean to you if you allowed yourself to believe it is true – not just as a mother or partner but as a woman?

Why?

This is a crucial question. It highlights the fears that may prevent her from feeling able to move forward. For example, many women think they will not be able to cope with the realisation that allegations may be true, that their life and relationships were not what they thought them to be, that they will not be able to deal with the consequences. To quote one mother whose husband was suspected of abusing their daughter, 'it's like being asked to jump off a cliff and not knowing if there's a safety net down there' (see the list of possible impact issues in Chapter 2). However, many women are stronger than they think they are and once the fears are identified they can be helped to manage them through a specifically designed intervention plan.

Would you know if your child(ren) was being abused in the future? What makes you think you would/would not know?

Why?

- If she answers 'no' that could be seen as a wrong answer when in fact it is a good answer, if it is because she is now aware that sex offenders lie and manipulate and she realises she needs a way to deal with that.

- Most mothers respond 'yes' because they expect that of themselves and because they have told the child(ren) to tell her. But most mothers do not know about how sex offenders groom and manipulate and if they have heard of grooming most women will have a simplistic view of it and think it will not happen to their child.

- Asking the question helps validate the need for resources for a follow-up intervention programme: how can we ask her to protect without providing her with the necessary knowledge to know what she is protecting a child from (both specific to the known/suspected offender and in general)?

What else is happening in your life?
Why?

- We need to put her reactions to the abuse in the additional context of other possible stresses and pressures in her life. For example: managing as a single parent; financial difficulties; other family problems; responses from family and/or local community; work-related pressures; religious or cultural issues (see the list of impact issues in Chapter 2).

- This helps us see if there is anything here that the known or suspected sex offender could still be manipulating to ensure her responses are favourable to him.

- This does not in itself make her a risky protector, but it identifies areas of further support that may be needed.

What kind of support do you have?
Why?

- It is likely she is receiving limited social support: child sexual abuse remains a social taboo and many women are reluctant to share personal information about it with others.

- If she has shared information, do her support systems share her views or have they been manipulated by the offender? (It is not uncommon for a mother/partner to believe the sexual allegations and to be ostracised by her extended family who continue to support him or, conversely, for a mother/partner to be shunned as a 'paedophile lover' by their local community (see Chapter 2).

What are your hopes for the future?
Why?

- It provides hope: at assessment the situation is likely to be in limbo and this gives the message things will move forward somehow.

- Asking the question gives her a say in that.

- It informs issues relating to child protection.

- It tells us of her perception of the needs of the child, her family and of herself and also the impact of the offender on all three, which needs to be addressed.

- It informs our recommendations and also any subsequent intervention plan.

What do you think you need to move forward?
Why?

- We can ask what she thinks she needs to help her be more aware in terms of protecting her child(ren) from sexual abuse. (We should not expect insight into offenders: why should she know this?)

- We can tell her we understand how men who are sex offenders operate, which we could share with her later (as part of an intervention plan) when there is more time. Would that help her? (She may react negatively at first – who would want to hear about this? – but it gives her time to think about it.)

Ending the interview

- We can thank her for her cooperation.

- We can give a commitment to completing our report as soon as possible and tell her that we or someone will go through it with her.

- We cannot say yet what we will be writing or recommending but we can make a commitment to be fair and to help move things on.

- We can explain that we never give a quick response to her question 'what do you think?' because we might change our mind when we analyse the information received during interviews.

- However, where there are concerns about her immediate ability to protect and remedial action is considered necessary, such as removing the child or young person or the known/ alleged offender from the family home, this should of course be explained to her and the reasons given.

Conclusions

This approach enables the interviewer to focus on the primary reason for the assessment, which is the alleged or known sexual abuse of a child or young person. Done sensitively it allows difficult and sometimes awkward or embarrassing questions to be asked in a way that is acceptable to the woman. It places the responsibility for known abuse where it belongs, that is, with the offender. Where abuse is alleged or suspected it registers concerns appropriately. It enables the woman to acknowledge her own responsibility in possibly having failed to protect a child, whilst beginning to free her from any inappropriate sense of guilt, blame and responsibility for the abuse, which is the responsibility of the abuser and not of her. It also helps us to recognise her other strengths and the possibility of moving on in a positive way.

Despite the many questions, with good planning this interview schedule can be completed in a total of six to eight hours.

All assessments require recommendations that should include, where appropriate, proposals for an intervention plan for work with the mother/partner based on the information received and devised to meet her particular needs. One of the most common questions women in this situation ask is 'how did he do that to the child, to me and to my family?' This is addressed in the next chapter.

CHAPTER 14

INTERVENTION
EMPOWERING MOTHERS AND PARTNERS TO ASSIST AND TO PROTECT THEIR CHILD AND FAMILY

All assessments require some kind of conclusion and recommendation. If we do not provide the means of helping the mother/partner to address whatever issues and needs have been identified in assessment then we are setting her up to fail, at the potential expense of her child and family and to the advantage of the offender.

In this chapter the focus is on putting knowledge of sex offenders into practice to assist in creating a short programme of direct work with the mother/partner specific to her individual needs, as identified during assessment. Whilst there may be a variety of issues to address, as with anything in life solutions need to be referenced back to the problem. In cases of child sexual abuse the core problem is not the child, the family or the mother or partner, but the known or suspected offender. Therefore, as in assessment, that is one of the places we can turn to for answers and for devising coping and preventative strategies. Finding the answers to the question 'how did he do that to me and to us?' opens doors to issues that can otherwise remain impenetrable and is a valuable additional tool to add to our range of other skills and knowledge.

This approach can be adapted to all situations, whatever practical decisions may have been made about child protection such as whether or not to take legal action and/or remove any of the parties from the family home. It can be used also in cases of suspected or alleged abuse where the child is believed; where there is little or even no additional specific information then general knowledge of sex offenders can be applied.

Every situation is different therefore the programme can be used either in its entirety or in part, according to need.

Planning an intervention programme

Follow-up intervention costs time and money and in a world of limited resources the most likely questions asked of the child protection practitioner by management and/or family court judges are:

- What comes next?

- What do you want to do?

- Why do you want to do it? (Prognosis? No outcome is guaranteed but is it viable?)

- Where will you do it?

- How will you do it?

- How long will it take?

- What resources will you need?

- When will it begin?

Given that a child's life may be on hold because long-term decisions about risk and safety are not possible until work with the mother/ partner has been completed, the answer to the question 'when will the work start?' should be 'as soon as possible'. With good planning and clear goals it is possible to undertake a core programme of work over a period of six to eight sessions in a limited time frame. As with assessment, there should be a balance between keeping gaps between each session to a minimum to ensure continuity, whilst also allowing enough time for the mother/partner to process her thoughts and feelings.

Core aims of intervention

Whilst every situation is different and there may be other problems to address, there are core aims common to most situations of child sexual abuse. At the very least these would be:

- to provide the mother/partner with information to help her understand about the abuse: to answer the question 'how did he do that to me, to the child and to the family?'

- to help the mother/partner to apply this information to help her understand and meet the healing needs of the child and family

- to help empower the mother/partner to protect by devising appropriate protective strategies relevant to her particular situation and against any threat posed by a specific offender and/or sex offenders and paedophiles in general

- to help the mother/partner make informed decisions about the future

- to help her to begin to resolve personal issues arising from the abuse that may otherwise impede her progress

- to inform child protection decision making.

Matching questions mothers and partners ask with knowledge of sex offenders and paedophiles

Table 14.1 demonstrates the questions mothers and partners commonly ask about known or alleged sex offenders who are their partners, relatives or close friends and how we can use knowledge of cycles and preconditions to offending (see Chapter 5) to help women find the answers.

TABLE 14.1 QUESTIONS AND ANSWERS

PARTNERS' QUESTIONS	STAGES OF CYCLE OF OFFENDING
Why do they want to do it?	Motivation – sexual arousal
Do they think it's OK?	Belief system/distorted thinking
If they know it's wrong how do they overcome this so that they can offend?	Excuse to offend
Do they think of it all the time?	Fantasy – types, patterns, frequency
Who do they choose?	Targeting
How do they get past people who might protect?	Grooming mother/partner and others
How do they get the child to comply and not tell?	Grooming child/young person

PARTNERS' QUESTIONS	STAGES OF CYCLE OF OFFENDING
What if the child tells? What does the offender do to keep the secret?	Post-assault/abuse grooming
Do they ever feel guilty?	It depends – belief system/distorted thinking
Do they all stick to the same pattern?	Patterns vary according to age, gender, intra-extra-familial cross-over or not?
Have all sex offenders committed lots of offences?	No – not necessarily
Do they do it all the time?	No – similar patterns/cycles but all different (all the same principle)

Adapted from Still *et al.* (2001)

Use and misuse of information about sex offenders

In Chapter 12 we argued against sharing too much offender knowledge and information during the assessment interviews because:

- those interviews do not allow enough time to help the mother/partner process information and deal with its likely painful consequences in a positive way

- the interviewer has not had sufficient time to analyse the information received from her and other sources

- conclusions and opinions prematurely expressed may later need to be adjusted and different conclusions reached, creating an unnecessary atmosphere of mistrust.

The aim here is to use knowledge and information and in a way that is helpful, positive and enabling to the mother/partner.

Who should do the work?

This work requires knowledge and sensitivity as well as skill on the part of the practitioner. We are all human and in many situations it could be difficult for a practitioner who is also working with the child or with the offender, as it may be also for some practitioners who are adult survivors of sexual abuse. It cannot be done by a practitioner who is experiencing unmanageable levels of anger with the mother/partner for failing to protect and/or with the known or suspected offender. Good supervision is required in an environment where it is acceptable to offload unhelpful feelings without fear of being judged and to regain an appropriate perspective.

Where should the work be done?

The same rules apply as for assessment. That is, this work needs to be done in a safe and comfortable environment away from the family home with minimum risk of interruption, especially from the known or suspected offender who may feel his control of the situation is threatened by what is happening.

Method

Depending on how and when it is done, talking about sex offenders to a mother or partner who has been affected by child sexual abuse can be either very helpful in giving her further insight into her situation or very unhelpful because it is too difficult and painful, pushing her into fight, flight or freeze mode. It is important to recognise that whilst talking about sex offenders and child sexual abuse may be part of our everyday work, to the mother/partner this is unknown territory and it would be natural at this stage for her to feel anxious, wary and even suspicious as to our motivation and objectives. Issues relating to the need for engagement and motivation as described in Chapter 10 are important and continue to apply. The following additional guidance can assist in keeping the mother/partner engaged:

- *'Come down this road with me'* usually beats 'you need to hear this'.

- *Start where she is now,* wherever she is on the spectrum of knowing/believing/acceptance (see Chapter 1). What matters is where she can progress to.

- *Use gradual exposure* when talking about sex offenders and paedophiles, moving from general information to how it might apply to a specific known or suspected offender (Deblinger and Heflin 1996; Still *et al.* 2001). This enables us to work in this way even where there is still disbelief or denial on her part because it can be used as an educational tool as to what to look for in future.

- *Hypothetical questions* of 'what if...?' can be helpful. Situations like this can often progress to her being able to examine the known or suspected offender more closely. Further information can be added later. If the known offender is or has been on a sex offender treatment programme this can provide valuable additional information as to the nature of his offending pattern.

- *Work with process as well as content.* Whilst part of the programme is factual and educational it is important to recognise her emotional as well as cognitive responses. If, for example, the mother/partner becomes angry and upset or feels blocked when focusing on a particular issue it is important to consider why that is and to help her resolve whatever difficult issues it raises for her.

- *Draw on her positives and strengths.* If she feels she has lost touch with them as a result of the sexual abuse, help her rediscover them.

- *Be aware of our own reactions, values, social values and belief systems.* We should not let them intrude if they do not pertain to our purpose or goals.

Mothers/partners who are higher up the 'did she know?' spectrum

In Chapter 2 we looked at the 'spectrum of knowing': at one end there is the woman who has no knowledge of the abuse and at the other end the minority of women who have been found to have been collusive in the abuse (aware but took no action) or even a co-offender, with different points in between. If a woman is higher up the spectrum and became collusive or worse, we need to understand how that came about. This is not to minimise the woman's behaviour but to inform decision making as to what is in the best interests of the child. Whilst it may be necessary and appropriate to remove the child and in some cases to prosecute the mother and end contact, there may be other issues to consider in the interests of the child. For example, if the woman was groomed into compliance against her wishes by a violent offender and if she did not know how to remove herself and her children from the situation, it may be that the child was aware of this and also of her reluctant participation. In such cases this can create many issues for the child that need to be addressed. These may include anger but also elements of grief for the subsequent loss of their mother and even an (albeit inappropriate) sense of guilt for 'causing' their mother this trouble. So whilst some children or young people in this situation may never want to see their mother again, for others their sense of loss may suggest the need for some form of continued contact. In such situations, instead of an occasional supervised meeting where neither dares speak of the past (or is allowed to) it may be better to use such contact as a therapy session to help the mother and child to talk, to help heal the child's pain – even if mother and child may never live together again.

Therefore some aspects of the proposed intervention programme can be used to work with the mother even in such circumstances, to provide more information to inform the child's therapy and to inform decisions about whether or not there should be contact and what type of contact that should be.

Inclusion of fathers and male carers

Child protection is the responsibility of both parents/carers. Whilst such work is commonly offered to the mother, where the abuse is by someone outside the family and there is no concern about the father or resident father figure, he can be included in the programme as appropriate. Good joint parental support will make it harder for any sex offender to target the child(ren) again.

Clarity about responsibility

We need to be realistic in our expectations. The welfare of the child is paramount and it is our job to do our best to help her to keep children safe. However, we should always remember that where there is further abuse, whilst the mother/partner needs to take responsibility for not protecting her child, the person who is responsible for the abuse is the offender. It is his responsibility not to reoffend and he should not be allowed to use anyone else as an excuse.

Whilst there is a need for appropriate sensitivity this should not blind the practitioner to possible concerns regarding the mother's/ partner's ability to protect if problems cannot be resolved.

Creating an intervention programme: guidelines

The following is not intended as a work manual but to provide ideas as to key issues that are common to many situations of child sexual abuse within a family or related context and how they can be addressed. Topics of discussion are presented in an order that begins with the need for engagement and builds on that session by session. This provides the building blocks to enable the mother/partner to develop her own knowledge, insight and also her personal confidence in addressing what can be extremely difficult problems, not only with the known or suspected offender and/or victim but also within the wider family. However, nothing is cast in stone and every situation is different. Some topics may be more important to the individual situation than others and as the work progresses flexibility is always required to adapt to the presenting situation. Topics and different scenarios are clearly headlined for easy reference. They can be used in their entirety to form a complete programme or in part, according to need.

Whilst some practitioners are experienced in working with child sexual abuse, in a world of generic practice others are less so. Also, with the many other demands placed on practitioners some elements of planning can be overlooked. Therefore, as with the assessment protocol, some guidance is provided to highlight common pitfalls and ways in which work of this type may be delivered to maximum effect. Some exercises are suggested and many of these are adapted from the Partners' Programme (Still *et al*. 2001).

Block one – getting started

Introductions and ground rules

If we are not the same person as the one who conducted the assessment then why should the mother/partner trust us? Introductions are necessary, simple explanations need to be given and ground rules need to be established. Special circumstances should be acknowledged, such as if the mother/partner has a background of her own abuse, and safety valves put in place including the need for breaks and time out.

The aim is to provide her with assistance to make informed decisions. It is not our job to tell her what to do and the aim of the work is not to make her break contact with the known or suspected offender, even though that may be what is hoped for. However, honesty and trust are early casualties in cases of known or alleged child sexual abuse. So whilst the formal assessment is now over and our objective is to help her, it is important to make it clear that if we hear anything further to suggest a child is at immediate risk and/or there has been further abuse that will be reported, as it will be if we have any concerns about her ability to protect that cannot be resolved. This can be phrased as an agreement rather than as a threat.

Establishing a starting point: update on her current situation

Have there been any significant changes since the assessment? For example:

- Who is living where? By court order, social services request or personal choice?

- If there are restrictions in terms of rules within the home or on contact visits, how are they working out?

- What is the continuing impact of the abuse on her, on the child, on the family and on relationships with the local community?

- What sources of support does she now have?

- How is she doing?

The list of common impact issues for the mother/partner in Chapter 2 can be referred to in advance to help anticipate the kind of problems she may be experiencing as well as any information from her assessment.

Questions and answers about the assessment(s)

No mother or partner will engage positively in an intervention plan if she has not had an adequate explanation as to what was recommended in assessment and why. This includes any decisions made about the known or suspected offender as to the level of risk he is or is not considered to present and any preventative action that may or may not have been taken. The mother or partner is entitled to know why that is, how such an assessment was made and by whom. If the assessment of the known or alleged offender was made by someone else it is preferable that person should explain it to her. If that is not possible then we need to do so and in an informed manner. This needs to be anticipated and planned for in advance by seeking appropriate information from the assessor, as described in Chapter 10.

Proposals for the programme of work

An outline of the proposed programme of work should be provided. It is especially important to explain early on that the approach we wish to adopt includes sharing information with her on how men who sexually abuse children and young people operate. This may seem a rather daunting prospect so it is equally important to explain the reason for this approach, which is to help her find the answers and solutions to any remaining unanswered questions and a way forward.

Working with adult survivors of sexual abuse

This is of particular importance when working with adult survivors of sexual abuse, for whom talk of sex offenders and paedophiles may be difficult in terms of resurrecting old memories and associated trauma. Whilst many women will have dealt with their abuse others may not have done so. In those circumstances, whilst we cannot say this programme of work will provide any or all of their counselling or therapeutic needs, when conducted with appropriate sensitivity we can suggest that it *can* provide positive assistance in helping her to make further sense of her own experiences as well as those of the child. Guidance can be given in seeking additional counselling where appropriate.

Hopes, fears, questions and brief intervention exercises

Although our goal is to assist and empower the mother/partner, at this stage the proposed programme of work is likely to be somewhat daunting to her. Also, we know that low self-esteem and loss of confidence among non-offending mothers and partners (see Chapter 1) is not uncommon following the discovery of child sexual abuse even if it was not an issue before. The following exercises can help her to reinforce the positive.

EXERCISE
HOPES AND FEARS

- What are her hopes for what she might gain from this work?
- What are her fears?
- What questions does she have that she would like to be answered?

It can be useful to record this on flipchart for future reference because it establishes a starting point from where overall progress can be recognised and validated by both parties, especially during more difficult sessions. Also, it creates a checklist for later, to ensure all bases are covered.

EXERCISE
STRENGTHS AND COPING STRATEGIES

It is pointless to try to engage anyone to do anything if they are preoccupied with possible negative consequences of doing so. Any associated worries and fears therefore need to be identified and coping strategies put in place. For example, take the following two common scenarios:

- 'I'm worried if I do this work it will make me feel even worse about being a bad mother because I let my child down.'
- **Response:** Ask her to list the ways (no matter how small) she is a good mother, or how other people would think she is a good mother.
- 'I'm worried that if I believe he did it, or if I hear more bad stuff about him, it will make me think I have to leave him. But I won't be able to cope as a single mother.'
- **Response:** Whilst we do not know that will happen, we can encourage her self-belief by asking her to list her personal strengths, sources of support (even if there are only one or two) and practical measures to take. These positive ideas can be reinforced and built on throughout the work programme.

EXERCISE
KEEPING A CHART FOR 'HOW AM I DOING?'

This is likely still to be a difficult time for the mother/partner, many of whom can feel their sense of autonomy has been usurped by outside agencies, perhaps by the courts and also by the known or suspected offender. It is important therefore for us to be aware at the beginning of each session of her current emotional state and any other difficulties she has to manage. However, this can often degenerate into a prolonged ventilation of blame and recrimination against the authorities, against the known or suspected offender and at this stage sometimes even the victim of the known or suspected abuse, especially if the victim is a teenager or not the woman's own child. This is not a signal to stop but an indicator of how important it is for her to undertake this work.

This situation can be made manageable with the use of a simple chart (see Figure 14.1) for the mother/partner to complete prior to each session, registering the date of the session and a rating of how she is feeling. There can then be a short discussion at the beginning of each session as to why she has rated her feelings that way before moving on to the business of the day. The additional benefit of providing a chart is that it provides visual evidence of:

- any consistent pattern to her 'highs' and 'lows' and with what thoughts, feelings or events they may be associated, which can then be discussed

- overall progress in her ability to meet her own objectives and ours.

How am I doing?	1	2	3	4	5	6	7	8
10								
9								
8								
7								
6								
5								
4								
3								
2								
1								

Session number (alter according to number of sessions)

Figure 14.1 How am I doing?
From Still *et al.* (2001)

EXERCISE
USE OF A DIARY AND/OR WORKBOOK

Some women find it easier to write than to talk so it may help her to keep a diary of what she did in each session, what she thought and felt, what she learned and questions she wants to address next time. A loose leaf folder and paper could be provided which could include any handouts, such as a copy of the 'how am I doing?' chart and of the offending cycle. This can help also to remind her of progress made when she may be feeling otherwise.

Cautionary notes

- It is her choice whether or not to do this.
- This should be her personal property and not part of any evaluation.
- She should be advised to keep it in a private place where it will not be found by children.
- Literacy levels are irrelevant so long as she can understand what she has written. Failing that, for example, some women can respond to simple drawings as a reminder of a session, with happy or sad faces or cartoon type scenarios comprising stick men, women or children, anything that can serve as an aide memoir, no matter how badly drawn.

Defining the problem

What is meant by the term 'child sexual abuse'? This question will have been asked of her in assessment and now needs to be revisited to avoid any misunderstandings. As we saw in Chapters 4 and 10, the term 'child sexual abuse' means different things to different people. For example, the simple answer of 'having sex with a child' can mean a myriad of behaviours to us as child protection practitioners and managers but to many mothers or partners it only means having sexual intercourse.

If the question of terminology and language was not fully addressed in assessment we can use the 'what if…?' example scenarios as proposed in the assessment schedule in the previous chapter as a basis for discussion.

The known or suspected sexual abuse: what does she now think happened?

This will have been addressed in assessment and now needs to be revisited.

- Has she had any more thoughts since the assessment?

- Has she received any more information?

- If so from where and from whom?

- How reliable is that information?

There may be much more for her to hear than she already knows and/or has allowed herself to hear or believe. It is as important for her to know the extent of his illegal sexual arousal and what he did and for us to now share whatever information we have honestly but with sensitivity. A whole range of human responses are possible: anger, upset, relief, blame, continuing denial or even no apparent reaction at all. Some of her responses may not be what we want to hear but that is not unusual at this stage; it is where she can move on to that matters.

EXERCISE
WHO DO I BLAME FOR THE ABUSE?

Ask the mother/partner to draw a large circle and to divide the circle into segments denoting the amount of blame they apportion to whom and why. Some women may blame the criminal courts and/or child protection agencies or even the child or young person.

Simply note responses now because it provides a quick way to ascertain her current position for later discussion and provides a marker against which progress can be gauged.

Block two – how did he do that to the child and to me? Helping the mother/partner to profile the known or suspected offender

Experience suggests that it is more empowering to let a woman work this out for herself than for us to tell her what we think she should hear. However, we can assist by providing her with the framework from which to work. Some women may be anxious about this because they do not know what they are going to hear and because their perception of sex offenders and paedophiles is likely to be the generally demonised view as portrayed in the media. The 'hopes, fears and questions' recorded in a previous session can be revisited and added to where necessary and addressed.

Planning this work requires the practitioner to be familiar with the contents of previous chapters on understanding sex offenders.

Demythologising sex offenders

Most people who are not sex offenders or paedophiles cannot understand how or why anyone would want to sexually abuse a child or young person, which can lead to the assumption that somehow such people are different from the rest of the world. This can be confusing when the person they know looks the same as everyone else. This is what prevents us from recognising a sex offender when we see one.

EXERCISE
CYCLES OF OFFENDING: NORMAL PROCESS, ILLEGAL AND ABUSIVE CONTENT

We can demystify sex offending by likening it to other everyday situations. This is not to minimise the seriousness of child sexual abuse but to help us to help the mother/partner understand it better. For example:

- Explain that we all do some kind of behaviour we know we should not do but we like to do it and so we keep doing it. That is, we have cycles of behaviour.

- Ask the mother/partner to give an example, such as smoking, drinking alcohol, eating chocolate, dieting, retail therapy, and so on. On days we feel good we can resist the temptation but at other times when we feel low we want something to make us feel better, so we think – a lot – about the drink of alcohol, the cake or chocolate, the cigarette (ask her for suggestions).

- What do we say to ourselves to make it OK? (I deserve it, I need it, I've had a bad day, I'll only have the one...)

- What if we had told everyone we were giving it up? Or if smoking, drinking or eating chocolate was against the law and if we were found out we would be sent to prison? (Don't let them find out, do it in secret, make sure we don't get caught, lie...)

- We enjoy the activity when we're doing it. But how do we feel afterwards when we know we shouldn't have done it? (Bad, guilty, disappointed in ourselves, let down...)

- What might we say to ourselves to make those bad feelings go away? (I only had the one when I could have had the whole packet, it wasn't so bad, it didn't do any harm really, I'll never do it again...)

- That might last for a short or long time but eventually we have another bad day and we need to do something to make ourselves feel better. (I feel like a cigarette, a drink, some chocolate, I deserve it, I'll only have the one...)

- And the cycle continues.

Explain that this is the same process, or cycle, that is common to most sex offenders who sexually abuse within a family or family-related situation. Whilst the content of his behaviour is illegal and abusive it is the sense of normality in the process that helps him to convince himself it is OK.

(Remember, for the paedophile it would be different in that he may believe his behaviour is acceptable and therefore there is no need to create the excuse of 'I need it, want it, deserve it, it will do no harm' and therefore there is no sense of guilt. However, that should not be used either by the mother/partner or the practitioner to minimise the seriousness of the situation in question, as in 'at least he's not as bad as a paedophile'.)

Explaining the simple frameworks for understanding sex offenders

Women do not need detailed knowledge of sex offenders but sufficient information to make sense of their situation and a framework on which to hang their questions.

- Language and concepts should be kept simple.

- Information in Chapter 2 can be used to give a simple explanation of the four preconditions to offending. Invite questions and discussion. Does this make sense to her? Is there anything there she can identify as possibilities in her particular situation?

- Information in Chapter 2 can be used to explain a cycle of sex offending, using Figure 5.1 on page 66. Relate it back to ordinary behaviours, as previously explained. Give a simple explanation of what each stage of the offending cycle means, how it works and how the timings of each stage vary from individual to individual. This is not a test but a simple educational tool. Keep it brief.

- With regard to grooming, highlight the different styles that can be used, for example Mr Nice Guy, Mr Nasty Guy (see Chapters 5 to 8).

Applying the four preconditions and the cycle of offending to the current known or suspected abuse

This information can then be related to her situation as a focus for discussion. Does this make sense to her? In hindsight is there anything she can see that could relate to her partner, friend or relative who is the known offender or against whom allegations have been made? There may be some small event, behaviour or conversation that niggled at the time but which she did not then associate with abuse; there may be more worrying things that she now realises she should have noticed and acted on but did not do so, for whatever reason. We can help her piece it together, step by step, drawing on her everyday knowledge and experience of him, as well as information from the investigation and from assessments of the child. The following are some examples of how this works.

Distorted thinking

It is important to talk about whether she ever heard him express inappropriate sexual attitudes about children or young people, or anything that did not worry her at the time but does so now. Any concerns about her own attitudes and beliefs can be discussed, bearing in mind the possible influence of a sex offender. The question 'what makes you think that?' can be helpful in identifying any such negative influence.

Fantasy

Sometimes the phrase 'sexual thinking' is more helpful than 'fantasy'. One question that worries many women in this situation is 'was he thinking about having sex with a child when he was having sex with me?' The only accurate answer to this has to be 'maybe': for some offenders that can be true and for others it is not true because they have sexual arousal to adults as well as to a child(ren) and they can draw a line between the two.

In those situations where we have detailed knowledge, for example, where a known offender is in treatment, is it vital for her to know everything? Some would regard telling her all about his abusive fantasies as being abusive of her, especially where she is his sexual partner; others would regard it as essential if she is to make decisions about her own relationship with him. Certainly the knowledge, for example, that a partner was fantasising about buggering young boys whilst having sex with her has been of focal importance for some women in deciding to separate from him. It is also true that abusive fantasy may in some cases be progressive and a rehearsal for the future and therefore a key indicator of risk that may be crucial for her to know. (See Chapter 12 for guidelines.)

Grooming

This is a concept that is now widely referred to in the media and is commonly associated with grooming the victim. But whilst she may have heard of grooming through the popular media it is not easy to hear about it in connection with someone who is a loved one or friend. And whilst knowledge is empowering we should not expect a mother or partner to be happy to hear he groomed her also – to get her out of the way and to ensure she did not know, suspect, believe or act on any suspicion or disclosure: 'you mean he manipulated me and lied to me as well as everything else he did?' However, it can also be the most fruitful area of discussion. For example, it can help her to understand how an offender gained secret access to the child and, if her child did not tell her, why not.

The value of the work

For some women this aspect of the work can feel liberating, answering many questions they have wondered about for a long time. However, it is also potentially difficult and distressing. It is for us to make it a useful and positive experience, reinforcing the value of the work. There may be a lot for the mother/partner to take in and we should not expect immediate and total revelations. Responses can vary from 'I always worried about that but didn't know why' to 'none of that relates to him'. Most women need time to go away and think about it.

For the small proportion of women who may have been aware of the abuse but failed to act, or worse, this is especially challenging. On the one hand, she may appropriately fear consequences such as her removal from the child's life and even prosecution. On the other hand, it is important for both her and us to understand the story behind her failure to act or even her collusion in the abuse because it can be vital in ensuring that it is used appropriately in decisions about residence, contact and also to inform what may need to be addressed for the child in therapy (see Chapter 7).

Block three – putting knowledge into practice with the child and family
Victim awareness and communicating with the child about the abuse

Child sexual abuse thrives on secrecy and if communication barriers persist then so do the dysfunctional family relationships, increasing the child and family's vulnerability to further abuse. Stress, worry, confusion and sometimes a divided sense of loyalty on the part of the mother or partner toward the (alleged) offender and victim can impede her capacity for victim awareness and/or empathy, even if unintentionally. This in turn can continue to inhibit the mother–child relationship, to the potential advantage of an offender.

This session is about helping the mother recognise and understand the impact of the whole abusive experience on the child, including the child's perception of the world, his/her relationships with siblings, with friends and his/her emotional, cognitive and possibly physical healing needs.

EXERCISE
HELPING THE MOTHER OR PARTNER UNDERSTAND THE IMPACT OF THE OFFENDER AND THE ABUSE ON THE CHILD

The contents of Chapter Seven relating to the possible impact of sexual abuse on children can be used to inform a discussion with her about the effects of the abuse on the child(ren) in question. For example:

- What impact has she seen the abuse have on the child(ren)?

- Is there anything else she is worried about for them?

- Using her knowledge of both the child and the known or alleged offender, use Figure 5.1 to help her work out what the offender did, or might have done, to produce that particular emotional and/or behaviour response in the child.

- At what age and stage of development was the child when the abuse (i.e. preparatory grooming) began? What else was happening in the child's life at the time?

- If the known or suspected abuse was by her partner or someone close and against someone other than her own child, this can be discussed on a hypothetical 'what if...?' basis and 'how do you think that child or young person may have been affected?'

Communication between mother and child

We often advise mothers to talk to their child(ren) about the abuse. This is good advice because failure to do so not only impedes her ability to understand the child but also because it maintains unhealthy secrecy and leaves the child vulnerable to the possibility of further abuse, either by the same offender or by a different offender who recognises the child's vulnerability.

But where to begin? This is especially difficult if the child or young person has no wish to talk and for whom communication is likely to be inhibited by whatever consequence was suggested or threatened during grooming. For example, if a child was told 'it will kill your mother if you tell' then maybe it will; if the offender's grooming of the child was to say that the abuse was about 'being in love' then the child may not want to talk to their rival for his affections, or hear that it was not love but abuse. Similarly, a well-intentioned mother can repeatedly reassure the child 'it was not your fault'. However, if the offender groomed the child into believing it *was* his or her fault then that is likely to be the more powerful message in the child's head, whilst reinforcing also the child's view that mother just does not understand. Mother–child communication can be further damaged by the child's continuing sense of betrayal at the mother's failure to protect.

These communication barriers do not disappear just because the abuse has been discovered. The information in Chapter 7 can be used to help a mother explore the impact of the abuse on her relationship with the child and how that came about. This does not absolve the mother of her responsibilities to protect but it places the responsibility appropriately with the offender.

EXERCISE
FACILITATING COMMUNICATION
BETWEEN MOTHER AND CHILD

These sessions can be used to practise the necessary conversations with the child. The following are examples of preliminary questions the mother/partner may have:

- What might my child want to say to me? (For example: why didn't you stop it? Why didn't you know? I don't believe you.)
- What do I want to say to my child?
- How might I say it?

Aim for the discussion to flag up a minimum of four possible answers to each question. These can be recorded on a flipchart followed by discussion as to the best way to go about it. **If the mother/partner is particularly nervous at the prospect it can be helpful to practise through role play, with the practitioner taking the part of the child.**

Linked work with the child

This process can be greatly assisted by feedback from whatever therapeutic work is being done with the child, to help the mother understand her child better. Some child care professionals balk at this idea, perceiving their work with the child to be confidential between them and the child. The only time such an attitude can make sense is when the assessment of the mother/partner has identified her as being a risk to the child in her own right. If there is concern that the mother/partner has not progressed sufficiently in her own work programme to be trusted to use the information appropriately, that may be simply a matter of timing. Otherwise, the message that is given to the child is 'your mother cannot be trusted', which undermines the mother and has the opposite effect of empowering her to protect.

We should anticipate some bumps along the road and it is important for the practitioner to be familiar with the contents of Chapters 7 and 8 in advance of these sessions.

Opening up communication within the family: what does my family need from me now?

Sexual abuse invariably has a damaging impact on the family as a whole, including on relationships with siblings. Inter-sibling rivalries and conflict are a common result of an offender's manipulations. The secrecy he imposed will have created additional stresses and tensions for individual family members, either because:

- they *know* the secret

- they *do not know* the secret (but are living with its impact)

- they *know* there is a secret *but they don't know what it is*

- *everyone in the family knows* the secret but everyone agrees (even if it is never discussed) that *no outsiders should know the secret.*

There are many possible variations as to sibling responses and many will relate back to grooming. For example, an offender may not have presented the same way to everyone: siblings may be split over what to believe; the victim may be blamed or disbelieved and/or scapegoated; jealousies can arise over what is perceived as favouritism, for example, where the victim receives gift and treats which siblings do not. Conversely, a victim who alleges their abuser was a Mr Nasty Guy may not be believed because everyone else experiences him as a Mr Nice Guy. The victim may defend the offender because he or she was groomed into thinking the abuse was about being in love.

Knowledge of sex offenders and the information in Chapter 7 can be used to help the mother facilitate open communication within the family, including with and between other siblings.

EXERCISE
FACILITATING COMMUNICATION
WITHIN THE FAMILY

A simple approach is to help the mother/partner make sense of the family dynamics, both before the abuse and now. The long case example in Chapter Seven of Jean and Ian can provide a reminder of some of the different possible permutations of family dynamics within the apparently same scenario of abuse, which can provoke different responses from individuals within a family. The following exercise follows the same principles using questions such as those below, which can prepare the mother/partner also for the necessary conversations with her family.

- Before the abuse, who was closest to whom and why (e.g. similar age, interests or personality and most supportive of one another) and who was least close and why?
- Since the abuse, has that changed?
- What does she think each family member thinks and feels about the abuse, about the victim and about the known or suspected offender – before and after the abuse?
- How does she think the (alleged) offender could have manipulated relationships within the family to protect himself and, given what she now knows, how might she guess he did that?
- What does she think her family needs from her now?
- Help her to use this insight to talk to her other children about this, whether individually or collectively: how she might do it, how she thinks they will react.
- Use role play to enable her to practise how she might manage these sessions, if that will help.

This approach can help repair unhelpful family conflicts and divisions and move on to 'how did he do that to **us**, individually and as a family unit?'

The impact of the abuse on the mother/partner

If resources are limited it is easy to focus on the child and to overlook the needs of the mother or partner. Sometimes this is reinforced by the mother/partner telling us she is fine and that we should concentrate on the child. She may be reluctant to tell us she is not OK for fear of being assessed as being a weak and unsafe protector. If she wants to talk about her own difficulties, sometimes this can be wrongly interpreted as her not being sufficiently focused on the child's needs. However, as we saw in Chapter 1, research shows the debilitating effect child sexual abuse can have on parents and carers and it is unlikely she is coping as well as she says she is.

Examples of the kind of difficulties that can arise for her are listed in Chapter 2. If we do not offer her time and a safe place away from the family to talk about and work through her own thoughts and feelings we jeopardise her chances of being able to make the most of this work programme. This is not long-term counselling but a simple brief intervention to discuss the issues and help her to identify coping strategies.

EXERCISE
SIMPLE QUESTIONS FOR THE MOTHER/PARTNER TO ADDRESS

These may include, for example:

- How did the discovery of (alleged) child sexual abuse affect me – at the time? And since?
- What effect has it had on my relationships with others?
- How much do I need to tell other people about the abuse? Why?
- How have I handled other people outside the family knowing?
- How am I coping with it? What has worked and what has not?
- How have I moved on?

Note: If her situation is particularly difficult these questions may need to be addressed earlier on, before she can move on to other topics.

What would I like to say to the (alleged) offender? Empowering her to move on

Whilst it may be the ideal child protection solution for the women to have no further contact with the known or suspected offender that in itself is not always helpful in empowering her for the future or helping her to move on. Important questions remain unanswered; things are left unsaid to him by her that should be said. This session is about empowering the woman to move away from feeling like a victim herself and to reinforce the message that she will not let him ruin her life or the child's life, and that she can move on.

EXERCISE
WHAT I WOULD LIKE TO SAY TO HIM

This exercise again offers her the chance to clarify her own thoughts and feelings and to reinforce her belief in herself. If circumstances permit she can then decide whether to put the exercise into practice with the alleged or known offender.

- Ask the mother/partner to use her new understanding of sex offenders generally, or of the specific (alleged) offender, to make a list of questions she would like to ask him and things she would like to say to him about what he has done – or is believed to have done – to the child(ren) and to her.
- Help her to think through how she would respond to his reactions and deal with any further attempt by him to manipulate and groom her.

- Ask her to list ways in which she feels she has moved on and how she could tell him this.

- If it will help, create a scenario of that meeting and let her practise out loud what she would say, possibly using role play with us putting ourselves in the role of the (alleged) offender. If she gets stuck or upset it is important to explore why that is. It is likely to be related to fear of the consequences for her or the child or family. There can then be discussion as to how she could deal in real life with whatever problem she fears, for example, whether they are emotional, practical or financial.

A joint session with a known or convicted sex offender (optional)

Where the offender has been charged and/or convicted and/or where he is or has attended a sex offender treatment programme, it is appropriate for him to take responsibility for explaining his own behaviour: why should we do it for him? If the mother/partner wishes to meet with him to hear what he has to say, the above exercise enables her to prepare for that face-to-face conversation.

It is vital that such a joint session should be planned carefully and preferably be supervised. This should include discussion with the offender's probation officer, psychologist or therapist who should also be present, because they would be better placed to spot any manipulation or grooming that might otherwise be missed and to intervene appropriately. It would also help avoid other possible pitfalls, especially if the offender is only part way through a treatment programme. For example, whilst the obvious worry is about grooming, conversely, having made sufficient progress to know that secrecy and manipulation are unacceptable he may go into honesty overdrive which can also be abusive. For example, it is never helpful for the woman to hear something like 'I only did it because you didn't like anal sex', which may be what he now knows he told himself at the time but which is still not the truth.

When handled well, such joint sessions can be fruitful in helping the mother/partner move forward.

A cautionary note

This direct approach may be inadvisable where the known or suspected offender is known to be violent and suitable safeguards cannot be put in place.

Block four – moving on: decision making, recognising potential risk and developing protective strategies

There is no such thing as total protection against sexual abuse. The best a mother, partner or carer can do is to make informed decisions, set preventative measures in place and maximise her ability to recognise and respond to risk situations.

It is primarily the responsibility of the mother or partner to make the right decisions to keep the child(ren) safe and child protection agencies should step in only when she fails to do so. However, it is not just about what she wants. As we saw in Chapters 7 and 8, situations are often complex and whatever decisions she makes will impact on others within the family. The aim of this section is to help her find her way through those complexities.

Decision making: issues for the mother/partner and for child protection agencies

Options for her to consider may include, for example: if he is my partner do I remain with him as my partner? Should we separate? Could I cope as a single parent? Should I stay in contact or break contact? Could I ever risk another partner? (Some women may feel they will never trust a man again, which would be further victimisation of her.) What is best for the child? What will be the repercussions for everyone else? What if they all want me to do something different? If I say he goes, or have no contact, will that harm the other children in the family who love him and who were not sexually abused by him? How much of that was real and how much might be grooming? Does it make any difference that he is not my partner but a non-resident relative/friend?

Note the following:

- The mother/partner can only make good decisions based on the best available information about presumed sexual risk and likely harm. Assessment of known sex offenders is undertaken within the criminal justice system and in Chapter 10 we looked at the kind of questions we should ask not only about the outcome of the assessment but also how it was done. It is important in these situations for basic information to be shared with the mother/partner.

- Information in previous chapters will assist.

- Her own assessment and that of the child are also important sources of information.

EXERCISE
WEIGHING UP THE PROS AND CONS

How risky is he? Ask the mother/partner to consider, on the information available:

- What do I now think the known or alleged offender did?
- How big a risk do the authorities think he is, to whom and why?
- What do I think? Do I think he has changed? If so, how and why?

What does the victim want (where the situation is deemed 'safe enough')? Ask the mother/partner to list at least two reasons why:

- the victim may *want* the offender to return/stay/have contact
- the victim *may not* want that
- the victim could *say* it but not *mean* it?

Are those responses thought to be genuine or still the result of grooming – for example, the child still believes the abuse was about love, the child is still fearful of saying no, the child does not want mum to be upset any more, the child has been groomed into thinking mum cannot cope without him?

What do other family members want? Is that going to be the same as what the victim wants?

- Repeat the same questions for other immediate family members.

Are any children still vulnerable to abuse? Ask the mother/partner to list:

- five things I think have changed for my children since the abuse that has made them safer.

Taking the above into account, ask the mother/partner to list:

- any reasons why I might want him to come home/stay/have contact
- any reasons why I might not want that
- what *I want* for my child, my family and for me.

Questions to ask about the (alleged) offender

If someone is a known sex offender, perhaps with an ancient conviction, but where there is good reason for him to remain in a family home or to have contact with the child(ren), he is the one who should take primary responsibility not to reoffend. Therefore the questions that should be asked of *him* would be:

- How will you we know you are at risk of reoffending?
- How will other people know that?
- How will you stop yourself from reoffending?

If he is unable to answer these questions that would suggest he has little self-awareness and therefore little idea of how to control himself. The answer 'I am not a risk' and 'I'd never do it again' would also be worrying, even when said with apparent remorse and good intentions, because it suggests he is unable to recognise that illegal sexual arousal can return and cannot describe a plan for stopping himself from reoffending. In the absence of his own inner control mechanisms the child's safety would therefore rely disproportionately on the mother/partner and on the child. If the sexual risk is assessed as low and the mother/partner is a strong protector that may be sufficient. If not, the situation would be unacceptable.

Recognition of risk and prevention of abuse

Failure to help a mother/partner understand the nature of risk, including what to look for and how an offender operates, can set her up to fail and lead to an over-reliance on children having to learn how to protect themselves.

Conversely, it is not unreasonable for any woman whose child has been sexually abused and/or whose partner or someone close has been identified as a known or suspected sex offender to become suspicious and over-protective, seeing risk everywhere. However, that is not healthy for her or for her child(ren) and is likely to lead to other problems. The aim of this section is to help the mother/partner find a healthy, well-informed and realistic balance between protecting her child and allowing her child an age-appropriate level of freedom and autonomy. By using information gained from previous sessions we can help the mother/partner formulate an alert list relevant to the situation.

There is no such thing in life as 'no risk' so the task is to minimise the risk as much as possible. There are two ways to look at this: worrying signs in the adult and worrying signs in the child.

Recognising worrying signs in the adult

EXERCISE
LOOKING FOR ALERT SIGNS AND
FACTORS IN COMBINATION

Where a known or suspected offender is still living with a family or in contact, it is primarily his responsibility to recognise if and when he has moved into a risk state. However, we should not rely on his ability to do so. Therefore it is helpful to revisit the earlier session with the mother/partner on preconditions to sex offending and cycles of offending, and to revisit in particular the session where we helped her to profile the (alleged) offender. This in turn will help her know what to look for in terms of any worrying factors in combination, including attitudes, moods and behaviours that could signal when he could be in the build-up of an offending cycle. For example, if previous discussion has suggested that he uses a mood state of 'poor me' as an excuse to move on into an offending cycle then alarm bells should ring if and when she sees that in him again. They should ring louder if combined with other potentially worrying behaviours that could suggest targeting, grooming and/or abusive attitudes and/or behaviours. This information can be augmented by information that is available from the child and other sources such as the police investigation, his probation officer and where relevant his sex offender treatment programme.

If the offender is no longer on the scene, she may still need to know how to be alert to the possibility of other sexual predators.

Some examples of possible alert signs in the adult

The following list is not comprehensive but provides examples by way of a guide to the kind of situations that could be warning signs that a sex offender, or someone who is believed to be a sex offender, could be moving into an active offending cycle. Whilst none of these individually would necessarily be cause for concern they would be if there were factors in combination or if they were known to be linked to his offending:

- mood changes, anxiety, depression, stress

- becoming withdrawn or evasive

- use of pornography

- long unexplained periods of computer use

- loss of control of other behaviours (e.g. smoking, drinking, drug use)

- changes in sexual behaviour/preoccupation with sex

- involvement in child or youth-centred activities

- poor privacy boundaries

- unexplained absences

- taking on a child or young person's sex education

- buying age-inappropriate clothing for a child

- spending excess time with one child, favouritism

- taking an excessive interest in a child's personal hygiene

- inappropriate play with a child; inappropriate touch

- isolating a child away from mother or other carer

- taking on excessive responsibility in day-to-day parenting/ discipline

- undermining the mother or carer

- provoking rejection by others (inducing a 'poor me' state of mind)

- verbal and/or emotional and/or physical aggression

- encouraging a child to watch age-inappropriate TV material or video games.

Recognising worrying signs in the child

If the mother/partner has already failed to protect then trust needs to be rebuilt and the child will need some solid indication that it is safe to have faith in her. Even if the mother/partner has told her children to tell her if anything is amiss this should not be relied on. The safest option is to assume the worst and to arm the mother/partner with an awareness of some of the signs and symptoms of sexual abuse that have been observed in children and young people. Information from Chapter 7 can assist.

EXERCISE
SHARING INFORMATION ON POSSIBLE SIGNS AND SYMPTOMS OF SEXUAL ABUSE IN THE VICTIM

Every situation is different. However, the following can provide some guidance to the mother/partner as to the kind of things that should ring alarm bells. Not all victims show all these symptoms. Not all these symptoms mean it is sexual abuse. Again, where there is nothing specific we may be looking at factors in combination.

Physical and medical evidence

Most sexual abuse does not leave any physical or medical evidence, making it hard to detect and to prove. However, the following are some examples that should raise questions: a child has pain or itching in the genital area; has difficulty walking, sitting; frequent urinary tract infections; vaginal discharge; painful urination; bruises or bleeding in the genital area; abnormalities to the vagina or anus; presence of semen; sexually transmitted disease; pregnancy.

Possible emotional and behavioural problems

These can include any of the following: sleep disturbance and nightmares; clinging; bedwetting or soiling; eating problems; sudden mood changes; fear of a particular person; frequent crying; becoming withdrawn, quiet, emotionally flat and disinterested and isolated; becoming hyperactive; becoming aggressive, throwing temper tantrums; problems with self-control; poor concentration; possible cruelty to animals or other children; running away or staying away from home a lot; school problems – poor attendance and/or poor school work; sexually inappropriate behaviour, for example open and excessive masturbation, sophisticated or unusual sexual behaviour or knowledge, touching other children sexually; self-harm; possible abuse of drugs and/or alcohol; psychosomatic illnesses; unusual fears, for example fear of baths, fear of going to bed, fear of closed doors.

Some children show none of these signs

They may do exceptionally well at school and/or in their other hobbies and interests. This can be their way of coping, by keeping one part of their life that is separate from the abuse where they are determined to find some sense of normality. This can cause other problems, for example they may focus on this part of their life to the exclusion of other normal social activities.

Timing

Some of these effects may immediately follow the abuse or they may be delayed, triggered by, for example an event, a person or a place. Some victims of abuse cope through what is called 'dissociation', by blanking everything off. Some may appear to be coping well until some external stimuli triggers an extreme response of unregulated stress.

The action the mother/partner should take is:

- to talk to the child or young person
- if in doubt, to seek professional advice.

Developing protective strategies

'Keep Safe' work with children is a valuable protective tool but it is no substitute for adequately empowering the mother/partner to protect. The work done in the previous session on victim awareness and communication, combined with work done elsewhere with the child or young person, will have hopefully begun to rebuild trust within the mother/child relationship.

EXERCISE
STRATEGIES FOR PROTECTING MY CHILD(REN)

Building on the above, the following can be used to provide further guidance to the mother/partner:

- Know the importance of listening to your child and hearing and understanding not only what is said but also the non-verbal messages such as body language and mood. Ask questions but in a way that does not make the child afraid to talk

- Anticipate that if the child has been sexually abused, the offender will have done or said something to prevent the child from telling. He could have done that by being Mr Nice Guy, Mr Angry Guy, Mr Nasty Guy, the 'Sulker', and so on or a mix of these.

- Know the signs of sexual abuse.

- Know the signs of possible grooming.

- It is unhelpful to punish your child for sexual behaviour. If it is inappropriate and/or abusive to other children, seek professional help. If a child or young person has been taught by the offender that certain sexual behaviour is normal and acceptable when it is not, seek professional advice on how to help the child unravel the confusion.

- Help your children to learn about appropriate privacy, 'OK to touch' and 'not OK to touch' but do it in a way that still leaves them feeling good about their own bodies. Make it fun, to minimise the danger of the child becoming over-anxious. Seek out related books written for this purpose. If you have difficulty, get professional advice.

- Tell your child to tell you if anyone ever does anything to make them feel uncomfortable.

- Reassure the child that you can hear whatever it is they may tell you and that you will do what is right to protect them.

- Know where your children are and who they are with. If you have worries about other people, use your knowledge of sex offenders to work out if any such concerns are justified.

- Know your child's friends.

- Talk to your child regularly – ask them about their day.

- If your child goes away, for example on an overnight sleepover, ask your child on his or her return 'how did it go?'

- If your child goes to nursery, day care or a club check it out first. What are their staff selection and vetting procedures? What safeguarding policies are in place?

- Help your child to identify trusted adults. This allows the child to have options of others to talk to besides you.

- Additional strategies to add? Every situation can throw up new ideas.

Where there is contact or continued residence with an (alleged) offender – establishing a child protection plan: conditions and restrictions

Where there is contact or where an (alleged) offender is to remain in or return to a family home, it is common practice for the authorities to devise a protection plan whereby conditions are laid down as to what he may or may not do and where he may or may not go. In the absence of offender knowledge such protection plans often use a scattergun approach with little relevance to the particular situation, which in some cases can place potentially harmful restrictions to children's development and impede healthy family relationships. Sometimes such plans can even inadvertently play into the hands of the offender by making it easier for him to offend.

EXERCISE
MAKING THE ALERT LIST INTO A CONTRACT

In the previous session we looked at using all the knowledge and information about the (alleged) offender that is now available to help the mother/partner identify factors relevant to the individual situation in question that should raise concern.

Where there is an offender in contact or in residence, that alert list should be used to inform what conditions and restrictions need to be put in place, relevant to the particular situation. This becomes the basis for an individualised child protection plan, by setting out the basic conditions of a contract with which both he and the mother/partner must comply. If there are good reasons for additional restrictions to be set that should be accepted, with a re-assessment of potential risk when necessary. This enables mothers/partners and the relevant agencies to work in partnership.

Joint sessions

Such a contract cannot be devised with the mother/partner alone, neither should it be left to her alone to tell him about the contract and then to enforce it: the known or suspected offender has to be an active party to it. This would require a joint session with both of them, supervised by us, with a clear message as to any consequences of failure to comply. If he has a probation officer and/or is attending a sex offender treatment programme they should be actively involved in the making of the contract and in the joint session. This would minimise the chances of the offender manipulating the situation.

EXERCISE
EXPLAINING THE 'DOS AND DON'TS' TO CHILDREN

Sometimes restrictions can seem strange to the children in the family, especially if they represent a change from previous behaviour. For example, if the (alleged) offender used to be very cuddly and now he is not; if he used to bath them and now he does not; if he used to 'teach' them about sex and now he does not; if he used to be the one to discipline them and now he is not; if he used to spoil a particular child and now he does not, and so on. Some children may like the changes and be pleased to see their mother taking control but others may not. For some it can leave them with a sense of loss and rejection, thinking they must have done something wrong.

It can be helpful to discuss the following with the mother:

- How will you explain the changes to the child(ren)?

- How could you do it in an age-appropriate way?

- How would you do it without scaring the child(ren) or making them feel guilty that they caused the changes to be made?

EXERCISE
HELPING THE MOTHER/PARTNER TO CONFRONT HIM

There needs to be confidence that the mother/partner can confront the known or suspected sex offender and say to him 'you may not be worried about you but I am' and not to be sucked back into his grooming. These sessions can be used to help her practise. For example:

- Ask the mother/partner to identify a situation in the family home that might cause her concern.

- How would she approach her partner/relative about it?

- If she thinks he is reverting to grooming either the child and/or her, how will she deal with it? (What would his style be: Mr Nice Guy, Mr Nasty Guy, Mr Seductive, other?)

- What would she do next? (e.g. talk to him, talk to her social worker/his probation officer for advice, talk to the child, report anything that suggests abuse or unmanageable risk).

Responding to abuse and suspicion

Every mother/partner doing this work will have had experience of a sexual abuse investigation and many will have found it painful. This could deter her from reporting any known or suspected abuse in the future. It is important to anticipate this possibility and to deal with it head on.

EXERCISE
WHAT MIGHT STOP ME REPORTING ANY ABUSE OR SUSPICION OF ABUSE?

Responses from the mother/partner to this question could include, for example:

- It's best if I handle it myself.
- I don't want my child to be medically examined.
- I don't want the child to go through all that (perhaps for some children that would be a second time).
- Past experiences of conflict or frustration with social workers, police, doctors.
- I don't want my family to be upset again.
- I want life to get back to normal.

Many of these responses are understandable in human terms. However the follow-up question needs to be asked: 'what happens if you don't report it?' Discussion should cover issues such as:

- It betrays the child.
- It leaves the child open to further sexual abuse.
- The (alleged) offender stays in control.
- It gives him a message it's safe to abuse the same child and/or move on to another.
- It makes her vulnerable to having her child(ren) removed.

It is important to provide the mother/partner with clear information on the need to report any suspicions of abuse or any known abuse of a child or young person.

We should provide her with details about who to contact, how to contact them and how such a report would be dealt with.

Where the offender has no further contact: using knowledge to protect the child from abuse by other offenders

The knowledge gained from previous sessions can be used to assist the mother/partner in creating an awareness of any potential risk from any other sex offender or paedophile in the community or online.

Moving on

The aim is to help the mother regain a normal life without the involvement of outside agencies and for children to be safe.

EXERCISE
REINFORCING THE POSITIVE

Where the discovery of child sexual abuse has had a damaging effect on the mother's/partner's self-confidence and self-esteem, even when that was not a problem before, this can disempower the woman and give her children the message that she is not strong enough to protect them. It is important that she now shows that she has regained what was lost.

In this exercise we focus on the positives by asking the woman to identify:

- five positive qualities about herself
- five things she has changed for her child(ren) since the abuse that make her child safer.

EXERCISE
WHAT HAVE I LEARNED?

This is not a test, simply a summing up of what she thinks she will take away from the programme.

EXERCISE
BUILDING A SUPPORT NETWORK

It is not uncommon for the woman to have become isolated from family, friends and the local community, either as a result of the offender's manipulations or for fear of other people's responses to knowledge of the abuse. Some of their responses could have been unfriendly and even hostile. It is important for her to build a support network of people she can trust. The following are questions she may be asking herself and which can now be discussed in a positive way:

- How do you know who you can trust? What are the qualities you should look for?
- Can you name at least one personal friend and/or relative to whom you can talk relatively openly.
- Who could you add to the list?
- Which agencies would you go to and for what kind of help?

EXERCISE
BUILDING FUN INTO LIFE

Many women in this situation feel guilty about allowing themselves to enjoy life and so their lives become defined by the problem of sexual abuse. This can also be a problem for children. But laughter is good for mental health and recovery and also sends a message to her children that mum is OK, she does not need protecting or looking after and that life can be fun. Help her to identify:

- things she enjoys that can be built into her day (no matter how simple)
- outside activities she would enjoy (these need not cost money or be expensive)
- anyone she could do these activities with, for companionship.

Discuss how this can be fitted in around child care obligations and who could help her.

Conclusions

Such an intervention programme has the capacity to provide a mother/ partner with the information she needs to make better informed decisions, to empower her to protect a known victim and any other child in her care and to put this information into practice to help her, her child and her family to recover from child sexual abuse.

Where there is a decision to remove a child(ren) from the family home such a programme can be implemented to explore the possibility of making the home situation safe enough for the child(ren) to return, as well as informing decisions about the nature of contact and adding to our understanding of the therapeutic needs of the child.

References

Deblinger, E. and Heflin, A.H. (1996) *Treating Sexually Abused Children and their Non-offending Parents: A Cognitive Behavioral Approach.* Thousand Oaks, CA: Sage.

Still, J., Faux, M. and Wilson, C. (2001) *The Thames Valley Partner's Programme.* The Home Office, London. Crown Copyright 2001.

SUBJECT INDEX

AUTHOR INDEX